HENRY VAUGHAN

THE BRECKNOCK BEACONS

HENRY VAUGHAN

A LIFE AND INTERPRETATION

BY

F. E. HUTCHINSON

D.Litt., F.B.A.

SOMETIME
FELLOW OF ALL SOULS COLLEGE

OXFORD
AT THE CLARENDON PRESS

Oxford University Press, Amen House, London E.C.4

GLASGOW NEW YORK TORONTO MELBOURNE WELLINGTON
BOMBAY CALCUTTA MADRAS KARACHI LAHORE DACCA
CAPE TOWN SALISBURY NAIROBI IBADAN ACCRA
KUALA LUMPUR HONG KONG

FIRST PUBLISHED 1947
REPRINTED LITHOGRAPHICALLY IN GREAT BRITAIN
AT THE UNIVERSITY PRESS, OXFORD
FROM SHEETS OF THE FIRST EDITION
1962

PREFACE

THE main source of this book is the material collected by Miss Gwenllian Morgan and Miss Louise Guiney for a life of Vaughan. When Miss Morgan, the survivor of the two, died nine weeks after the beginning of the late war, her friends asked me to review the collection and advise what could be done with it. It consisted of many notebooks, files, genealogies, copies of legal documents, magazine articles, and hundreds of letters that had passed between the two ladies during the twenty-four years of their collaboration. After sorting and analysing this large collection I was obliged to report that there was nothing in it ready for printing and that the only service I could render would be to write a book of my own planning, which should scrupulously preserve all that was of value in the collection and also incorporate the results of my own researches. I trust that the book as it now stands will honour the memory of two women who discovered more about the poet they loved than any previous scholars have done. To measure the extent of their findings we have only to compare the slight account of Vaughan which was all that Henry Francis Lyte could compile a hundred years ago.

There are still important facts in the poet's life which have baffled all inquirers—notably the dates of his two marriages and of his beginning to practise medicine, and the source and date of his medical degree. There is no portrait of Vaughan and no contemporary account of his character and habits. If only his cousin John Aubrey had given us a few of such intimate details about Vaughan as he gave about Milton and Hobbes!

Miss Gwenllian E. F. Morgan came of a family that had been settled for three centuries at Devynock, nine miles from Brecon. When she was twelve years of age her father became rector of Llanhamlach, the nearest parish to Llansantffraed, and after his death in 1868 she lived the rest of her long life at Brecon. From early years she interested herself in the history of the county, its people and traditions. At a time when there was little local interest in the Silurist, she carried her investigations into every likely quarter. She was specially successful in tracking the poet and his kinsfolk in the unprinted matter in the Record Office, Lambeth Palace library, the British Museum, and Somerset House, besides exploring local probate registries and the records of the Brecknockshire Great Sessions and Quarter Sessions in the National Library of Wales. As Miss Morgan commonly employed professional aid for transcripts and digests of legal documents, I have not thought it necessary to re-examine them. Her lifelong acquaintance with Welsh country life gave her an insight into Vaughan's poetry and she was quick to detect his often cryptic allusions to the persons and events of his time. She lacked, however, the uninterrupted leisure necessary for writing a book. Her time was generously given to municipal and philanthropic work, as Poor Law guardian, governor of schools, town councillor, and magistrate. She was the first woman in Wales to serve the office of mayor, and, a devoted church-woman, she was for a time warden of Brecon Cathedral (the Priory Church). In 1925 the University of Wales conferred on her the honorary degree of M.A. in recognition both of her civic work and of her researches into the life of Vaughan. After Miss Guiney's death in 1920 Miss Morgan still hoped for her part to write the poet's life, but advancing age and constant suffering frustrated her cherished intention. She died at Brecon in her 88th year on 7 November 1939.

Miss Louise Imogen Guiney was born in 1861 near Boston, three months before the first shot was fired in the Civil War. Her father, of English, Irish, and French descent and married to a Scotswoman, was among the first to respond to President Lincoln's appeal for recruits in the northern army, and he won distinction in the war. His daughter was proud that Guiney's Station, where Colonel Guiney's regi-ment had been quartered, was marked on the map of Virginia. In early years Miss Guiney became known as a poet and she also contributed articles on literary subjects to American magazines. Already in 1894 an essay of hers on

Henry Vaughan appeared in the *Atlantic Monthly*, and she included it, with other essays, in *A Little English Gallery* (1894). At the close of 1895 her correspondence with Miss Morgan began, and within a twelvemonth an American publisher announced as 'in preparation' an edition of Vaughan's poetry, with biographical essays, by Miss Guiney and Miss Morgan. Similar announcements appeared in the press for the next forty years, but all that Miss Guiney finished, besides several magazine articles relating to Vaughan, was the editing of *The Mount of Olives*. She was hampered throughout life by the need of supporting herself by more remunerative work and by periods of ill health. With an ardent love of England and a romantic devotion to the royalist cause and its poets, she came to this country whenever her means allowed, and for the last ten years of her life she made her home here. She had had the good fortune to find a copy of the very rare *Thalia Rediviva* in a Boston bookshop and she generously gave it to the Bodleian Library, where she spent many of the happiest hours of her life. She greatly assisted her colleague in research and brought to their common task her poetic sensibility and her extensive knowledge of the English poets of the seventeenth century. After a long and disabling illness, with the possibility of completing the *magnum opus* ever receding from her grasp, she died at Chipping Campden on All Souls Day, 1920.

For my part, before dealing with *Silex Scintillans*, I have sought to give the poet a firm setting in his time and place by relating all that has been discovered about his circumstances, his kinsfolk and neighbours, and the countryside. I have set out the background of contemporary Breconshire life in its political, military, and ecclesiastical aspects, since these greatly affected Vaughan's life and feeling. If he judges the Puritans hardly, I am more concerned to understand why he felt as he did than to justify his opinions. For the religious history of Wales I owe much to the carefully documented books of Dr. Thomas Richards. It has been a great advantage to have the use of Professor L. C. Martin's scholarly edition of Vaughan's works; his annotations and those of

Sir Edmund Chambers have been very useful. American scholars, too, have in recent years added to our understanding of Vaughan. Mr. E. L. Marilla is preparing a fuller bibliography of Vaughan than is yet available.

With much diffidence I have included a chapter on the influence of Welsh language and poetry on Vaughan. No previous writer has made more than a passing reference to this theme. I was persuaded of its importance and have said what I could, *ne taceatur*, and in the hope that some competent Welsh scholar may be moved to improve upon my tentative exploration of the subject. Sir Harold Idris Bell and Professor Henry Lewis gave me much help, but they have not seen what I have written and are not responsible for any mistakes I may have made.

Mr. J. Goronwy Edwards, the Vice-Principal of Jesus College, gave me access to the college Buttery Books. Most gratefully I acknowledge also the help I have had from Professor R. I. Aaron, Mr. Donald Attwater, the Rev. R. Trevor Davies, Miss Elizabeth Holmes, the Rev. Professor Claude Jenkins, Dr. W. Pagel, the Rev. T. M. Parker, Dr. Percy Simpson, the Bishop of Swansea and Brecon, the Rev. G. O. Williams, Professor F. P. Wilson, and the Rev. G. H. M. Worthing, rector of Llansantffraed. I am specially indebted to Miss K. M. Lea, Fellow of Lady Margaret Hall, for reading the proofs and for many valuable suggestions. My readers will be as grateful as I am to Mr. Siegfried Sassoon for allowing me to end the book, more gracefully and fittingly than I could hope to do in prose, with his sonnet, 'At the Grave of Henry Vaughan'.

F. E. H.

OXFORD

All Souls Day, 1946

CONTENTS

ILLUSTRATIONS

WORKS OF HENRY VAUGHAN

PUBLISHED IN HIS LIFETIME

Poems, with the tenth Satyre of Iuvenal Englished.
Printed for G. Badger. 1646.

Silex Scintillans: or Sacred Poems and Priuate Eiaculations.
Printed by T. W. for H. Blunden. 1650.

Olor Iscanus.
Printed by T. W. for Humphrey Moseley. 1651.

The Mount of Olives: or, Solitary Devotions.
Printed for William Leake. 1652.

Flores Solitudinis. Collected in his Sicknesse and Retirement.
Printed for Humphrey Moseley. 1654.

Hermetical Physick. By Henry Nollius. Englished by Henry Vaughan.
Printed for Humphrey Moseley. 1655.

Silex Scintillans. The second Edition, In two Books.
Printed for Henry Crips, and Ludowick Lloyd. 1655.

The Chymists Key to open, and to shut: or the True Doctrine of Corruption and Generation. [Translation of Nollius' *De Generatione,* 1615.]
Published by Eugenius Philalethes.
Printed by E. B. for L. Lloyd. 1657. [Possibly 1655: see below, p.183.]

Thalia Rediviva. With some Learned Remains of the Eminent Eugenius Philalethes.
Printed for Robert Pawlet. 1678.

Olor Iscanus. [A reissue of the 1651 edition.]
Printed, and are to be sold by Peter Parker. 1679.

ABBREVIATIONS
USED IN FOOTNOTES

B.M.   = British Museum.

Cal. S.P.D. = Calendar of State Papers Domestic.

Chanc. Pro. = Chancery Proceedings, Bills and Answers, before 1714.

Chambers   = *Poems of Henry Vaughan*, ed. E. K. Chambers, 2 vols., 1896.

D.N.B.   = *Dictionary of National Biography.*

Grosart   = *Complete Works of Henry Vaughan*, ed. A. B. Grosart, 4 vols., 1870–1.

Lyte   = *Sacred Poems and Private Ejaculations*, by Henry Vaughan, ed. H. F. Lyte, 1847.

M   = *The Works of Henry Vaughan*, ed. L. C. Martin, 2 vols. (paged continuously), 1914.

M.L.N.   = *Modern Language Notes.*

M.L.R.   = *Modern Language Review.*

O.E.D.   = *Oxford English Dictionary.*

P.M.L.A. = *Publications of the Modern Language Association of America.*

R.E.S.   = *Review of English Studies.*

Richards i = *A History of the Puritan Movement in Wales, 1639–53*, by Thomas Richards, 1920.

Richards ii = *Religious Developments in Wales, 1654–62*, by Thomas Richards, 1923.

Theo. Jones = *History of Brecknockshire*, by Theophilus Jones, 2 vols. 1805–9; ed. Bailey, 4 vols. 1909–30. (The latter is referred to, unless the former is expressly mentioned.)

Waite   = *The Works of Thomas Vaughan: Eugenius Philalethes*, ed. A. E. Waite, 1919.

I
THE VAUGHANS OF TRETOWER

HENRY VAUGHAN'S relation to the ancient family of the Vaughans of Tretower is proclaimed in the coat of arms on his tombstone in Llansantffraed churchyard—a chevron between three boys' heads, each with a snake wreathed about the neck. No Welshman of Vaughan's time and breeding could have been wholly unmindful of the privilege of honourable ancestry. In no country were family ties so highly regarded and remembered as among the Welsh. Giraldus Cambrensis remarked upon his countrymen's esteem for generous descent and upon their tenacious memorizing of their lineage. Five centuries later Defoe was struck by the persistence of this Welsh characteristic: 'They value themselves much upon their Antiquity: The Antient Race of their Houses, and Families, and the like; and above all upon their Antient Heroes.'[1] The historian of Cardiganshire has, however, pointed out that the Welshman's pedigree 'was his title-deed, by which he claimed his birthright in the country', and that 'he was affected with respect to legal process in his collateral affinities through nine degrees'.[2] The late Sir David Brynmor-Jones stated that even in fairly recent times, if a witness in court was asked 'Are you a relative of the defendant?', it was not unusual for him to reply, 'Not related within the ninth degree.' We shall find that Henry Vaughan and his correspondents stretched cousinship to include kinsfolk of more remote degrees than would have been usual in England. It was an amiable habit which helped to maintain the sense of kinship in a small community bound together by innumerable family ties of blood and affinity.

Henry Vaughan shows something of an aristocratic mind in a passage in his *Life of Paulinus*, where he does not appear

[1] *Tour through Great Britain*, 1725, ii. 466.
[2] Sir S. R. Meyrick, *Hist. and Antiq. of the County of Cardigan* (1810), edn. 1907, p. 30.

to be quoting from his principal source, *Vita Paulini*, but commenting upon what he finds there:

> Certainly extraction and a virtuous descent (let popular flatterers preach what they will to the contrary,) is attended with more Divinity, and a sweeter temper, then the indiscrete Issue of the multitude.[1]

He often reveals his dislike and mistrust of what he calls 'the populacy',[2] and has almost nothing of the current democratic feeling. But he is also well aware of the vanity of earthly distinctions. Just as George Herbert had commented on the inevitable crumbling away of tombs and epitaphs 'in dustie heraldrie', and bids himself 'learn here thy stemme And true descent',[3] so Vaughan, in his poem 'Retirement', echoes Herbert's words about church monuments:

> A faithful school where thou maist see
> In Heraldrie
> Of stones, and speechless Earth
> Thy true descent.[4]

In his 'Elegie on the death of Mr. *R. W.*' he urges that the lowliest office of affording 'a Cheap pillow to thy quiet head' at the burying

> can do more
> To keep thy name and memory in store
> Than all those *Lordly fooles* which lock their bones
> In the dumb piles of Chested brasse, and stones.[5]

In translating a poem of Boëthius he enlarges upon the text, adding four lines which may be taken to express his own mind, with their anachronistic reference to contemporary heraldry:

> O why so vainly do some boast
> Their *Birth* and *Blood*, and a great *Hoste*
> Of Ancestors, whose *Coats* and *Crests*
> Are some rav'nous *Birds* or *Beasts*![6]

And in translating another poem of Boëthius, though he keeps closer to the Latin, he gives it an English turn:

> The Darke grave scorns your brightest glorie.
> There with Nobles beggers sway,
> And Kings with Commons share one dust.[7]

[1] M 363.   [2] M 270, 322, 363.   [3] *The Temple*: 'Church-monuments'.
[4] M 463.   [5] M 51.   [6] M 634.   [7] M 84.

In his poem 'To Lysimachus' he scoffs at those who brag of their acquaintance with 'This *Lady*' and 'such a *Lord*', and asks 'How much of *Blood* was in it?' He bids his friend instead ask himself

> what is't to thee,
> Who canst produce a nobler Pedigree,
> And in meer truth affirm thy Soul of kin
> To some bright *Star*, or to a *Cherubin*?[1]

Izaak Walton allows that, if George Herbert in his Cambridge days 'exprest any Error', it was that 'his cloaths seem'd to prove, that he put too great a value on his parts and parentage'; but no such vanity is detected in Vaughan. He expressed a strong dislike of finery and foppish manners, whether in men or women. He finds the 'artless looks and dress' of 'the sheep-keeping *Syrian* Maid' a braver show than the 'gay, alluring wear' of the fashionable world.[2] For himself, he is well content with 'this corse fleece I shelter in', by contrast with the 'curl'd, puff'd points' of the gallants, and he intends to bequeath no wardrobe except of home-woven stuff.[3] He and his friend Lysimachus may be pointed at as country cousins by the young fops they meet in the London streets, but they can afford to laugh at them:

> Saw not, *Lysimachus*, last day, when wee
> Took the pure Air in its simplicity,
> And our own too: how the trim'd *Gallants* went
> Cringing, & past each step some Complement?
> What strange, phantastic *Diagrams* they drew
> With Legs and Arms; the like we never knew
> In *Euclid, Archimed.*[4]

His twin brother (who, indeed, may have been Lysimachus) shared this feeling, and professed to have learnt it from the river Usk which wears 'the same simple vesture all the year':

> I'le learn *simplicity* of *Thee*, and when
> I walk the *streets*, I will not *storme* at *Men*,
> Nor *look* as if I had a *mind* to crie,
> It is *my valiant Cloth of Gold, and I.*[5]

[1] M 612.   [2] 'The Ornament' (M 507).
[3] 'Content' (M 422).   [4] 'To Lysimachus' (M 612).
[5] *Anima Magica Abscondita*, 1650, p. 54. Reprinted in *The Works of Thomas Vaughan: Eugenius Philalethes*, ed. A. E. Waite, 1919, p. 117.

Henry Vaughan had a very sober regard for ancestral privilege; he does not undervalue it, but neither will he presume on it. It will dictate to him an inner code of honourable conduct, but not an arrogant outward behaviour. It will be something to keep to himself as a spur to noble living, but he will make no display of it in speech or bearing. He could never have used such language as Rowland Vaughan, of the Bredwardine line, used in the dedication of a book of his to William Herbert, fourth Earl of Pembroke:

It is necessary your Lordship warrant my descent from *gladis de gam* Daughter of Sʳ *David Gam* slaine in the vanguard of the battell of Agincourt; who being sent by *Henry* the fift to discover the force of the *French*; Answered, *they were a-now to be slaine, e-now to be taken prisoners, e-now to run away*: which speech continues to his everlasting praise; this *Gladis* being mother to your Lordships *Ancestors* and mine: the *Earle of Pembrook, Sir Richard Herbert, Vaughan* of *Bradwardin, Hergest,* and *Vaughan* of *Tretowr* hir 5 sons al 5 brethren and al 5 overthrowne at *Banbury* field. Five such brethren out of one woman, the 13 shires of Wales hath seldom yielded: my Lord, I am by *Gladis* kin to most of the Old Nobility; which aged descent is almost worn out, yet not so worn, but either by consanguinity, or affinity, I can light on a *Howard,* a *Herbert,* a *Somerset,* a *Carew,* or a *Knowles.*[1]

Coleridge humorously complains that in Wales 'all V's are Vaughans', and, since the use of surnames developed slowly in the Principality, the name Vaughan often denoted no more than a cadet branch of a family. The poet's family can, however, be traced for many generations, though the genealogies are often inconsistent with one another. The field of Agincourt had special associations for the Vaughans and links them with the rival family of Herbert; they have a common ancestress in the daughter of the famous warrior Dafydd ap Llewellen, commonly known as David Gam from a nickname which means 'squinting'. He is said to have been knighted on the field of Agincourt shortly before he was killed, though, as Professor Tout points out,[2] the contemporary chroniclers in noticing his death describe him

[1] Rowland Vaughan, *The Water-Workes of Herefordshire,* 1617, Dedication.
[2] *D.N.B.* s.v. David Gam.

as 'esquire'. In Shakespeare's *Henry V* the king reads from the herald's list the names of the slain including 'Davy Gam, esquire'.[1] It has sometimes been suggested that Shakespeare modelled his Captain Fluellen on Dafydd ap Llewellen, but he does not identify him with the famous Welshman, as Fluellen is present when Henry V reads the list of the fallen.

David Gam's daughter, Gwladys, was married first to Roger Vaughan of Bredwardine, who, like his father-in-law, is said to have been knighted on the field and killed at Agincourt. His effigy is in Bredwardine church, and he is the reputed ancestor of the branches of the Vaughan family, settled respectively at Bredwardine, Hergest, and Tretower. After Sir Roger Vaughan's death, Gwladys took a second husband, William ap Thomas, known also as Sir William Herbert, lord of Raglan.[2] The effigies of Gwladys and her second husband are in the Herbert chapel in St. Mary's, Abergavenny. A son of theirs was the first Earl of Pembroke in the Herbert line, and another son was the ancestor of George Herbert. The older poet is fifth in descent from Gwladys Gam, and Henry Vaughan is eighth. But the younger poet, for all his veneration of George Herbert, and in spite of the remarkable freedom with which the Welsh have extended the degrees of cousinship, is not known to have claimed him as a kinsman.

There is another member of the Vaughan family for whom Henry and his brother Thomas may have had some regard, although he was not their direct ancestor. Sir Thomas Vaughan, 'probably youngest illegitimate son of Sir Roger Vaughan of Tretower'[3] (a son of the first Sir Roger and Gwladys), was prominent on the Yorkist side in the Wars of the Roses, and was with the young prince at Ludlow when the news came of Edward IV's death. With Rivers, Grey, and others, he set out for London with Edward V in their charge, but at Stony Stratford they were arrested on the orders of Richard and Buckingham, and

---

[1] *Henry V*, IV. viii. 109.
[2] *D.N.B.* s.v. William Herbert, Earl of Pembroke (*ob.* 1469).
[3] *D.N.B.* s.v. Sir Thomas Vaughan (*ob.* 1483).

sent as prisoners to the north. At Pontefract they were
tried, sentenced to death, and executed on 23 June 1483,
two days before Richard declared himself king. A scene in
the third act of *Richard III* represents Sir Richard Ratcliff
before Pomfret Castle, 'with halberds, carrying Rivers,
Grey, and Vaughan to death', and in the last act Vaughan's
is among the ghosts who trouble Richard's sleep on the
night before the battle of Bosworth Field.[1] Henry Vaughan
may have had these associations in mind when he wrote his
'Elegie on the death of Mr. R. *Hall*, slain at Pontefract,
1648'. His brother, who had not perhaps the same interest
in Hall, wrote no less than five poems on the siege of
Pontefract.[2]

Through his paternal grandmother Henry Vaughan was
descended from the Somersets of Raglan, the most powerful
house in south Wales throughout the poet's lifetime. *Thalia
Rediviva* was dedicated by its editor 'J. W.' to Henry Somerset,
third Marquess and seventh Earl of Worcester, grandson of
the indomitable defender of Raglan. In 1684 he made an
almost royal progress through Wales, soon after he had
been created Duke of Beaufort. Henry Vaughan's grandfather, William Vaughan of Tretower, married Frances,
daughter of Thomas Somerset, third son of the second Earl
of Worcester.[3] In some genealogies Frances is given as a
natural daughter, and this would seem to be correct.[4]
Thomas Somerset is not known to have married, and in

---

[1] *Richard III*, III. iii. 1, and v. iii. 143.
[2] Waite, pp. 465–7. It is worth pointing out that the *D.N.B.* article on
Sir Thomas Parry (*ob.* 1560), controller of Queen Elizabeth's household, is
mistaken in stating that Henry Vaughan was a descendant. This account of
Parry's progenitors differs at almost every point from that given in the
D.N.B. article on Sir Thomas Vaughan (*ob.* 1483). If the former account
were correct, the poet would be descended from the man who was executed
at Pontefract, but the evidence does not bear examination. This Sir Thomas
is confused with his contemporary, also Sir Thomas, the poet's ancestor, who
was still alive in 1491.
[3] Frances Somerset had previously married Roger Vaughan of the Porthaml
family, from whom was descended Roger Vaughan of Trephilip, who was
high sheriff of Breconshire in 1646, with the poet's father as under-sheriff. See
below, p. 12. Cf. Chanc. Depositions, 659. 17, 12 June 1612, *Jones* v. *Vaughan*.
[4] Col. J. A. Bradney, *History of Monmouthshire*, 1911, vol. II, part i,
pp. 25–6.

his will made 'in our bulwarke belonging to the tower of
London' on 5 April 1586, and proved on the following
27 May, there is no mention of wife or children.[1] For
twenty-four years, almost without intermission, he had been
a prisoner in the Tower for his adherence to the old faith.
He was originally committed to the Fleet on 10 June 1562
'for translating an oratyon out of Frenche, made by the
Cardinall of Lorraine, and putting the same without authority in prynte'.[2] He was allowed leave of absence for a few
weeks from 28 February 1581/2 'for the following of certain
suites in lawe triable betwene him & others at the next
Assizes in divers sheirs in the Province of Wales', on
bonds and sureties being given.[3] He did not return by the
appointed day because he was 'of late fallen into some
extremity of sicknes', and was granted an extension of
leave 'untill he shall have recovered his health', but he was
to spend the last four years of his life in the Tower. In the
inventory of Cardinal William Allen's debts, made at Simancas
soon after his death at Rome on 16 October 1594, there is
mention of a loan of 2,000 scudi made by Thomas Somerset
'cattholico gentil'huomo Ynglese' for the maintenance of
the English College at Rheims.[4] The cardinal in his will
considers his executors bound to provide for the repayment
of the loan, so soon as may be, 'to the heirs of the said
Thomas on demand'.[5] The descent of Henry Vaughan from
a devoted recusant is more interesting than his aristocratic
connexion with the Somersets on the wrong side of the
blanket. He was connected by kinship or friendship with
many recusant families, and, though he remained throughout life a loyal son of the Church of England, he was
notably free from any prejudice against reading widely in
the writings of adherents of the old faith.[6]

Henry Vaughan's grandfather died on 12 June 1617, but
his grandmother Frances was still alive when he reached
boyhood. The children of William and Frances Vaughan

[1] Somerset House, C.T.C., Windsor 28.
[2] Acts of Privy Council, 1558–70, p. 108, and B.M. Harl. MS. 360, f. 34.
[3] Acts of Privy Council, 1581–2, p. 336.
[4] *Records of the English Catholics under the Penal Laws*, 1882, vol. ii, p. 378
[5] Ibid.   [6] See below, pp. 131–4.

were Charles, the eldest son, Thomas, the poet's father, Margaret, who married John Walbeoffe, for whose son Charles the poet was to write an elegy in 1653, and perhaps others.[1] Charles Vaughan, the inheritor of Tretower, married in 1604 Eleanor Norton, whose mother was a daughter of Dr. William Aubrey, the eminent civilian, great-grandfather of the Oxford antiquary with whom Henry Vaughan corresponded. She died on 10 August 1636,[2] and almost at once Charles Vaughan took as second wife Ursula, daughter of Sir William Coningsby of Hampton Court in the county of Hereford. He may have hoped to mend his broken fortunes, as her father, by his will made in 1616, had devised £3,000 to her. If so he was disappointed, as he was himself dead by the end of the year or in the first month of the next year,[3] and his widow in the following May was suing her brother Fitzwilliam Coningsby for the £3,000.[4] Charles Vaughan, for some unascertained reason, bequeathed Tretower and all his manors, not to his son William, married to Margaret Gunter, but to their son Edward, an infant aged 7 years.[5] Administration of the will was granted to William, and he instituted proceedings on 27 April 1637 on behalf of his infant son to discover and obtain the testator's estate. Ursula Vaughan was still living fifteen years after her husband's death, and her stepson William, by his will proved on 10 May 1654, devised that his daughter Margaret should 'have other property upon the death of Ursula Vaughan my stepmother'.[6] Since Ursula Vaughan is described in a lawsuit of 1652[7] as residing at Walton in the county of Salop, she is likely to have had little or no contact with the poet's family. It may be presumed that Henry Vaughan had some early acquaintance with his uncle

[1] For the reasons for regarding William Vaughan as the poet's grandfather, not great-grandfather (as some genealogies give him), see Appendix A, p. 243.
[2] Chancery Proceedings, Bills & Answers, before 1714: Bridges 88. 53.
[3] His will was proved 23 Jan. 1636/7: Prerogative Court of Canterbury, Goare 8.
[4] Chanc. Pro., Car. I, 10 May 1637, U 15. 46. Also, 24 June 1637, U 16. 10.
[5] Chanc. Pro. Car. I, U 9. 51 and U 14. 61.
[6] Will made 25 Feb. 1653/4, proved at Westminster 10 May 1654.
[7] Chanc. Pro., Collins 151. *Vaughan* v. *Vaughan*, 29 Apr. 1652.

and aunt, Charles and Eleanor Vaughan, as they lived till
he was fifteen years of age. His uncle's fortunes were
seriously embarrassed; in an action which he brought on
6 February 1625/6 against his 'near kinsman' William
Gunter of Treveynon and Blanche Parry, the defendants
demur that the plaintiff ought not to be answered as he has
been 'outlawed for debt',[1] and in his will he states that he
needs the Coningsby legacy 'towards the payment of my
debts'.

Henry Vaughan could not fail to have some interest in
Tretower, which had been his father's early home, but no
mention of it is found in any of his extant letters. It lay
only some six miles, in the direction of Crickhowell, from
the poet's home, Newton in the parish of Llansantffraed.
John Leland, the King's Antiquary in Henry VIII's reign,
thus described it :

Tretour, a smaulle Village stonding on a litle Brooke, and
within half a Mile of Wiske. Ther is a pretty Castel longging now
to the King, and therby also in the Village is a faire Place of
Henry Vehan Esquier.[2]

The Early-English round tower of the Castle is still a striking
feature of the landscape, but the usefulness of the Castle
either for defence or for residence was long past. The
Vaughans' home was Tretower Court. Its north range
was built by John Picard about 1300. The Vaughans,
acquiring it 150 years later, enlarged and remodelled the
structure. The house encloses a courtyard which is an
irregular quadrangle. Even in its present decay it preserves
much of its original dignity and beauty, especially in the
gatehouse and, on the opposite side, the great hall, which
still retains its fine timbered roof.[3] It remained in the

---

[1] Chanc. Pro., Car. I, U 9. 39.
[2] *The Itinerary of John Leland*, ed. T. Hearne, 1710–12, vol. v, p. 59. 'Wiske'
is the river Usk. The Henry Vaughan of Henry VIII's reign was a great-
grandson of Sir Roger and Gwladys Vaughan, and a direct ancestor of the
poet.
[3] There is an architectural article on Tretower by J. H. Parker in *Archaeologia Cambrensis*, 4th series, vol. vii, 1876. The Ministry of Works, which is
engaged on a conservative restoration of Tretower Court, has published an
admirable Guide, *Tretower Court*, by C. A. Ralegh Radford, 1938, with many
illustrations.

possession of the Vaughans until near the end of the eighteenth century, although they had long ceased to live there after acquiring a more modern house at Scethrog. Henry Vaughan was born at Trenewydd (*Anglice*, Newton), a house in the hamlet and manor of Scethrog, in the parish of Llansantffraed and hundred of Pencelli. It had become the home of his father Thomas on his marriage in 1611 to Denise, the only child and heiress of David Morgan of Llansantffraed. A record in the Court Leet of Scethrog Manor shows David Morgan paying chief rents in 1584 to 'Mrs. Blanche Parry owner and lady of the same manor'. She was a lady-in-waiting and keeper of the jewels to Queen Elizabeth. The tombstone of Denise's father is the oldest surviving from the old church, and is now in the south transept of the new church, built in 1884.[1] The inscription runs: 'Heare lyeth the bodie of David Morgan David Howel who married [Gwenllian] William of Llanhamolch, and they had issue one daughter [called] Diennis. He died 2d June 1598.'[2] At the time of his death he was possessed of 'goods and chattels to the value of £400'. Although his wife Gwenllian survived him, he left the Trenewydd estate to his daughter. In his will, made on 9 June 1598, after bequeathing sixpence 'to the Cathedrall church of Sainct Davis' and 'my forgotten tithes three shillinges fouer pence' to the rector, and sundry minor legacies of land in other parishes, he ends: 'I doe make and ordaine [and] constitute my welbeloved daughter Denize vg David sole executrix'.[3] As Denise was only five years old, it is not surprising that, on 16 November following, a commission was issued to her mother Gwenllian to administer the property during her minority. The mother's rights were, however, limited. In an Inquisition held on 13 September 1599 it was found that David Morgan had held certain lands of the

---

[1] S. W. Williams, 'Llansaintffread, Llanhamlach and Llanfigan Churches', in *Arch. Cambr.*, 1887.

[2] S. W. Williams, op. cit. The Christian name Gwenllian is illegible, but is supplied from legal documents. The word preceding 'Diennis' is also undecipherable. Perhaps it should be 22d, as the will is 9 June.

[3] Prerog. Court of Canterbury, Lewyn 96. The abbreviation 'vg' represents the Welsh word for daughter.

Queen by knight's service, and that consequently Denise
was a ward of the Queen.[1] The wardship was granted to Sir
David Williams, sergeant-at-law. Sir David allowed Denise's
mother to occupy Newton and to collect the rents and profits
for the use of her daughter during her minority. In 1606,
when Denise was twelve years old, her mother married
Madoc ap John of Llansantffraed, and till his death in May
1612 she and her husband administered the estate.

Meanwhile the little heiress had been twice married.
First, in August 1608, when she was only fifteen, she was
married to Thomas Jenkin, son and heir apparent to Jenkin
Thomas of Llandefalle. After barely two years he died on
18 July 1610,[2] intestate and without issue, and in the
following year Denise, at the age of eighteen, took for her
second husband Thomas Vaughan, who was perhaps about
seven years her senior.

The young married pair appear to have had much difficulty for several years in securing their rights, and at no
time in his life was Thomas Vaughan averse from going to
law. He and 'Dyonis his wife' commenced Chancery proceedings against her first husband's father for detaining
moneys received from Sir David Williams in respect of the
Newton estate. Jenkin Thomas denied that his son had
received any such sum, and, besides, preferred a prior claim
as his son was in debt to him at the time of his death. Nor
was this the only action. The young pair also sued Gwenllian's stepson, Thomas Madoc, because his father had died
without rendering account of his stewardship of Newton,
and because the son, although inheriting enough to discharge his father's debts, 'out of a covetous mind and
disposition, seeking to enrich himself and intending most
unreasonably to deceive and defraude your Orators of the
rents and profits', refused to account for the said profits.[3]
Litigation continued: as late as 1627 Thomas and Denise
Vaughan sued Jenkin Thomas ap Jevan of Llanfigan for

---

[1] Chanc. Inq. p.m. 41 Eliz., vol. 257, no. 51.
[2] Date on the tombstone in Llandefalle church, as recorded in Theophilus
Jones, *History of Brecknockshire* (1809), ed. Bailey, 1911, iii. 24.
[3] Chanc. Pro., Jac. I, U 2. 58 and 59.

a debt of £500 on a bond dated 18 December 1595.[1] For one reason or another Thomas Vaughan seems to have been constantly behindhand in his payments. On 30 January 1612/3 the list of Insoluts of the Lay Subsidy payable on the marriage of James I's daughter to the Elector Palatine includes 'Thomas Vaughan of Newton and his mother-in-law Gwenllian Madocks widow, 6s'.[2]

It is not known that Thomas Vaughan followed any profession, although the Newton estate was not more than enough to maintain him and his family. He was liable to the usual obligations of a country gentleman. In an undated Muster Roll of '100 footmen, drawne and elected out of the hundreds of Crickhowell and Penkelly, being the trayned bande comitted to the conduct and leadinge of Charles Vaughan of Tretowre, Esqre' there appears the entry 'Thomas Vaughan, gent., Lieuftenant',[3] and a similar entry is found with the date 3 October 1632.[4] In a list of Pikemen, dated 1617, Charles Vaughan is down for two muskets, and Thomas Vaughan of Newton for one.[5] Thomas Vaughan appears as a Justice of the Peace in 1624, when he was commissioned, with Charles Vaughan and two other magistrates, to examine 'Gwenlyan vg Madocke', widow, in the matter of a suit brought against her by Edward Games of Buckland for alleged unlawful intrusion into a messuage in Llansantffraed.[6] Although a magistrate, Thomas Vaughan appears not to have been of sufficient importance and substance to be made sheriff of the county, but he was under-sheriff in 1646 when his kinsman Roger Vaughan was sheriff.

A Jacobean window-head from the old church, which has been built into the inside wall of the vestry of the new

[1] Brecon Plea Rolls, 56, m. 6d (1627).
[2] Ibid., Lay Subsidy, 219. 62.
[3] B.M. Sloane Add. MS. 10609, f. 18.
[4] Ibid., f. 45.   [5] Ibid., f. 71.
[6] Chanc. Pro., Jac. I, Brecon G 13. 3, 12 June 1624. E. K. Chambers (*Poems of Henry Vaughan*, ii. xxvi) states that the name of the poet's father 'appears in a list of Breconshire magistrates for 1620', but, following the faulty genealogy given in Harl. MS. 2289, f. 81, he takes 'Henricus Vaughan' in that list to be Henry Vaughan's father, whose Christian name Thomas is given in many legal documents.

church, bears the date 1626 and the initials 'EG. TV. WT. WF. ID.'[1] It is likely enough that TV. stands for Thomas Vaughan, and that he was churchwarden in that year along with EG., who is probably Edward Games of Buckland, the plaintiff in the action of two years before.

[1] S. W. Williams, op. cit., who gives a picture of the window-head.

II
CHILDHOOD

IT is a little surprising that the twins, Henry and Thomas, were not born to Thomas and Denise Vaughan till about ten years after their marriage. But, at a time when the rate of infant mortality was very high, there may have been other children who died in infancy. Among the older children, if there were any, may be a daughter, whose Christian name has not survived; in a lawsuit of 1655 one William Parry, of whom nothing else is known, is named as a son-in-law of Thomas Vaughan.[1] There was also a younger son, William, born probably in 1628.[2]

The poet's own testimony is precise about the year of his birth, but there is no evidence about the month and day.[3] In answer to John Aubrey's request for details about himself and his twin brother, for Anthony Wood's use in his forthcoming history of Oxford and Oxford men, Henry Vaughan wrote on 15 June 1673: 'My brother and I were borne att Newton in the parish of St Brigets in the yeare 1621.'[4] Henry was the elder of the twins; he is described in a legal document of 1659 as 'heir at law to his father Thomas Vaughan' and 'heir apparent in the right of his mother' to Newton, and he did, in fact, inherit that estate.[5]

The exact hour of his birth, which was probably not quite the same as his twin brother's, would determine his horoscope. Henry Vaughan alludes to his horoscope, perhaps playfully in the poem 'To Master T. Lewes',[6] and with more seriousness in two other poems, which speak of the moon as the ruling feature at his birth. In 'The importunate Fortune', making his will in the manner of Donne's poem 'The

---

[1] See below, p. 96.   [2] See below, pp. 95–7.
[3] For reasons against the birthday being 17 Apr. 1622, based on a misreading of B.M. Sloane MS. 1741, which is given as the authority for this date in the *D.N.B.* s.v. Henry Vaughan, see Appendix B, p. 245.
[4] M 667.
[5] Chanc. Pro., Collins 579. 112: *Vaughan* v. *Jones*, 29 Apr. 1659.
[6] M 61.

Will', after bequeathing his 'dull Clay' to the earth, he continues:

My growing Faculties I send as soon
Whence first I took them, to the humid *Moon*.[1]

And he enlarges upon the 'Influence' of the moon on his early years in 'To Etesia looking from her Casement at the full Moon':

Above all others in that one short hour
Which most concern'd me, she had greatest pow'r.
This made my *Fortunes* humorous as wind,
But fix'd *Affections* to my constant mind.
She fed me with the *tears* of *Starrs*, and thence
I suck'd in *Sorrows* with their *Influence*.
To some in *smiles*, and store of *light* she broke:
To me in sad *Eclipses* still she spoke.
She bent me with the motion of her *Sphere*,
And made me feel, what first I did but fear.[2]

But he tells Etesia that 'when I came to Age, and had o're-grown Her Rules, and saw my freedom was my own', he had sought to direct the lines of his life by his natural reason. Few men of his day, even those of intellectual power and scientific mind, could entirely quit themselves of all belief in the influence of moon and stars on human destiny. Vaughan has a poem, full of technicalities, unintelligible to the uninitiated, and purposeless if it had no reality for himself, on the *Zodiac* of Marcellus Palingenius (Petro Angelo Manzoli), a Venetian student of the occult, whose work was translated by Barnabe Googe in the early years of Elizabeth's reign and enjoyed a long popularity.[3] Perhaps Vaughan outgrew this belief; in 'The importunate Fortune' he gives up 'my false *Magic*, which I did believe', though later in the same poem he asks 'And shall I then forsake the *Stars* and *Signs*?'[4] In one of his latest poems, 'Daphnis', commemorating his brother Thomas who died in 1666, he alludes to the stars at Thomas's birth.[5] So, earlier, in 'An Epitaph upon the Lady Elizabeth', who died on 8 September 1650 in her fifteenth year, he

[1] M 616. [2] M 625.
[3] M 611. *Zodiacus Vitae*, publ. *c*. 1531; Engl. tr. by B. Googe, Bks. I–III, 1560; I–VI, 1561; I–XII, 1565.
[4] M 614–17. [5] M 659, ll. 117–18.

alludes to her 'sad stars' which dispensed to her 'No Influxe, but Calamitie'.[1] Vaughan's older friend, Thomas Powell of Cantref, in his prefatory poem upon the twins in *Olor Iscanus*, plays prettily upon the planet that ruled their birth.[2] It may be noted that in all his extant letters to friends in England, and in the dedications and prefaces of his printed works, Vaughan always used the English forms of his address: not Trenewydd, but Newton, or sometimes 'Newton by Usk', or more fully 'Newton by Uske neare Sketh-Rock'; not Llansantffraed, but 'the parish of S. Brigets'. Llansantffraed is the native name of the place of St. Freda, Bride, or Bridget, the popular Irish saint, to whom Vaughan's parish church and some eighteen other Welsh churches were dedicated.

Some idea of the size and character of the house in which Henry Vaughan was born and lived almost the whole of his long life may be inferred from the inventory taken at his father's death in 1658. The 'prisers' or valuers were all men of substance in the village, and two at least of the three were Thomas Vaughan's kinsmen. Thomas Powell lived at the Tower, a farmhouse between Newton and Scethrog, and was of kin to Denise Vaughan. David Maddocks, steward of Scethrog Manor, was of a family long settled at Llanfrynach, and a cousin of the Aubreys; he died in 1685. John Watkins, grandson of a former Dean of Hereford, lived at Llansantffraed, close to the church, and his lands marched with the Newton estate; he was related to the Walbeoffes, to whom Vaughan also was related.

A true and perfect Inventorie of all the goods, cattell, and chattels of Thomas Vaughan of Newton, late deceased, prised by Thomas Powell, David Maddocks and John Watkin, gent. the five and twentieth day of June 1658.

Imprimis one table in the hall with 3 wainscoat benches and 3 chaires.
Item, one stuffe carpett.
    „   one standing bed in the little chamber over the entry with curtains.
    „   one table with a small frame to it in the great chamber over the kitchin.

Item, one chest or coffer in the s^d. chamber over the kitchin.

,, one green rug & two coverlets.

,, 4 payre of sheetes.

,, 2 table cloaths.

,, 1 feather bed.

,, 1 chaffe bed.

,, 1 feather bed in the little chamber over ye Entrie.

,, 9 pewter dishes of all sorts.

,, 7 pewter spoons.

,, 6 wooden piggins.[1]

,, of wooden trenchers of all sorts, 17.

,, 3 pewter flagons.

,, 1 pewter candlestick.

,, in the kitchin, 1 table & 2 benches, & 3 stooles.

,, in the Garrett one old chest, & an old coffer in the chamber over ye kitchin.

,, 2 spills & 2 small racks & 1 paire of little andirons & 1 gridiron & 1 frying pan.

,, 1 old brasse caldron & 1 old fire slice.[2]

,, 1 small brasse kettle, & 1 paire of tongs.

,, 2 wooden cannes.

,, 3 barrells & 1 salting tub.

,, 6 cheese fatts & 1 old presse for cloaths.

,, 1 little table in the buttery & 1 coffer.

,, 1 small flax wheele.

,, 1 little bed in ye study.

,, 1 old churning tub.

,, of oaten mault halfe a bushell.

,, 1 peck of barley mault.

,, of corporal apparell not given by himselfe before his decease, 1 riding coate & 1 payre of bootes.

,, 1 old faulchion & 2 forrest bills.

,, fower sheep & 1 ram & 2 lambs.

,, 8 acres or thereabouts of hard corn growinge in the field called y Llaworth y Ty.

All these forecited goods, cattells & chattells were prised by the forenamed Prisers to the value of Five Pounds of current English money.

Subscribed by us
THOMAS POWELL.
DAVID MADDOCKS.
JOHN WATKINS.

---

[1] Milking-pails.   [2] A fire-shovel.

On the ground floor were the hall, study, kitchen, and buttery; on the first floor, a 'little chamber' over the entry or porch, a 'great chamber' over the kitchen, and rooms over the hall and study; and there was also a garret. There would be, no doubt, outhouses or lean-to buildings, such as wash-house, brewery, and dairy, but altogether it was a modest house with no more than eight living-rooms, counting the kitchen but not the buttery. The hall, carpeted and wain-scoted, was the main living-room of the family in the medieval way. The '3 wainscoat benches' suggest that it was panelled with oak or other seemly wood, and had fixed benches of the same wood running round three sides of the room. The study is significantly so called, as one would expect it to be called parlour or withdrawing-chamber; no books are mentioned, but the books in the house were likely to be Henry's. The study contained 'a little bed'. The kitchen was large enough to have over it what is called a 'great chamber'. The porch also must have been of some size to have over it a 'little chamber', which contained both a feather bed and a standing bed, the latter being a high bed-stead on legs, as distinguished from a low truckle-bed on castors which could be wheeled underneath the standing bed when not in use.[1] There was probably another bedroom on the first floor, though it is not mentioned, with the second feather bed.

The valuation of the whole contents and of the livestock at five pounds is surprisingly low, but it must be remembered that there may have been other furniture and livestock be-longing to Thomas Vaughan's wife, who was an heiress.[2] The furniture and effects seem humble enough, but they

[1] In *The Merry Wives of Windsor*, IV. v. 4–7, Simple tells the host of the Garter he wishes to speak to Falstaff, and he replies: 'There's his chamber, . . . his standing-bed and truckle-bed.' There is much information, especially about the smaller houses, in Iorwerth Peate, *The Welsh House*, 1940.

[2] It may be well to add the list of furniture and effects belonging to Henry Vaughan's mother Denise, as cited in the suit of *Thomas and Denise Vaughan* v. *Jenkin Thomas* in 1612 (Chanc. Pro., Jac. I, U 2. 58): 'nyne payre of fyne hollond sheetes worth eighte poundes, one fetherbedde with all furniture worthe ten poundes, one table cloth of diaper worth twenty shillings, one table cloth of Holland worth twenty shillings and half a dozen of Turkye worke Cushions worth forty shillings.'

may be such as many of the poorer gentry in Wales possessed. There are many pewter vessels but no silver.[1] The 'small flax wheele' would be turned for converting yarn into thread, as was still the practice in most homes until the arrival of the spinning-machine in 1764. The small frame adjusted to a table would be one in which silk, muslin, or other material was stretched for embroidery. The forest bill was a bill-hook for lopping trees, brushwood, and hedges, and the falchion was a smaller wood-knife; they were not weapons of war but of husbandry. The large kitchen was more plentifully supplied than the living-rooms; the implements provide for dairy work, meat-curing, brewing, and bread-making. Everything points to the self-contained life which was usual in a country house of the time.

Perhaps most striking is the limited extent (if we are to judge from the inventory) to which Thomas Vaughan farmed his own lands; the livestock consists of a few sheep only, with no cows or horses. And there were but eight acres of 'hard corn', which was a common name for wheat and rye. It is hard to estimate the size of the Newton estate, as it varied from time to time by sale and purchase. Denise's father held at his death, as is stated in an Inquisition of 13 September 1599, '1 messuage, 20 acres of land, 6 acres of meadow, 6 acres of pasture, 3 acres of wood, &c., worth £4'—35 acres in all, besides lands in other parishes, some of which was devised by him to others than his daughter.[2] Perhaps the words 'worth £4' refer to the woods only, as Thomas Vaughan in a deposition of 25 November 1612 states that the lands which came to his wife Denise from her father were 'of the clear yearly value of £20'.[3] It is not safe to infer from much later descriptions of the Newton estate that it was in Thomas Vaughan's day or in his son Henry's day 'of about 200 acres'.[4] Thomas Vaughan may have added to what his wife inherited from her father, though this is unlikely, considering his generally impecunious condition.

---

[1] It is possible that the Vaughans had given their silver to support the King's cause in the early years of the Civil War.
[2] Chanc. Inq. p.m., 41 Eliz., vol. 257, no. 51.
[3] Chanc. Pro., Jac. I, U 2. 59.   [4] Chambers, II. xxiv.

He was forced by his later necessities to part with some land. Thomas Vaughan's condition seems to have been typical of the smaller gentry in Wales. The president of the Council of the Marches, in a letter to Thomas Cromwell, reports that 'there be very few Welshemen in Wales above Breknock that may dispende ten pounde lande'.[1] Few Welsh landowners were wealthy enough to be forced to buy baronetcies in the reign of James I or for long after. When Charles I, after dissolving Parliament in 1625, sought to raise money by instructing the Lords-Lieutenant to borrow money on Privy Seals from the rich men of their counties, £105 only was advanced by seven persons in the county of Brecon, although nineteen were approached.[2] The general condition of the Welsh gentry is summarized by Sir John Rhys and Sir D. Brynmor-Jones:

Speaking broadly, the estates of the gentry in Wales in the seventeenth century appear to have been small—possibly many may have been extensive in area but certainly from the point of view of annual value they were as a rule very small. Major General Berry, writing to Cromwell, says 'You can sooner find fifty gentlemen of 100*l*. a year than five of 500*l*.'[3]

Enough has been said to show that Henry Vaughan was not born to affluence or even to an assured competence, and this may have some bearing on his eventual decision to enter the profession of physic, especially if the estate suffered diminution by the fines and other penalties which were levied on 'malignants'.

There is another feature of the Newton home which left its enduring mark on the memory of Henry's brother Thomas. In 1658, after his father's death, Thomas Vaughan dreamed that his father and his younger brother, who had died ten years before, came to him as he lay 'full of sores in my feet . . . under the shelter of the great oak, which grows before the courtyard of my father's house'.[4] Perhaps Henry alludes to the same tree in 'Daphnis':

So, where swift *Isca* from our lofty hills
With lowd farewels descends, and foming fills

---

[1] *Cit. ap.* J. R. Phillips, *Memoirs of the Civil War in Wales*, 1874, i. 14.
[2] Ibid. i. 37. [3] *The Welsh People*, 1900, p. 449. [4] Waite, p. 448.

A wider Channel, like some great port-vein,
With large rich streams to feed the humble plain:
I saw an Oak, whose stately height and shade
Projected far, a goodly shelter made,
And from the top with thick diffused Boughs
In distant rounds grew, like a Wood-nymphs house.[1]

Henry Vaughan might have echoed the words of William
Wordsworth:

Fair seed-time had my soul, and I grew up
Foster'd alike by beauty and by fear;
Much favour'd in my birth-place.[2]

And the Usk may have done for Vaughan what the Derwent
did for Wordsworth:

the fairest of all Rivers lov'd
To blend his murmurs with my Nurse's song.
And, from his alder shades and rocky falls,
And from his fords and shallows, sent a voice
That flow'd along my dreams.

Palgrave remarks that the Usk 'seems to run through all
Vaughan's poetry with an undercurrent of peace and
music':[3]

Dear Stream! dear bank, where often I
Have sate, and pleas'd my pensive eye.[4]

He loved the Usk in all seasons and weathers; in the spring,
when primrose and bluebell adorned its banks and water-
meadows, as he describes in his Latin poem 'Ad fluvium
Iscam';[5] or when the floods were out in the Usk valley above
Newton, causing the river to look like a veritable sea and,
when so stirred, to have a distinct redness. His poem 'The
Storm' begins:

I see the use: and know my bloud
Is not a Sea,
But a shallow, bounded floud
As red as he.[6]

Miss Morgan writes to Miss Guiney on 29 July 1907: 'There

[1] M 657, ll. 43–50.   [2] *The Prelude*, i. 301–3 and 270–4.
[3] F. T. Palgrave, 'Henry Vaughan of Scethrog', *Y Cymmrodor* for 1890–1,
vol. xi, part 2, 1892, p. 199.
[4] 'The Waterfall', ll. 13–14 (M 537).   [5] M 92.   [6] M 423.

have been the reddest of red floods in the Usk: I never saw
him redder.'¹ It is significant that Vaughan chose (if we
may be allowed to think that it was the author's, not his
editor's, choice) the title, *Olor Iscanus*, 'The Swan of Usk', for
his principal volume of secular verse, placing at the head of
it his poem on that river, and should already in early manhood express his wish to be 'layd to rest hard by thy streams',
and in verse to celebrate it, as other poets have sung of their
native rivers, in such a way

> As shall from age to age thy *fair name* lead
> 'Till *Rivers* leave to *run*, and *men* to *read*.²

Aubrey and Wood, in writing to one another, alluded to
Vaughan as 'Olor Iscanus', though it is not known that he
desired this name for himself, but rather, as on his title-
pages, that of 'Silurist'. His brother shared his love for the
river, and the most attractive of Thomas's English poems
sings the praise of 'my crystal Usk'.³

The countryside about Llansantffraed is not only well
watered but also well timbered, and there are many poems of
Henry Vaughan that illustrate his love of trees and his
watchful observance of their growth. Like other lovers of
trees, he is struck to the heart at their needless felling. In his
translation of Boëthius ii. 5 he interpolates the third and
fourth of the following lines:

> The shadie Pine in the Suns heat
> Was their Coole and known Retreat,
> For then 'twas not cut down, but stood
> The youth and glory of the wood.⁴

And in one of the most beautiful of his poems, 'The Timber',
he describes feelingly the 'resentment' which even the dead
tree feels at the approach of such a storm as had laid it low.⁵
In his 'Prayer in time of persecution', one of the grudges he
bears against the Puritan régime is apparently that, to pay

¹ Cf. Aubrey, *Brief Lives*, ii. 328 (of Herefordshire): 'All the earth red, as
also all Wales from the Severn to the sea.' Vaughan may mean Llangorse;
Defoe notes the tradition that the river Llewini 'runs thro' it, and keeps its
Colour in Mid-Channel distinguish'd from the Water of the Lake'.
² M 39.   ³ Waite, pp. 116–17.
⁴ M 83, ll. 13–16.   ⁵ M 497.

indemnities or for other cause, some wooded parts of the Newton estate have been forfeited: 'Our wood is sold unto us.'¹

The other notable feature of the Llansantffraed scenery, the Breconshire Beacons, so clearly seen from the site of Vaughan's home, receives less explicit mention in his poems than one might expect, if one did not bear in mind that delight in mountains finds expression in English poetry much later in time than delight in more pastoral scenes—rivers and meadows, fountains and woodlands. In his translation of a poem of Ovid the introduction of 'Spring and Groves' is his own addition.² Yet we may detect an occasional allusion to his native hills, as when he compares his memory of those that are 'all gone into the world of light' to 'those faint beams in which this hill is drest, After the Sun's remove';³ as Miss Morgan says: 'The poem was probably written in view of the Allt, on the slope of which Newton stood, whilst its crest caught the last rays of the setting sun.' In the concluding words of the first poem called 'Mount of Olives'— 'this Hill Was then his Chaire'—there may be an allusion to Cader Idris, or to Pen y Gader, the highest peak of the Black Mountains, *Cader* meaning 'chair'.⁴ But, on the whole, Vaughan may have shared the contemporary awe of bare mountain heights; as Professor Judson has observed, he had a wholesome respect for their height rather than an admiration of their beauty.⁵

From early years the twins would have been attracted by Llangorse Pool (Llynsafadden), less than two miles over the Allt from their home. It may well be the 'drowsie Lake' from whose mists the shower came;⁶ a hot mist would rise from a lowland lake in cultivated country, whereas most of the Welsh lakes are clear mountain-tarns. Llangorse Pool is the home and breeding-ground of more wild birds, probably, than any other place in south Wales. Miss Morgan tells

---

¹ M 166, l. 23.   ² M 68, ll. 47–8.
³ M 484, ll. 7–8.   ⁴ M 415, ll. 31–2.
⁵ A. C. Judson, 'Henry Vaughan as a Nature Poet', *Publications of the Modern Language Association*, Mar. 1927. Perhaps he over-emphasizes the 'conventional' treatment of local scenery by Vaughan.
⁶ 'The Showre' (M 412).

of the birds seen there from time to time: the ringed plover, turnstone, redshank, greenshank, curlew, sheldrake, little grebe, moor-hen, pintail, shoveller, snipe, water-rail. Even the green sandpiper has been known to visit the lake, and in winter the widgeon and gooseander, the heron, the dunlin, and the bittern have been seen there. The charms of the lake would be heightened by 'the legend of the countrey people', which Aubrey discussed with 'My Cosen Hen: Vaughan' in 1656, that there 'was heretofore a Towne drowned by an Earth-quake'.[1]

There may be another reminiscence of childhood in the poem 'Vanity of Spirit', where Vaughan tells of

> A peece of much antiquity
> With Hyerogliphicks quite dismembred,
> And broken letters scarce remembred.[2]

An old cromlech, named Ty Illtyd (home of St. Illtyd), remains on the hill in Llanhamlach, the next parish to Llansantffraed; it consists of three upright stones with a slanting fourth stone for a roof, covered with rude crosses, circles, and other 'hieroglyphics'.[3]

Henry Vaughan was, indeed, fortunate in his birth-place and he would not have questioned Wordsworth's view of the influence of natural beauty upon the growing child. At first it would be an unconscious or only half-conscious perception of 'beauty old as creation'; then, a conscious and passionate delight in river, waterfall, rocks, and trees; and, in the sober, maturer years, the 'auxiliar' reflections which trouble and spiritual growth supplied, till they ripened in that 'sense sublime' to which his mystical insight brought him. The translator of Giraldus the Welshman says of the valley of the Usk that it 'may vie with all others in Wales for extent of beauty, and is, perhaps, nowhere so much diversified as between Brecknock and Abergavenny'.[4]

Like Wordsworth, too, and unlike most of Vaughan's

---

[1] Bodl. MS. Gen. Top. c. 24, f. 230; Monum. Brit., part I.
[2] M 419, ll. 22–4.
[3] Theo. Jones, iv. 17. There is an illustration of the inscriptions on the Ty Illtyd stones in E. Gibson's edition of Camden's *Britannia*, 1695, p. 594.
[4] Sir R. C. Hoare, *The Itinerary of Giraldus de Barri*, 1806, ii. 368.

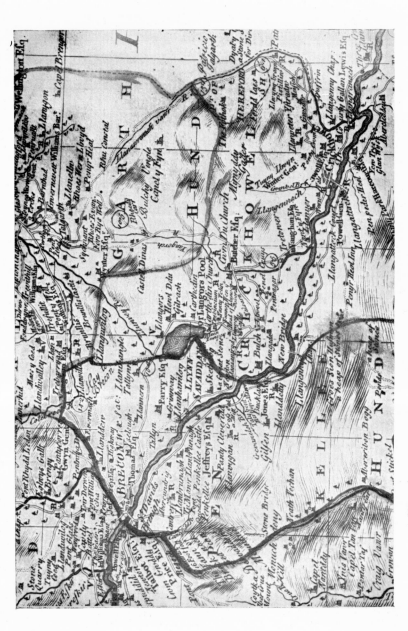

THE VALLEY OF THE USK BETWEEN BRECON AND CRICKHOWELL
From *A new Map of South Wales* drawn from actual surveys by Thomas Kitchin, 1777

contemporaries, the poet cherished throughout life a high
regard for childhood and its innocence:

> Happy those early dayes! when I
> Shin'd in my Angell-infancy.[1]

It was the 'Dear, harmless age', 'An age of mysteries', that
he dwells upon in his poem 'Childe-hood':

> I cannot reach it; and my striving eye
> Dazles at it, as at eternity.
> Were now that Chronicle alive,
> Those white designs which children drive,
> And the thoughts of each harmless hour,
> With their content too in my pow'r,
> Quickly would I make my path even,
> And by meer playing go to Heaven.[2]

In the poem 'Looking back' he speaks of 'morning-glories'
that 'cannot dye', and apostrophizes the scenes of his
infancy:

> Fair, shining *Mountains* of my pilgrimage,
> And flow'ry *Vales*, whose flow'rs were stars:
> The *days* and *nights* of my first, happy age;
> An age without distast and warrs.[3]

His brother Thomas had the same high regard for childhood. He says of his 'first youth':

Nature, whose pupill I was, had even then awaken'd many
Notions in me, which I met with afterwards, in the *Platonick
Philosophie*. . . . This *Consideration* of my self, when I was a Child,
hath made me since examine Children, namely, what thoughts
they had of these *Elements*, we see about us, and I found thus much
by them, that *Nature* in her simplicity, is much more wise, than
some men are with their acquired parts, and *Sophistrie*. . . . A Child,
I suppose, *in puris Naturalibus*, Before education alters, and ferments him, is a Subject hath not been much consider'd, for men
respect him not, till he is companie for them, and then indeed they
spoile him.[4]

---

[1] 'The Retreate' (M 419).   [2] M 520.
[3] M 640. L. C. Martin contributes a valuable study, 'Henry Vaughan and
the Theme of Infancy', with many allusions to earlier and contemporary
reflections on childhood, in *Seventeenth Century Studies presented to Sir Herbert
Grierson*, 1938, pp. 243–55.
[4] *Euphrates* (1655), pp. 19–21 (Waite, p. 396). Cf. Traherne, *Cent. Med. iii. 7.*

A matter affecting Vaughan as poet is his mother-language, and on this his twin brother gives precise evidence. In the penultimate paragraph of *Anthroposophia Theomagica*, which appeared in 1650, the same year in which the first part of *Silex Scintillans* was published, Thomas Vaughan makes 'one request' for the reader's indulgence: 'I would not have Thee look here for the *Paint*, and *Trim* of *Rhetorick*, and the rather because *English* is a *Language* the *Author* was *not born to*.'[1] In the same book occurs a sentence which provoked a comment on his use of English from his antagonist, Henry More, the Cambridge Platonist, writing under the name 'Alazonomastix Philalethes'. Thomas Vaughan, who used the pen-name 'Eugenius Philalethes', had written:

> But my *Peripateticks*, following the Principles of *Aristotle* and *Ptolemie*, have imagin'd so many wheeles there with their small diminutive *Epicycles* that they have turn'd that regular *Fabrick* to a rumbling Confused *Labyrinth*.[2]

Henry More, quoting the last four words, comments:

> 'Tis only *Erratum Typographicum*. I suppose you mean, a rumbling Wheel-Barrow, in allusion to your Wheel-work and Epicycles aforementioned. But why small diminutive Epicycles? *Eugenius!* you are so profound a Magician, that you are no Astronomer at all.[3]

Thomas Vaughan, returning to the charge in this interminable and vituperative controversy, answers More's 'Observation 13':

> 'Nobody', saith he, 'will say the Heavens or a Labyrinth doth rumble, but such as are no Englishmen, as you say somewhere you are not, and so doe not understand the language.' For my part, I *professe* I am no *Englishman*, neither would I be *taken* for *such*, though I *love* the *nation* aswell as *thy self*: And for their *language*, if I did not *understand* it, yet I might understand *Labyrinth*, for it is not *English*, but *Greek*.[4]

Yet it will be noticed that Henry Vaughan, in his poem to

---

[1] *Anthroposophia Theomagica*, p. 65 (Waite, p. 60).
[2] Ibid., p. 14 (Waite, p. 20).
[3] *Observations upon Anthroposophia Theomagica*, by Alazonomastix Philalethes, 1650, p. 20.
[4] *The Second Wash: Or the Moore Scour'd once more*, by Eugenius Philalethes, 1651, p. 119.

Thomas Powell 'upon His Translation of Malvezzi's *Christian Politician*', begins:

> Wee thank you, worthy Sir, that now we see
> *Malvezzi* languag'd like our Infancie.[1]

This suggests that the Vaughan children were bilingual; it is
probable that their father, a scion of the house of Tretower
and a magistrate, spoke English, but that their mother was
Welsh-speaking; her ancestors, says Miss Morgan, 'were
Welsh from the earliest times'. Palgrave remarks that when
Henry Vaughan came to practise as a country doctor he
'must have spoken far more Welsh than English'.[2] The
effect of his lifelong familiarity with the Welsh language on
his English poetry will be considered in Chapter XII.

Henry Vaughan, with his brother Thomas, 'was educated
in Grammar Learning in his own Country for six Years
under one *Matthew Herbert* a noted Schoolmaster of his
time'.[3] This statement of Anthony Wood is borne out by
Vaughan's autobiographical poem, 'Ad Posteros':

> then I went
> To learned Herbert's kind encouragement,
> Herbert, the pride of our Latinity;
> Six years with double gifts he guided me.
> Method and love, and mind and hand conspired,
> Nor ever flagged his mind, nor his hand tired.
> This was my shaping season.[4]

The years would be from 1632 till 1638 when the brothers
went to Oxford. Matthew Herbert was more affluent than
most Welsh parsons; he had been from 1621 rector of
Llangattock with its attached chapelries of Llanelly and
Llangenny, and was as well rector of Llanfihangel-Cefnllys
in the county of Radnor, with total profits of £400 a
year,[5] besides holding a prebendal stall in the collegiate
church of Brecon. The rectory of Llangattock was leased
by a former rector, Hugh Rawlins, with the permission of

---

[1] M 60.   [2] *Y Cymmrodor*, vol. xi, part 2, p. 196.
[3] *Athenae Oxonienses*, 1721, ii. 926.
[4] M 32. Mr. Edmund Blunden kindly allows me to use his translation
(*On the Poems of Henry Vaughan*, 1927, p. 9).
[5] Hist. MSS. Comm. 7th Report, Appendix, part i, p. 96: House of
Lords MSS. Papers relating to the Act of Indemnity.

the then Earl of Worcester, the patron, in 1555 to Thomas Somerset, Henry Vaughan's great-grandfather, for 99 years at £60. 18*s*. 8*d*. a year. On the expiry of the lease, Matthew Herbert in July 1655 begged the discharge of this sequestration.[1] He was married to Joan, daughter of John Price of Crickhowell. Llangattock was reached from Llansantffraed by following the Brecon–Crickhowell road, down the steep Bwlch hill, and crossing the Usk at Crickhowell, a distance of about nine miles.

Wood's description of Herbert as 'a noted schoolmaster' suggests that he kept school or had other pupils besides the Vaughans at his rectory, but nothing is known of this, nor is it known whether he was a graduate.[2] It was an honourable tradition for poets to dedicate verses to their former preceptors. So Camden had been honoured by Jonson, Saravia by Sylvester, and less notable schoolmasters by Randolph and Wither. The Vaughan brothers paid several handsome tributes to Matthew Herbert. Thomas has two Latin poems addressed to him, besides prefixing to *The Man-Mouse taken in a Trap* an Epistle Dedicatory 'To my Learned, and much Respected friend, Mr. Mathew Harbert', which begins oddly: 'Sir, I know you are not *Great*, there's a *better title*, you are *Good*.'[3] Henry, in a Latin poem 'To his old Schoolmaster and ever honoured Mr. Matthew Herbert', even contrasts the physical life he owes to his father, a life which will soon pass away and be forgotten, with the enduring life which will preserve both the poet's name and his schoolmaster's in the poetry that blossomed from Herbert's training.[4] We may also recognize Herbert in 'Daphnis' as 'old Amphion',[5] named after the Theban ruler who harped with

---

[1] Calendar of the Committee for Compounding, Domestic, 1643–60, part iii, p. 1713.

[2] Matthew Herbert's name is not in Foster's or Venn's *Alumni*.

[3] Waite (p. ix) suggested that Matthew Herbert is Seleucus Abantiades, to whom Thomas Vaughan dedicates *Aula Lucis* (Waite, p. 311): 'Our *Acquaintance* began with my *Child-hood*', he says, but he does not explain the fanciful name which he gives to his 'best and noblest Friend'. Miss Morgan thought that Seleucus was Sir George Vaughan, who, she says without giving her reasons, was a noted alchemist.   [4] M 93.

[5] Cf. 'Lycidas', l. 36: 'And old *Damoetas* lov'd to hear our song.' *Old* is a natural term of affection.

such skill that his music drew the stones into their places to form the city walls. After a description of the pastoral scene, the poet continues:

> And many times had old *Amphion* made
> His beauteous Flock acquainted with this shade;
> A Flock, whose fleeces were as smooth and white
> As those, the wellkin shews in Moonshine night.
> Here, when the careless world did sleep, have I
> In dark records and numbers noblie high
> The visions of our black, but brightest Bard
> From old *Amphion's* mouth full often heard;
> With all those plagues poor shepheards since have known,
> And Ridles more, which future times must own.[1]

So then, besides being well grounded in Latin by one whom Henry apostrophizes as '*Latiae* gloria prima *Scholae*', the boys learned from Herbert something of the legends and prophecies of Merlin, the Black Bard. It may be, too, that to him they owed their first interest in astrology and the occult, and even in alchemical experiment. Thomas Vaughan, at any rate, in discussing the action of fire on water, remarks: 'This *Speculation* (I know not how) surpris'd my first youth, long before I saw the University.'[2] It is probable that Henry, to some extent, for many years shared his brother's interest in such subjects, though later he turned from them.

Everything points to the happiness of those years at Llangattock and to the good fortune or wise choice which placed the Vaughan boys under a wise and sympathetic teacher who developed their minds and won their lifelong affection.[3] They were ripe for Oxford when they had reached their seventeenth year.

---

[1] M 657, ll. 55–62. [2] *Euphrates*, p. 19 (Waite, p. 395).
[3] For the later events in Matthew Herbert's life, see below, pp. 109–10, 201–2.

III
OXFORD AND LONDON

THOMAS VAUGHAN was matriculated from Jesus College on 14 December 1638, and it has hitherto been assumed that he and his brother Henry went up to Oxford in that month. But, as is shown in the surviving Buttery Books of the college, he had been admitted to the college seven months earlier, on 4 May, and was continuously resident, except for vacations, from that date, being charged each week with 'battels', the term for sums due to the college for provisions. There is no written record of Henry's matriculation or of his membership of Jesus College. His studying at Oxford rests primarily upon his own statements. When Aubrey wrote to him on 10 June 1673 to obtain facts about himself and his brother in the interest of Anthony Wood, whose Oxford history was due to appear next year, Vaughan answers that Thomas continued at Oxford 'for ten or 12 years', but 'I stayed not att Oxford to take any degree'.[1] He tells Aubrey of his own and his brother's books, and Wood made use of this information. If Henry Vaughan had not studied at Oxford, he would have had no rightful place in Wood's book, which has for its sub-title in the fuller English edition 'An Exact History of all the Writers and Bishops Who have had their Education in The University of Oxford'.[2] He is humbly grateful that he and his brother should find a place in the forthcoming history. 'I am highly obliged to you', he tells

---

[1] M 667. Chambers (II. xxvi–xxviii), writing in 1896, questioned Henry Vaughan's membership of Jesus, but, after the appearance of extracts from his letters in A. Clark's edition of Aubrey's *Brief Lives* in 1898, he allowed that the evidence of Vaughan's having studied at Oxford was satisfactory (*Athenaeum*, 29 Mar. 1902).

[2] Wood's Latin work, *Historia et Antiquitates Universitatis Oxoniensis*, published at Oxford in 1674, was followed in 1691–2 by a fuller history in English under the title *Athenae Oxonienses*. A posthumous edition of *Ath. Oxon.*, for which Wood had collected additions and corrections, appeared in 1721, and P. Bliss re-edited it in 4 vols., 1813–20. My references are to Bliss's edition, unless I have cause to name one of the earlier editions.

Aubrey, 'that you would be pleased to remember, & reflect
vpon such low & forgotten thinges, as my brother and my
selfe: I shalbe ever ready to acknowledge the honour you
have done vs.'[1]

Henry Vaughan considered himself an Oxford man. For
instance, in the poem 'On Sir *Thomas Bodley's* Library; the
Author being then in *Oxford*' he uses the first person
repeatedly—'We are bound to thee', 'Thy safe, discreet
Expence on us did flow', 'all our fame Meets here to speak
one *Letter* of thy name'.[2] As for the last phrase, no editor
has yet offered any explanation of 'one *Letter* of thy name'
or seen its bearing on the date of the poem. When Bodley
enlarged Duke Humphrey's Library by adding the Arts
End, an eastern wing at right angles to the original building,
the whole assumed the shape of the letter T, the initial of
Bodley's Christian name. Upon his death in 1613 a volume
of commemorative verses appeared under the title *Justa
Funebria Ptolemaei Oxoniensis*, in which several of the epi-
grammatists seized upon the fact of his library being
constructed in a T shape. One of the epigrams may be
Englished thus: 'A single book contains ever so many
little letters; here's a single letter which holds innumerable
books.'[3] The jest was by Vaughan's day a hoary one, and
would be obsolete by 1640, when the addition of the
Selden End balanced the Arts End and the whole assumed
the shape of H. Vaughan is likely, therefore, to have
written this poem in his undergraduate days, before the
construction of the Selden End.[4]

The fact that Henry Vaughan's name is not to be found
in the university matriculation lists is not fatal to the view
of his having been an Oxford undergraduate. In the first
place, the extant lists are defective, as Anthony Wood often
complains. For example, Thomas Hobbes was entered by
his uncle at Magdalen Hall in January or February 1602/3

[1] M 669.   [2] M 614, ll. 37, 43, 51.
[3] Some of the poems of 1613 are reprinted with annotations in the *Bodleian
Quarterly Record*, vol. i, no. 4, pp. 96–101.
[4] Miss Guiney took Vaughan's poem 'To my Ingenuous Friend, *R. W.*'
(M 3) to be also written in these years: see her article 'An Oxford Poem',
Academy, 15, 22, and 29 Apr. 1911.

and proceeded to the B.A. degree five years later, but there
is no record of his matriculation.[1] Furthermore, if a student
did not intend to take a degree, matriculation was often
dispensed with. Kenelm Digby, gentleman commoner of
Gloucester Hall for two years from 1618, did not matriculate.
'This', says Andrew Clark, 'was by no means infrequent
all through the seventeenth century.'[2] Wood remarks of
Vavasor Powell, afterwards to be the most active Puritan
preacher in Wales: 'Whether he was matriculated, or avoided
it to save a little money, as many have done that intend to
take no degree, I know not.'[3] Henry Vaughan's father may
have intended from the beginning that his eldest son should
proceed, as early as he was fit for it, to the study of the law
in London without completing a degree course at Oxford,
whilst a full university course was proper for the second
son, who was destined for holy orders. An exactly parallel
case with that of Henry Vaughan was George Wither, who
spent two years at Magdalen College, from the age of 16 to
18, and then settled in London to study law. It may be our
Henry Vaughan who appears in the Register of the Chancellor's Court at Oxford:

10 Maij 1639. Acta habita est . . . coram venerabili viro Accepted
Frewen . . . Willelmus Taylor contra Henricum Vaughan. Mylles
Procurator. Stet.

The only other Henry Vaughan resident in the university
in that year was a young clerical Fellow of Jesus. It was not
unusual for an Oxford tradesman to sue an undergraduate
for debt in the Chancellor's Court, and there are many
references in Vaughan's early poems to debts and duns
and money difficulties.

That Henry Vaughan was an Oxonian may be taken as
certain, but his membership of Jesus College is less certain
though probable. The college Buttery Books have survived
for the year 1638 (but not for 1639), for 1640, for the second
half of 1641, and the first half of 1642, after which there is a

---

[1] *D.N.B.* s.v. Thomas Hobbes.
[2] Aubrey, *Brief Lives*, ed. Clark, i. 225, editorial note.
[3] *Ath. Oxon.* iii. 911.

gap till Michaelmas 1647. Andrew Clark remarks that in the seventeenth century undergraduates 'trickle into college by units at all indeterminate dates, instead of coming up by batches at the beginning of the term'.[1] He reckons that in 1638 there were 99 men on the books, though not all of them were in regular residence. In the Buttery Books the names are arranged by seniority in categories—Principal and Fellows 18, Scholars 17, Noblemen 4, Doctors and M.A.s 6, Fellow-Commoners 11, B.A.s 5, Commoners 18, Battelers 7, Servitors 13. Of this total of 99, 38 were from south Wales, 11 from north Wales, 10 from the Border counties—i.e. 59 from Wales and its borders, 6 from the rest of England, 3 from the Channel Isles (a connexion which began in that year and still continues), and 31 whose place of origin is not recorded.

There are no less than 6, if not 7, Vaughans in the Buttery Books for the years 1638 to 1642, but none of them can be our Henry Vaughan. Among the Fellows are James and Henry Vaughan, elected to their fellowships in 1637 and 1638 respectively. The absence of the poet's name is the more disappointing as his brother's record is complete for 4 years; Thomas Vaughan 'of Brecon' (i.e. the county), plebeian, was admitted on 4 May 1638 and matriculated on the following 14 December, was promoted from Commoner to Scholar in May 1641, took his B.A. degree on 18 February 1641/2, and, continuing to hold his scholarship, remained in residence until the record ends. Except for absence from August to December 1641 he has weekly accounts charged against him throughout these years, and it is interesting to note that they are consistently higher than for most of the undergraduates except for some of the Fellow-Commoners.[2] Edward Vaughan was elected Scholar in 1639. 'Mr. Herbert Vaughan' appears among the Noblemen in 1640: he is probably not to be identified with a Vaughan (without Christian name) among the Fellow-Commoners of 1641,

[1] Andrew Clark, 'Yearly Lists for Jesus College compiled from the College Buttery-Books' (Bodl. MS. Top. Oxon. c. 173).
[2] Possibly the twins shared a room and battels, but Thomas Vaughan's battels do not decrease on Henry's leaving for London.

since both names are found on the same pages concurrently. There appears to be a Vaughan (without Christian name) among the Commoners of 1641, for the first time, but this is too late for the Silurist, who by this time had probably passed on to London.

There are, however, a few other possible indications of the Silurist's membership of Jesus College. In a collection of academic verse, *Eucharistica Oxoniensia*, commemorating Charles I's safe return from Scotland on 25 November 1641, there is an English poem signed 'H. Vaughan. Ies. Col.'[1] Earlier in this volume are Latin verses signed 'Hen. Vaugh. Ies. Soc.', and the subscription to the English poem may distinguish the undergraduate from the Fellow of the same names. But the English poem might be the work of the Fellow-Commoner who signs his contributions to two preceding volumes of academic verse 'Herbertus Vaughan, Equ. Aur. Fil. Unicus Coll. Iesu Soc. Communalis';[2] as, however, Herbert Vaughan had already twice used this distinguishing description of himself, he would be likely to use it again, and therefore the contributor of the English poem in *Eucharistica* may be the Silurist. Aubrey, who was in closer connexion with Henry Vaughan than Wood was, expresses himself hesitatingly: 'Eugenius Philalethes was of Jesus College. Whither Henry was I have forgotten.'[3] But Wood is definite, whether he had the information from Aubrey or not. His account of Henry Vaughan in his *Historia et Antiquitates Universitatis Oxoniensis* (1674) comes after he has dealt fully with the life and writings of Thomas Vaughan:

Fratres erant gemelli *Thomas* hic noster & *Henricus*, cognomento *Silurista*; is autem primogenitus cum esset, ac proinde Legum Angliae municipalium studio à patre destinatus, *Oxoniae* (eodem enim in Sodalitio Artibus ingenuis aliquamdiu vacavit) spatio temporis exiguo commoratus est.[4]

Wood means Jesus College by *Sodalitium*, as he has already

[1] The poem is printed in Martin, p. 665.
[2] *Horti Carolini Rosa Altera*, 1640, commemorates the birth of Henry, Duke of Gloucester, and Προτέλεια *Anglo-Batava*, 1641, celebrates the marriage of Charles I's eldest daughter Mary to William of Orange.
[3] *Brief Lives*, ii. 269.　　　　[4] *Hist. et Antiq.* ii. 321.

used this word in mentioning Thomas Vaughan's membership of that college. It will be noticed that Wood is embody-
ing the information given by Henry Vaughan in his letter
to Aubrey of 15 June 1673,[1] but neither in that nor in any
other letter of his is his membership of Jesus College mentioned. Henry Vaughan certainly saw what was written
about himself and his brother in Wood's Latin history,
because, in writing to Wood on 25 March 1689, he calls
attention to some mistakes and omissions, which he desires
to be corrected: 'If you intend a second Edition of the
Oxford-historie, I must give you a better account of my
brothers books & mine; wch are in the first much mistaken,
and many omitted.'[2] The fact that Henry Vaughan asks for
no correction of Wood's assigning him to Jesus College is
sufficient proof that Vaughan accepted it as correct, and
it seems to me conclusive. Strangely enough, in spite of
both Aubrey and Wood having collected information from
Vaughan for use in the fuller history in English, *Athenae
Oxonienses* (1691–2), Wood does not include the sentences
of the 1674 edition about Henry Vaughan's life and writings,
but merely mentions him incidentally. At the end of his
very long account of Thomas Vaughan, he says of him:
'He hath also left several Lat. Poems behind him, which are
in the hands of his Brother *Henry*, called by some *Olor
Iscanus*, esteemed by many fit to be published.'[3] Also he
says of John David Rhesus that he had written, besides his
Welsh Grammar, 'other excellent things, but are lost, as I
have been assured by Olor Iscamus' [sic].[4] In his account
of William Cartwright he states that his *Poems* were 'usher'd
into the world by many copies of Verses, mostly written
by *Oxf*. men; among whom were . . . *Hen. Vaughan* the
Silurist and *Eugenius Philalethes* his brother, both of *Jesus*
Coll.'[5] But in the second edition of *Athenae Oxonienses*,
which appeared in 1721, 26 years after Wood's death, a
fuller account of Henry Vaughan than he had included in
1674 is added, giving some facts which are not to be found
in his letters. It should, therefore, be given here in full:

---

[1] M 667. [2] M 674. [3] *Ath. Oxon.*, 1692, ii. 254.
[4] Ibid. i. 304. [5] Ibid. ii. 18.

Henry Vaughan, called the *Silurist* from that part of Wales whose Inhabitants were in ancient times called *Silures*, Brother Twin (but elder) to *Eugenius Philalethes*, alias *Tho. Vaughan*, . . . was born at *Newton S. Briget*, lying on the River *Isca* commonly called *Uske* in *Brecknockshire*, educated in Grammar Learning in his own Country for six Years under one *Matthew Herbert* a noted Schoolmaster of his time, made his first entry into *Jesus* Coll. in *Mich.* Term 1638, aged 17 Years: where spending two Years or more in Logicals under a noted Tutor, was taken thence and designed by his Father for the obtaining of some knowledge in the municipal Laws at *London*.[1]

There is some slight corroboration of Henry Vaughan's membership of Jesus College in the fact that Aubrey's inquiries of him on Wood's behalf concern former members of that college only, although it is also true that most Welsh Oxonians who were writers since the end of the sixteenth century had been educated at Jesus. There is as well Aubrey's remark, in a letter to Wood on 19 March 1680/1, that Vaughan had borrowed from Jesus College a copy of Rhesus's Welsh Grammar.[2] On the whole it seems probable that, although there is no evidence of his residing in the college and drawing 'battels' as his brother did, Henry Vaughan was a member of it and was taught by one of its tutors.[3] In any case he was likely to have become familiar with his brother's college and with some of its members.

Jesus College answered to James Howell's description of it as a 'national college'. Welshmen of all classes were in residence at it when the Vaughans came to Oxford. George Stradling, son of a Glamorganshire baronet, was admitted Scholar on 27 April 1638. He had many social gifts and was 'a rare lutenist'; later he was for many years a Fellow of All Souls and was at the end of his days Dean of Chichester. Five weeks after Thomas Vaughan was admitted, James and John Herbert, the third and fourth sons of the Earl of

[1] *Ath. Oxon.*, 1721, ii. 926. From Wood's collections for the 2nd edn. which he did not live to see through the press. He could have learnt about T. Vaughan's poems from Henry's letter to Aubrey (M 667).

[2] *Brief Lives*, ii. 201, and Bodl. MS. Aubrey 8, f. 11.

[3] Much the same conclusions are reached by Mr. J. Goronwy Edwards, 'Henry Vaughan and Jesus College', *Jesus College Magazine*, June 1937.

Pembroke, High Steward of the University and Visitor of Jesus College, were admitted. In the humbler category of Battelers was Andrew Watkins from the Vaughans' native village, admitted on 17 October 1638, and among the Servitors a few months later was Jenkin Jones of Llandetty, who was to be a leader of the Puritan cause in Breconshire. Another future Parliamentarian, commander-in-chief and member of the Saints' Parliament, Bussey Mansell, was admitted in the category of Noblemen in October 1640.

The Principal, Dr. Francis Mansell, third son of Sir Francis Mansell, baronet, of Muddlescombe in Carmarthenshire, 'spent his life in and for the college', as devoted a head as any that the college had yet had. When he was evicted by the Parliamentarians he went for a while to the house of Sir John Aubrey, whose mother was a Mansell, at Llantrithyd in Glamorganshire. Here he taught a few young men and brought to help him a young Jesus man, who was afterwards, as Sir Leoline Jenkins, to succeed him as Principal.

The Fellows, of whom about nine or ten were generally resident, were mostly young men. But there were two older men who come into Henry Vaughan's later life. Thomas Powell, the Vaughans' neighbour as rector of Cantref, and Henry's closest literary friend, was a resident Fellow of Jesus during most of 1638. William Thomas, a future Bishop of St. Davids, was from his election as Fellow in 1635 Praelector Dialecticae or Logic Reader, whose duty it was to lecture three days a week and to hold classes in the hall for undergraduates every day; it may well be that Henry's 'noted tutor in Logicals' was his future diocesan. The name of Archbishop Ussher, 'Jacobus Armaghanus', is in the Buttery Books from July to the end of November in 1640.

Jesus College, officially styled 'of Queen Elizabeth's foundation', was incorporated by letters patent of 27 June 1571 on the petition of its real founder, Hugh Price, D.C.L., Treasurer of St. Davids, who is buried in Brecon Priory Church. The original statutes gave no special privileges to Welshmen, but all its early Principals were Welsh, and the funds for its endowment were chiefly raised in the Principality. For the first fifty years of its history the new college was hampered by insufficient endowments and inadequate buildings, but in the first half of the seventeenth century great strides forward were made until the Civil War interrupted its progress. Before the end of James I's reign the hall and chapel were added, and Sir Eubule Thelwall, a wealthy and generous lawyer from Denbighshire, who was Principal from 1621 to 1630, completed the front quadrangle by adding at his own cost the Principal's Lodgings with the beautiful wainscoted drawing-room. Thelwall's successor, Dr. Mansell, raised further funds in Wales and, with bountiful additions from his own purse, 'had Contributions sufficient in view to finish and perfect' the inner quadrangle. Among those who had promised help was Sir George Vaughan of Fallerston in Wiltshire, a distant cousin of the Vaughans of Tretower, who was soon to present Thomas Vaughan to the rectory of Llansantffraed. He had expressed his intention of finding the money to build the west side of the projected inner quadrangle, but Mansell was able to complete only the eastern portions of the north and south sides before 'all those pious Designes and Contribucions were lost by the Dispersions and Ruines that by the Warr befell those who intended to be our Benefactors'.[1]

The general appearance of the college, as the Vaughans saw it, and as Loggan depicted it in 1675, must have been in many respects more picturesque than it is since its later alterations. The buildings of the outer quadrangle were of two stories only, with attics and gabled dormer-windows; the substitution of a third story for the attics and the rather stiff embattled parapets were later additions. Only two years before the Vaughans came to Oxford Dr. Mansell had enlarged the chapel at both ends, carrying it a further bay west, and bringing its east end flush with the front in Turl Street and adorning it with 'a fayre east window'. The drastic restoration of 1864 cleared the chapel of its Jacobean panelling and stalls, and all that remains of the interior

[1] Bodl. MS. Wood F 30, 32: a *Life of Mansell*, attributed to Sir Leoline Jenkins. Privately printed in 1854.

fittings are the handsome wooden pulpit and the black and white marble steps. The hall happily retains its panelling and the fine screen at the south end, but a plaster ceiling has for two hundred years hidden the open timber roof and its hammer beams.[1]

Some of the most notable of the university buildings were only completed shortly before the Vaughans' arrival in Oxford, and must have therefore aroused comment. For example, the Convocation House behind the Divinity School was finished in 1635, and the Canterbury quadrangle of St. John's College was being built by Laud, the Chancellor, from 1631 to 1636. A Jesus man, Morgan Owen, one of Laud's chaplains, who was soon to be Bishop of Llandaff, was the donor in 1637 of the new porch of the church of St. Mary the Virgin, with the 'very scandalous statue' of the crowned Virgin and Child which was to attract the hostile notice of the Long Parliament.

According to Wood, as we have seen, Henry Vaughan spent only '2 years or more' in Oxford before his father sent him to London to study municipal law. If the two years are reckoned from the date of his brother's entering Jesus College, Henry would arrive in London in the summer or autumn of 1640, and would remain till his father recalled him home on the outbreak of the Civil War in August 1642.

In very much the same way, nearly a century and a half before, Sir John More had removed his son Thomas from Oxford, after less than two years there, and entered him at an Inn of Chancery, although he was only in his seventeenth year. Oliver Cromwell, after little more than a year at Cambridge, 'seems to have left the university and betaken himself to London to obtain the general knowledge of law which every country gentleman required'.[2] As in Cromwell's case, Vaughan's father may have desired for his eldest son and heir a 'general knowledge of law' such as

[1] *An Inventory of the Historical Monuments in the City of Oxford*, Royal Comm. on Hist. Monuments, 1939, p. 62, and E. G. Hardy, *Jesus College*.
[2] C. H. Firth in the *D.N.B.* s.v. O. Cromwell.

would equip him to deal with the duties of a small land-
owner, rather than that he should make the law his profession. George Herbert, who regarded idleness as the worst
fault of the well-to-do, recommended that their sons should
pursue 'the study of the Civill Law', 'read Books of Law,
and Justice; especially, the Statutes at large'.[1] The Welsh
in that age were so much given to litigation, and Henry
Vaughan's father was himself so frequently concerned in
lawsuits, either initiated by himself or brought against
him, that this general knowledge may have been all that
was intended. A contemporary writer expresses just such
an intention:

I am not of the opinion of some of our Nobility and Gentry,
who, when their sons leave the Universities, omit the Innes of
Court, and send them beyond the Seas. Travail is a necessary
Accomplishment of a Gentleman, and an especial part of his
Education: but what is it to be conversant abroad, and a stranger
at home? These Innes of Court are vertuous and fruitfull
seminaries for the breeding of youth, where they study the
known Lawes of the Land and other noble exercises.[2]

Membership of one or other of the Inns was 'a certificate
of education and gentility equivalent to a university degree'.
Sir James Mackintosh says of the Inns in the sixteenth
century:

It was not then a metaphor to call them an university: they had
professors of law; they conferred the characters of barrister and
serjeant, analogous to the degrees of batchelor, master, and doctor,
bestowed by universities; and every man, before he became a
barrister, was subjected to examination, and obliged to defend
a thesis.[3]

Henry Vaughan's name cannot be found in the books
of any of the Inns of Court; nor indeed can Cromwell's,
though Heath says that he became a member of Lincoln's
Inn. In any case Vaughan's sojourn in London was not
long enough to procure him any considerable knowledge

[1] 'A Priest to the Temple', *Works of George Herbert*, Oxford English Texts,
1941, pp. 276–7.
[2] William Higford, *Institutions: or Advice to his Grandson*, Oxford, 1658,
pp. 58–9.
[3] *Life of Sir Thomas More*, 1831, p. 10.

of the law, and he was never called to the Bar. Whether he
studied the law seriously or not, it is evident from his
early poems, with their many reminiscences of the London
years, that he was principally interested in his introduction
to literary society and in the political events of the time,
which find a larger place in his writings than has been
generally recognized.

The latter half of 1640 was an exciting time for a young
man to make his first acquaintance with the greater world.
The atmosphere was charged with electricity and critical
events followed one another in quick succession. On 22
October the Court of High Commission met for the last
time, when a mob broke into the court-room and sacked
it. On 3 November the Long Parliament met and almost at
once proceeded to impeach Strafford on 11 November and
Laud on 18 December; Strafford was committed to the
Tower on 25 November and Laud on the following 1 March.
A commission was issued to deface and demolish images
and altars, the Commons passed the Bishops' Exclusion
Bill on 1 May 1641, and the Root and Branch Bill was
read in the Commons on the 27th. The Bill of Attainder
against Strafford, having passed the Commons on 21 April,
still awaited the decision of the Lords and the King, when
on 3 May a mob beset the House of Lords clamouring for
Strafford's blood. Five days later the Lords passed the
attainder, the King gave his assent on 10 May, after the
mob had howled outside Whitehall and threatened violence,
and on 12 May Strafford was executed on Tower Hill. The
part played by the mob is described by Sir Philip Warwick,
who was 31 years old at the time of Strafford's execution:

And to shew how mad this whole People were especially in and
about this then bloody and brutish City; in the evening of the daye
wherein he was executed, the greatest demonstrations of joy that
possibly could be exprest rann thro' the whole Town and
Countries hereabout; and many that came up to Town on purpose to see the execution rode in triumph back, waving their
hatts, and with all expressions of joy, through every Town they
went crying, 'His head is off! His head is off!', and in many
places committing insolencies upon, and breaking the windows

of those persons who would not solemnize this Festival with a bonfire. So ignorant and brutish is a multitude.[1]

The passage is quoted to show the kind of feeling which possessed young Vaughan. His detestation of 'the populacy', which is constantly found in his secular and even in his religious verse, dated from these events of 1641. Strafford's fate may even have occasioned, or at least affected, Vaughan's translation of Juvenal's tenth satire. Miss Guiney convinced herself that the long passage about the 'tumultuous fate' of Sejanus, which Vaughan elaborates, was in the translator's mind paralleled by Strafford's. The Duke of Buckingham had been compared to Sejanus by Eliot, speaking in the Commons' House in 1626,[2] but his assassination in 1628, when Vaughan was but 7 years of age, would have meant little to him. It was otherwise with the trial and execution of Strafford, the most arresting incident in Vaughan's short residence in London. A very obscure poet, S. Sheppard, in his poem 'On the Death of Strafford', apostrophizes him:

> Second Sejanus! In thy fall we see
> *Nosce teipsum* was not known to thee.[3]

It may, however, be objected that so fervid a royalist as Vaughan would have been slow to compare Strafford with a character so odious and disloyal as Sejanus, and still slower to hint at King Charles's ignoble sacrifice of his devoted minister. There was little resemblance between Strafford and Sejanus except that they were subjects who grew 'prodigious high' and that their sudden destruction was the occasion of wild popular rejoicing. Yet, without naming Strafford, the ardent young royalist could give to discerning readers an expression of his hatred of the Parliament and of popular passion. In the preface to *Poems*, in which the Satire appeared, Vaughan expressly relates his translation to 'the distractions of our own' state, and hopes that in its English dress it may wake his countrymen from that 'Nap'

---

[1] *Memoires of the Reigne of King Charles I*, 1701, p. 163. Warwick wrote his *Memoires* between 1675 and 1677.

[2] S. R. Gardiner, *Hist. Eng. 1603–42*, edn. 1883–4, vi. 105–7.

[3] *Epigrams*, 1651, book iv, Epigr. 39.

which they would have had, 'had it been still Latine'.[1]
Samuel Johnson could effectively substitute Wolsey for
Sejanus in his version of the same Satire, but Vaughan
means his friends to see its topicality.

Whether or no there is any contemporary allusion in his
Juvenal, Vaughan's preoccupation with political events is
clearly seen in the longest original poem in his first collection of verse. Besides the importance of 'A Rhapsodis.
Occasionally written upon a meeting with some of his
friends at the Globe Taverne'[2] for the light it throws on
Vaughan's literary associations and ambitions, it witnesses
also to his excited political feeling. The poem begins with
a description of the inn with its painted ceiling; it was
probably not the Globe in Southwark, but another tavern
with the same sign in Fleet Street, which is marked in
Hollar's map of 1647, and the allusions in the poem to
'Fleet Street, & the Strand' support this view. The poet
proposes three toasts, none of them literary as one might
have expected in a company which resembles that of the
'sons of Ben', but all of them highly political, though
couched in the safe obscurity of Roman history. The first
toast 'is to him That made his horse a Senatour'; contempt
for the Parliament could be no more outrageously expressed
than in recalling Caligula's memorable affront to the Senate.
The second is to Julius Caesar 'that like fire broke forth
Into the Senates face' and sent 'the dull gray beards & furr'd
gowns' flying into the city to take counsel—a rough and
none too historically accurate analogy to Charles I's attempt
on 4 January 1641/2 to arrest the five members, three of
whom were 'furr'd' lawyers of the Inner Temple, and the
flight of the Parliament men to renew their deliberations
in one obscure place after another away from the king's
observation. The last toast is to 'brave Sylla'. 'Why should
it be sed, We drinke more to the living, then the dead?'
There is little resemblance in the characters of Sulla and
Strafford, but it was enough for Vaughan that Sulla was
the upholder of the patrician class against the *populares*.
Clarendon was, later, to draw at any rate one comparison

[1] M 2.   [2] M 10.

to Sulla, when he wrote of Strafford's contempt for 'the People':

In a word, the Epitaph which *Plutarch* records that Sylla wrote for himself, may not be unfitly applied to him, 'That no man did ever exceed him, either in doing Good to his Friends, or in doing Mischief to his Enemies; for his acts of both kinds were most notorious'.[1]

Vaughan, besides having little historical sense, had, in early years at least, no political moderation; the young Welshman takes fire and expresses his hot indignation in the reckless language of a partisan. A similar passionate tone will appear in later secular poems and will even disturb the remote air of *Silex Scintillans* and his religious meditations in prose.

The 'Rhapsodis' has an even greater interest in revealing Vaughan's literary ambitions. At Oxford he may already have fallen under the spell of William Cartwright, a much admired poet, lecturer, and preacher. Jonson had said: 'My son Cartwright writes all like a man.' His play, *The Royall Slave. A Tragi-Comedy*, performed before the king and queen in Christ Church hall in 1636, was twice printed during Vaughan's Oxford years. He died of what was known as the camp disease, while serving the office of Proctor, in 1643 at the age of 32. Henry Vaughan's poem, 'Upon the *Poems* and *Playes* of the ever memorable Mr. William Cartwright',[2] appeared with very many others, including one by his brother Thomas, in the preliminary pages of Cartwright's *Poems* in 1651. Henry Vaughan had no personal acquaintance with him; his poem begins 'I did but *see* thee', echoing Ovid's *Virgilium vidi tantum*, but he may have heard him lecture, as Thomas certainly had, who says of his lectures: 'When he did read, how did we flock to hear.'[3] Henry borrowed many lines from Cartwright in his early poems, as from others of his contemporaries.

London would bring opportunities of meeting a larger circle of writers. Thomas Vaughan alluded to his brother's literary friends when, in his commendatory poem to *Olor Iscanus*, he begins by saying that the poet might have sum-

[1] *History of the Rebellion*, 1702–4, i. 204.   [2] M 55.
[3] 'On the Death of Mr. William Cartwright' (Waite, p. 476).

moned many others to introduce the volume to the world,
had he not been too proud to ask their help:

> I write not here, as if thy *last* in store
> Of learned *friends*, 'tis known that thou hast *more*;
> Who, were they told of this, would find a way
> To rise a guard of *Poets* without *pay*,
> And bring as many *hands* to thy *Edition*,
> As th' *City* should unto their *May'rs* Petition,
> But thou wouldst none of this, lest it should be
> Thy *Muster* rather, than our *Courtesie*.[1]

Almost all the contemporary poets whom Henry Vaughan
most admired and imitated may be counted among the
'sons of Ben'—Randolph, Cartwright, Cleveland, Davenant,
Habington, Carew. Of these Randolph alone was dead, and
Vaughan may have met any of the rest in London. He
may also have made the acquaintance of his fellow country-
man, James Howell, son of a Welsh clergyman. Howell,
Vaughan's senior by some 27 years, had been elected a Fellow of Jesus in 1623, though he did not reside after election.
It may have some significance that George Badger, who published Vaughan's first book, was probably related to Thomas
Badger[2] who printed Howell's first book, *Dodona's Grove*
(1640), for Humphrey Moseley, and Moseley was later to
publish three of Vaughan's books. There is, however, no
evidence of Vaughan's having met Howell; Howell never
mentions him in his *Familiar Letters*, and Vaughan never
mentions Howell.[3]

There can be little doubt that Vaughan's association with
other poets in London quickened his desire to 'commence
author', even if as yet he had little to write about, and was
content for a while frankly to imitate the poets of the day.
The slender volume, *Poems*, published in 1646, has many
borrowings, especially from Randolph, Cleveland, Cartwright, and Habington. Of the love-poems to Amoret more
will be said later, but even they are largely conventional.

[1] M 37.
[2] H. R. Plomer, *Dict. of Booksellers and Printers*, pp. 10–11.
[3] In spite of the absence of any evidence, Miss Guiney was disposed to
take Howell to be addressed in Vaughan's poem 'To his friend ——', beginning 'I wonder, *James*' (M 44).

'A Rhapsodis' shows that the poet had, at this stage of his life, some attraction to the congenial company of kindred spirits who 'After full Cups have dreames Poeticall' and look for inspiration to 'royall, witty Sacke, the Poets soule':

> Drink deep; this Cup be pregnant; & the wine
> Spirit of wit, to make us all divine,
> That big with Sack and mirth we may retyre
> Possessours of more soules, and nobler fire.[1]

This may be something of a pose, and he will soon leave all such life behind him without expressing any regret.

Besides the lively description of the disorderly London streets at night in 'A Rhapsodis', there are other humorous reminiscences of his London days in later poems. In a poem, probably written not earlier than 1646, 'Upon a Cloke lent him by Mr. *J. Ridsley*', he asks his friend:

> have you for two pence e're
> Seen King *Harryes* Chappell at *Westminster*,
> Where in their dustie gowns of *Brasse* and *Stone*
> The Judges lye, and markt you how each one
> In sturdie Marble-plets about the knee
> Bears up to shew his legs and symmetrie?[2]

Actually there are no monuments of judges in Henry VII's Chapel, but in the neighbouring Chapel of St. Paul are the Elizabethan lawyers, Sir Thomas Bromley and Sir John Puckering; they are in long gowns which show 'legs and symmetrie' hardly at all. Perhaps Vaughan remembers Donne's lines:

> At Westminster,
> Said I, The man that keepes the Abbey tombes,
> And for his price doth with who ever comes,
> Of all our Harries, and our Edwards talke,
> From King to King and all their kin can walke:
> Your eares shall heare nought, but Kings.[3]

It is likely enough that the theatre attracted Vaughan, though his poems on Fletcher's and Cartwright's plays need not mean that he had ever seen them acted. His poem 'Upon Mr. Fletchers Playes, published, 1647'[4] is a tribute

[1] M 10–12.   [2] M 53–4.
[3] Donne, *Sat.* iv. ll. 74–8 (Grierson's edn., i. 161).   [4] M 54.

to the plays at a time when the playhouses were closed by the Puritan government, and the allusion to actors—' 'Tis but for Field's or Swansteed's overthrow'—is historical rather than from Vaughan's own experience. He may have seen Elyard Swanston act, but Nathaniel Field died in 1633. Another well-known actor in Jonson's and Fletcher's plays was Barkstead, and it is possible that 'Swansteed' is Vaughan's inaccurate amalgam of Swanston and Barkstead.

There are few allusions to the law in Vaughan's poems, fewer than in Herbert's, and he gives no indication of its having any particular attraction for him. In any case, he was recalled home before he could have got far in its study.

IV
RETURN TO BRECONSHIRE

AUBREY has described what it meant to him to be fetched home from 'beloved Oxon' by his father because of the Civil War and his having had smallpox, and his feelings may not be unlike those of Henry Vaughan in similar circumstances:

> My father sent for me into the country again; where I conversed with none but servants and rustiques and soldiers quartred, to my great griefe (*Odi prophanum vulgus et arceo*), for in those dayes fathers were not acquainted with their children. It was a most sad life to me, then in the prime of my youth, not to have the benefitt of an ingeniose conversation and scarce any good bookes—almost a consumption. This sad life I did lead in the country till 1646, at which time I gott (with much adoe) leave of my father to lett me goe to the Middle Temple.[1]

Henry Vaughan was a little older than Aubrey, and he may have had more congenial neighbours than he, and, to judge from his wide reading, more access to books. But from what Aubrey says about the contemporary relations of fathers and children, it is to be feared that Vaughan did not find much companionship in his father. As has been already shown, his praise of his old schoolmaster appears to be at the expense of his father.[2] His brother Thomas was mostly in Oxford during these years, but the youngest brother William was at home, and to him Henry was greatly attached.

In answering Aubrey's queries thirty years later Vaughan has little to say of his life immediately after abandoning his legal studies 'which the sudden eruption of our late civil warres wholie frustrated'.[3] He says nothing of soldiering or other employment except for the books which he had published, omitting to include the *Poems* of 1646; at the time at which he writes, in 1673, he has practised physic 'now for

---

[1] *Brief Lives*, i. 38. [2] See above, p. 28, and M 93. [3] M 667.

many years'.[1] Wood, in his Latin history of 1674, perhaps
having nothing more to go upon than Vaughan's letters to
Aubrey, also does not mention any campaigning but describes him in words which may be Englished thus: 'Wholly
devoting himself to poetry and humane studies (*rei poeticae
et literarum humaniorum studio omnino deditus*) he ultimately
showed that those hours passed in the gardens of the
Muses were not utterly wasted, since he was able to show
his poetic faculty in certain specimens, one of which is
called *Olor Iscanus*.'[2] This account is omitted from the first
edition of *Athenae Oxonienses* (1691–2), but in the second
edition, 1721, Wood repeats the words of 1674 in an English
version, adding nothing further about those years. In both
accounts Wood states that 'afterwards' (*deinceps*), that is,
presumably, some time after publishing *Olor Iscanus* in 1651,
Vaughan turned to the study of medicine. But this idyllic
account of Vaughan's life in his twenties must be corrected
from what can be learnt from other sources.

Aubrey says of Vaughan that 'he was a clarke sometime
to Judge Sir Marmaduke Lloyd'.[3] Lloyd, son of a former
precentor and treasurer of St. Davids, had been appointed
in 1636 Chief Justice of the Great Sessions of Brecknockshire, Radnorshire, and Glamorganshire, that is, of the
Brecon circuit. Like most of the Welsh judges, he was an
active royalist, and was taken prisoner at the siege of Hereford in December 1645, heavily fined, and discharged from
his office as judge. His devotion to Church and King would
have appealed to young Henry Vaughan. He remained faithful to the Church even in her affliction, as is shown in his
will, proved in 1651: 'I hope onlie to bee saved in vera fide
Christiana Ecclesiae Anglicanae in qua natus fui *puer*; in
eadem vera fide *morior senex*.'[4] Vaughan's secretaryship to
Lloyd can only have been at longest from 1642 to 1645. It
has been suggested that he was prothonotary and Clerk of
the Crown, the recording officer at the Sessions, but it is

---

[1] M 668.   [2] *Hist. et Antiq.*, 1674, ii. 321 and *Ath. Oxon.*, 1721, ii. 926.
[3] Letter to Wood, 14 Mar. 1671/2 and *Brief Lives*, ii. 269.
[4] *Lloyd Records and Pedigrees*, ed. Theakston and Davies, 1912, p. 30, *cit. ap.*
T. Richards, *A History of the Puritan Movement in Wales*, p. 138.

known that this office was held by one Thomas Hughes
from 1634 till his death in 1664.[1] Vaughan's youth (he was
only about 23) and his slender knowledge of the law would
hardly have qualified him for such a responsible position.

To the first few years after his return home belongs the
preparation and publication of his first volume, *Poems*,
which was registered at Stationers' Hall on 15 September
1646. So slight a volume need not, indeed, have occupied
much of his time or prevented him from secretarial or
military duties. Apart from 'Iuvenals tenth Satyre Englished', which takes up almost half the book, there is
little enough in it to employ his time. Some of the poems,
as has already been shown, belong to his Oxford and
London years, especially the two longest, the opening poem
'To my Ingenuous Friend, *R. W.*', which refers either to
Oxford or London, and 'A Rhapsodis' which deals with
London. The remaining eleven poems are all of love and
courtship. The tone of the defiant little preface is exclusively
literary. There is no allusion to the war, and he could only
speak of 'these dull Times' if at the time of writing he was
taking no active part in the war. He is contemptuous of the
criticism of the general public and asks indulgence only of
the inner circle of poets and scholars who know Plato and
the literature of ancient Rome; 'It is for you only that I have
adventured thus far, and invaded the Presse with *Verse*.'[2]

The love-poems are almost all addressed expressly to
Amoret. It was a name much used by the poets for a lady-
love. Browne wrote of his 'lovely Amorett', Lovelace has
his Chloris and Amoret, and Spenser has Amoret for a
heroine. Lodge in his *Rosalynde* would 'pass away the time
in these woods with writing amorets'. Edmund Waller,
Vaughan's senior by fifteen years, included in his *Poems*

---

[1] W. R. Williams, *Hist. of the Great Sessions in Wales*, 1899, p. 156; cf.
Cal. S. P. D. 1653–4, p. 458. 'Two Petitions of Mr. Vaughan and Mr. Jones for
Two Prothonotaries Places' were sent by the Lords to the Commons on
3 Jan. 1645/6 (*Journal of the House of Commons*, iv. 395). It is unlikely that so
uncompromising a royalist as Henry Vaughan would have petitioned the
Parliament, and the Vaughan who petitioned in 1645/6 is almost certainly
the Rice Vaughan who petitioned successfully on 16 Mar. 1653/4 for the
office of prothonotary in the counties of Montgomery and Denbigh (Cal.
S.P.D. 1653–4, p. 94). [2] M 2.

(1645) a poem entitled 'Amoret! the Milky Way'; its fifth line 'Amoret! my lovely foe!' is perhaps responsible for Vaughan's using the words 'my lovely foe' in his first poem to Amoret, although this notion of the loved one being cruel was a convention followed by Carew, Suckling, and others. There are also borrowings from Randolph and Felltham.

Far more remarkable is Vaughan's indebtedness to William Habington's *Castara*.[1] The older poet, protesting 'the innocency of a chaste Muse', had expressed in his preface his adherence to strict chastity of thought and word:

In all those flames in which I burnt, I never felt a wanton heate, nor was my invention ever sinister from the straite way of chastity.

Vaughan gave a similar assurance in his preface:

You have here a *Flame*, bright only in its owne *Innocence*, that kindles nothing but a generous *Thought*; which though it may warme the Bloud, the fire at highest is but *Platonick*, and the *Commotion*, within these limits, excludes *Danger*.[2]

Vaughan's later manner of adopting or imitating George Herbert's fanciful titles is anticipated in his following of Habington's. His titles are remarkably close to those used by Habington, who has, for instance, 'To Castara, upon a sigh', 'To Castara, Looking Back at her Departing', 'Upon Castara's Absence', 'To Castara, Weeping', 'To Castara: How Happy, though in an Obscure Fortune', 'To Castara, being to Take a Journey'.[3] But his likeness to Habington goes far beyond a following of titles and themes. Habington had broken with the Petrarchan tradition of celebrating in verse some lady other than the poet's betrothed or his lawful wife. Mary Herbert was already his wife before he published *Castara*, and it is probable that Vaughan's *Poems* celebrate not only his courtship of Catherine Wise but also his marriage.

The likeness to Habington is increased if we may identify the Amoret of *Poems* with the Etesia to whom love-poems are addressed in *Thalia Rediviva*, which certainly contains

---

[1] *Castara*, parts I and II, 1634; 'corrected and augmented', 1635; with a third part, 1640. [2] M 2. [3] Cf. M 5, 8, 13, 626-7.

much of Vaughan's early work. The tone in the Amoret and Etesia poems is the same, and often even the circumstances are similar or identical, and the expression the same. In 'To Amoret, Walking in a Starry Evening'[1] he compares her face to a star that 'had shin'd from farre', and in 'The Character, to Etesia' he declares

> Thou art the dark worlds Morning-star,
> Seen only, and seen but from far.[2]

There is a much more remarkable parallel. The last of the poems in the 1646 volume, 'Upon the Priorie Grove, His usuall Retyrement', begins:

> Haile sacred shades! coole, leavie House!
> Chaste Treasurer of all my vowes,
> And wealth! on whose soft bosome layd
> My loves faire steps I first betrayd.[3]

And later in the poem he addresses the Grove as the place where 'Thou first didst eye our growth, and birth'; that is, it witnessed the beginning and the culmination of their attachment. Evidently it was while he lay on the 'soft bosome' of the Priory Grove lawns that his future wife's 'faire steps' approached him unawares, and there later they plighted their troth, so that the Grove will be for ever 'sacred' to him. In 'To Etesia going beyond Sea' he tells her that in her absence

> Now to those happy *Shades* I'le go
> Where first I saw my beauteous Foe.
> I'le seek each silent *path*, where we
> Did walk, and where you sate with me
> I'le sit again, and never rest
> Till I can find some *flow'r* you prest.[4]

It is an almost inevitable inference that both poems celebrate the poet's first meeting with his future wife in the Priory Grove and the plighting of their troth in its walks. The Priory Grove is the extensive ground, still richly wooded and with the Honddu flowing through it, belonging to the house of Brecon Priory, the home of the Prices. Colonel Herbert Price's ancestors had acquired the Priory, except

[1] M 7.   [2] M 624.   [3] M 15.
[4] M 626–7. Vaughan had called Amoret also 'my lovely foe' (M 5).

the church, which became the parish church, at or soon after the Dissolution. His wife Goditha was a daughter of Sir Henry Arden of Park Hall in the county of Warwick, a near neighbour and perhaps a kinsman of Richard Wise of Gilsdon Hall, Coleshill. Vaughan was to marry in succession Catherine and Elizabeth, daughters of Richard Wise and his wife Lucy, daughter of Sir Charles Egerton. It may be significant of relationship between the Egerton and Arden families that Richard Wise also had a daughter Goditha, whose baptism in 1640 and burial in 1658 are recorded in the Coleshill parish register. It is not known how Vaughan became acquainted with the Warwickshire family, but it is a reasonable surmise that he first met Catherine Wise when she was staying with the Prices at Brecon Priory. We may also note that the Priory Grove would hardly be 'His usuall Retyrement' unless he was at the time residing in the county town. Possibly his duties as secretary to Judge Lloyd took him there, though there is no apparent reason why the judge of a circuit including three counties should have his office or a house at Brecon.

Some of the verses in *Poems* are as frigid as Habington's, and read like early exercises on conventional lines with the thought that the loved one's cruelty will be the death of him ('her beauty murther'd mee'). Other poems take a warmer tone, and 'To Amoret gone from him'[1] is delightful. In 'To Amoret, Walking in a Starry Evening' he expresses his growing conviction that 'Twixt thee, and me' there is 'some predestin'd sympathie'.[2] Even if he should die and his loved one should accept another suitor, he declares his fidelity in 'A Song to Amoret', not at all in the light tone of a Suckling:

> Fortune and beauty thou mightst finde,
>   And greater men then I:
> But my true resolved minde,
>   They never shall come nigh.
>
> For I not for an houre did love,
>   Or for a day desire,
> But with my soule had from above,
>   This endles holy fire.[3]

[1] M 8.   [2] M 7.   [3] M 9.

Just so Habington had told his Castara:

> But there was something from above
> Shot without reasons guide, this fire.[1]

And in another poem he declared that 'vertuous love is one sweet endlesse fire'.[2]

It is arguable that Vaughan's resemblance to Habington goes farther still, in celebrating married love as well as courtship. 'Etesia absent'[3] seems to be addressed to a wife, and still more does 'To Amoret Weeping', in which, after admitting and facing his lack of worldly goods, Vaughan concludes:

> I envy no mans purse or mines; I know,
> That loosing them, I've lost their curses too;
> And, *Amoret*, (although our share in these
> Is not contemptible, nor doth much please)
> Yet whilst Content, and Love we joyntly vye,
> We have a blessing which no gold can buye.[4]

The words 'our share' are more naturally used of those who have already joined their fortunes than of those who only intend to do so. If this inference is rightly drawn, Henry Vaughan was already married to Catherine Wise before he published his *Poems* in 1646. In a Chancery action brought by Thomas, his only son by this first marriage, nearly fifty years later the son alleged that his father sought the hand of Catherine Wise 'well knowing her to have a considerable marriage portion as well in money as in plate, jewels, etc.'[5] Whether this statement, made at a time when the son was at law with his father, was justified or not, there are no means of judging. Besides their son Thomas, Henry and Catherine Vaughan had three daughters: Lucy, Frances, and Catherine. The exquisite little poem, 'The Burial of an Infant',[6] may commemorate the loss of a child who died in infancy.

---

[1] William Habington, *Castara*, ed. Arber, 1895, p. 24.
[2] Ibid., p. 80.   [3] M 627.   [4] M 14.
[5] Chanc. Pro., Mitford 355. 174, 5 July 1693.
[6] *Silex Scintillans*, 1650, M 450.

V

MILITARY SERVICE

THE question whether Henry Vaughan bore arms in the Civil Wars has been much discussed ever since his first modern editor, Henry Francis Lyte, a hundred years ago, inferred from the autobiographical poem 'Ad Posteros', prefixed to *Olor Iscanus*, that the poet 'expressly asserts that he had then nothing to do with open warfare' and 'conscientiously abstained from meeting in the field his infatuated countrymen', though he would advocate his sovereign's cause 'by every means which he deemed legitimate'.[1] Sir Edmund Chambers suggests that 'Ad Posteros' may have been written before 1645, but this would hardly excuse Vaughan's allowing it to be printed without alteration in 1651, if since writing it he had actually engaged in military service.[2] And if, as Sir Edmund also suggests, Vaughan means only that he had no part in bringing about the Civil War, it would be a superfluous disavowal by one who was only twenty-one when the war began.

In 'Ad Posteros', after describing his childhood and schooling, Vaughan alludes to the *tempora dura* in which his early manhood was spent, when 'the raging furies of presbyter and people' had destroyed English unity, ravaged the fair and peaceful countryside, and laid low 'the sacred Rose' —a description of King Charles often used by Cavaliers. He

---

[1] *Sacred Poems and Private Ejaculations*, by Henry Vaughan. With a Memoir by the Rev. H. F. Lyte, 1847, p. xviii. Lyte deserves to be remembered with gratitude for having reintroduced Vaughan's sacred poems, which had not been reprinted since 1655. The facts of the poet's life were little known to Lyte and his contemporaries. The opinion that Vaughan was a combatant has recently been well argued by E. L. Marilla, 'Henry Vaughan and the Civil War', *Journal of English and Germanic Philology*, Urbana, Illinois, Oct. 1942. Before seeing his article I had marshalled the evidence in a similar way, with necessarily the same instances, except that I had added the references to blood-guilt in Vaughan's later writings, which Mr. Marilla did not include in his survey.

[2] *Poems of Henry Vaughan*, ed. E. K. Chambers, 1896, II. xxx.

wishes posterity to know where he had stood in the great
national crisis and he concludes:

> Duret ut *Integritas* tamen, & *pia gloria*, partem
>   Me nullam in tantâ *strage* fuisse, scias;
> Credidimus nempè insonti *vocem* esse Cruori,
>   Et *vires* quae post funera *flere* docent.
> Hinc *Castae fidaeque* pati me more *parentis*
>   Commonui, & Lachrymis *fata* levare meis;
> Hinc nusquàm horrendis violavi *Sacra* procellis,
>   Nec mihi *mens* unquàm, nec *manus* atra fuit.
> Si *pius* es, ne plura petas; *Satur* Ille recedat
>   Qui *sapit*, & nos non Scripsimus *Insipidis*.[1]

The last two lines indicate that he writes, not for fools whom
he despises, but for understanding friends who can read
between the lines; and, to escape hostile notice or prosecution, he is being deliberately obscure. If he intended obscurity, he certainly succeeded, as the interpretation is far
from clear. If it were not for evidence, yet to be considered,
the natural interpretation of the first four lines here quoted
is that Vaughan is glad to have borne no part in 'that great
overthrow' (*in tantâ strage*) of Charles and the Church and to
have shed no 'innocent blood'. Recalling the Divine reproof
of Cain—'What hast thou done? the voice of thy brother's
blood crieth unto me from the ground'—he avows his own
belief that 'innocent blood had a voice to speak and a power
to draw tears after death'.[2]

The view that Vaughan congratulates himself on having
himself caused no bloodshed, even of the king's enemies,
receives some support from the many allusions which he
makes in later writings to his horror of blood-guiltiness. The
final prayer in *The Mount of Olives*, 'A Prayer in adversity, and
troubles occasioned by our Enemies', includes these words:

Thou seest, O God, how furious and Implacable mine Enemies

---

[1] M 32.
[2] Mr. Blunden's translation of the second line, 'In this great ravenous heat
I had no part', seems hardly to give full weight to *strage*, which is likely to
mean the overthrow of the established order in Church and State. Mr. Marilla
translates it 'I was no part of so great an overthrow', and he thinks that, to
the friendly and initiated, it might also convey a suggestion of the 'slaughter'
of King Charles.

are, they have not only rob'd me of that portion and provision which thou hadst graciously given me, but they have also washed their hands in the blood of my friends, my dearest and nearest relatives. I know, O my God, and I am daily taught by that disciple whom thou did'st love, that no murderer hath eternal life abiding in him. Keep me therefore, O my God, from the guilt of blood, and suffer me not to stain my soul with the thoughts of recompense and vengeance, which is a branch of thy great prerogative, and belongs wholly unto thee.[1]

This may mean no more than that Vaughan, with his new and deepened sense of Christian ideals, puts from him any thoughts of such revenge as a renewal of war might effect, although he has suffered grievous losses by the Puritan victory. The words must not, however, be given too slight a meaning, because his horror of bloodshed is repeatedly expressed in *Silex Scintillans*, especially in the second part, 1655, when he had had time to reflect more deeply upon the nature of civil war. Already in the first part, 1650, in 'The Constellation', the phrase 'Thus by our lusts disorder'd into war', based on James iv. 1, appears by his use of the word *our* to throw the blame not on the Puritans alone.[2] Towards the end of the second part the theme of blood-guilt keeps recurring in a series of poems. In 'Righteousness' he answers the question 'Who is the man that walks in thee?' by saying that it is one 'Who spills no blood', 'Who knows earth nothing hath Worth love or wrath', and

> Who seeks and follows peace,
> When with the ease
> And health of conscience it is to be had.

> Who bears his cross with joy
> And doth imploy
> His heart and tongue in prayers for his foes.[3]

In 'Abel's blood' he is thankful to have been 'kept From bloody men'.[4] In 'The Men of War', after quoting from Revelation xiii. 10—'He that killeth with the sword, must be

[1] M 167.   [2] M 470, l. 45.   [3] M 525, ll. 34–9.
[4] M 524, l. 28.

killed with the sword. Here is the patience and the faith of the Saints'—he continues:

> Were not thy word (dear Lord!) my light,
> How would I run to endless night,
> And persecuting thee and thine,
> Enact for *Saints* my self and mine. . . .
> Thy Saints are not the Conquerers; . . .
> The sword wherewith thou dost command
> Is in thy mouth, not in thy hand,
> And all thy Saints do overcome
> By thy blood, and their Martyrdom.[1]

A similar horror of bloodshed is expressed in 'The Rainbow' ('the first sin was in *Blood*') and in 'Jacobs Pillow, and Pillar'.[2] Vaughan may, indeed, mean that the shedding of 'innocent blood' was the crime of the Puritans only, who offend him the more by arrogating to themselves the name of Saints, and that the blood of the king's enemies, shed in the Civil War, was not 'innocent' but rightfully spilt in a just cause. It is noteworthy that Thomas Vaughan, though he bore arms for the king, uses almost identical language, when, in defining the Christian way of life, he says: 'Above all Things, avoyd the *Guilt of innocent Blood*.'[3] Upon the morrow of the Civil War there was, no doubt, a fairly widespread revulsion of feeling among those who had taken part on either side in the slaughter of their fellow countrymen, and who in retrospect wondered if there could not have been a better way of determining civil disputes. Charles I had no more loyal adherent than Lord Capel, who, when he died on the scaffold five weeks after his royal master, uttered these words:

God Almighty stench, stench, stench this issue of blood. This will not do the business! God Almighty finde out another way to do it![4]

Some writers have (wrongly, I think) believed themselves to find evidence of Henry Vaughan's indifference to the national contention. It must be admitted that there is a rather strange aloofness in his first book, published in the

[1] M 516.   [2] M 509 and 527. Cf. 'The Bee', ll. 63–78 (M 653).
[3] *Anima Magica Abscondita*, 1650, p. 52 (Waite, p. 115).
[4] *Royall and Loyall Blood*, 1662, p. 28.

fourth year of the war. The theme of most of the poems
being courtship, there is no occasion for introducing the
national cause. Except for the possible allusions in the
translation of Juvenal, which have already been discussed,[1]
there appears to be only one reference: in 'To Amoret
Weeping', after referring to his having lost his means of
support, he thanks Heaven for its having at any rate saved
him from the responsibilities of wealth:

> For I (had I been rich) as sure as fate,
> Would have bin medling with the King, or State,
> Or something to undoe me.[2]

And in the preface the air of detachment is marked. If anyone finds fault with his pursuing his 'more calme *Ambition*,
amidst the common noise', this young man of less than five
and twenty scorns to answer: 'If any shall question that
Courage that durst send me abroad so late, and revell it thus
in the *Dregs* of an Age, they have my silence.'[3] There is
a similar detachment in a much later poem, written within
a few weeks of the king's execution. He invites a friend to
'steal A Revell in the Town':

> blith (as of old) let us
> 'Midst noise and War, of Peace and mirth discusse.
> This portion thou wert born for: why should wee
> Vex at the times ridiculous miserie?
> An age that thus hath fool'd it selfe, and will
> (Spite of thy teeth and mine) persist so still.[4]

These lines have drawn upon Vaughan the grave censure of
Whittier, writing during the American Civil War:

> Olor Iscanus queries: 'Why should we
> Vex at the land's ridiculous miserie?'
> So on his Usk banks, in the blood-red dawn
> Of England's civil strife, did careless Vaughan
> Bemock his times. . . .
> Not thus we trifle with our country's tears
> And sweat of agony.[5]

Courthope, too, finds in the tone of Vaughan's poems the
'epicurean indifference' of 'a mere spectator' of the troubles

---

[1] See above, pp. 42–3. [2] M 14, ll. 43–5. [3] M 2.
[4] 'To his retired friend, an Invitation to Brecknock', ll. 75–80 (M 47).
[5] *Poetical Works*, Oxford edn., 1915, p. 364. From *In War Time*, 1863.

of the time, and the marks of 'a bad citizen'.[1] But this is
heavy-handed criticism of so light-hearted a *poème de circon-
stance*. It will be no small part of my portrayal of Henry
Vaughan to show from his own words how passionately
concerned he was with the fortunes of Church and State,
but there are occasions when he must find relief from
despondency in the society of an equal and hide his griefs.
His attitude in 'An Invitation to Brecknock' is not unlike
Michael Drayton's:

> Because I loosely tryfle in this sorte,
> As one that fain his sorrowes wo'd beguile,
> You now suppose me al this time in sport
> And please yourself with this conceipt the while. . . .
> Where other men in depth of passione cry,
> I laugh at Fortune, as in jest to dy.[2]

It was worth while to consider these occasional utterances
of Vaughan, which seem to indicate both an initial dis-
inclination to bear arms, and, when the war was over, the
misgivings which overtook him like many other English-
men, but they cannot stand against the evidence of the war-
poems in *Olor Iscanus*. Here he praised unreservedly those
who took up arms for the royal cause, and censured those
who abstained from such action, profiting by 'The sweat
and tears of others',[3] and those who 'quitted action, to their
shame'.[4] Almost certainly he saw military service, at any
rate in the autumn and early winter of 1645. There are two
elegies on friends of his who fell fighting. The first commemorates the 'loyall upright life, and gallant End' of R.W.,
who died, before reaching the age of twenty, in the royalist
defeat at Rowton Heath, near Chester, in September 1645.
The poet did not receive confirmation of his friend's death
till a year later, and the manner of his death remained unknown.[5] In the field R. W. had displayed the utmost dash;
he moved like lightning, and

> like *shott* his active hand
> Drew bloud, e'r well the foe could understand.

---

[1] *Hist. of English Poetry*, iii. 237–8.   [2] *Poems*, 1605: 'Idea', sonnet xxiv.
[3] 'An Elegie on the death of Mr. R. W.', l. 43 (M 50).
[4] 'An Elegie on the death of Mr. R. Hall', l. 31 (M 58).
[5] M 50, ll. 50–65.

'In all the doubtfull way *Conscience* and *Honour* rul'd him.'
Vaughan modestly hopes that his verse may 'do more To
keep thy name and memory in store' than the monument
which he lacked; but his name is unfortunately lost to us,
and no research has succeeded in identifying R. W.[1]

The second elegy is for R. Hall who was killed at the siege
of Pontefract, perhaps some little time before its surrender
on 22 March 1648/9, during one of the famous sallies made
by men of Colonel Morris's garrison. A report dated before
the surrender states: 'From Pontefract I heare the valiant
Cavalliers act their Parts to the Rebells admiration: they
take constant sallies and beate up their Guards daily.'[2] It is
just such a sortie that Vaughan describes:

> Nor is't a Common valour we deplore,
> But such as with *fifteen* a *hundred* bore,
> And lightning like (not coopt within a wall)
> In stormes of *fire* and *steele* fell on them all. . . .
> The fair and open valour was thy *shield*,
> And thy known station, the *defying field*.[3]

Vaughan portrays his friend as one in whom '*Piety* and
Learning did unite', who yet deserted books for arms, and
crowned his service with 'Martyrdome'—'In thy own bloud
a *Souldier* and a *Saint*'.[4]

---

[1] The R.W. of this elegy is not the same as the R.W. to whom the opening
poem of the 1646 volume is addressed. The latter is an Oxford contemporary
of Vaughan's, who would be about 24 in 1645, while the R.W. killed at
Rowton Heath is less than 'a full score' (l. 27). The latter is a 'deare wit',
the R.W. of the elegy 'possess'd a solid skull'. There is no evidence of any
R.W. of suitable age in the families of Wise, Walbeoffe, or Wynter. Other conjectures, which do not seem to me probable, are named in Chambers, ii. 338.

[2] *Mercurius Pragmaticus*, no. 44, 17 Feb. to 5 Mar. 1648/9.

[3] M 59, ll. 37-40 and 47-8.

[4] Among the sallies from Pontefract described in a letter dated 8 Oct. 1648
(T. Carte, *A Collection of Original Letters*, 1739, i. 177), is the following: 'A
party of 16 horse charged and routed 140 of the Enemies horse and killed
and took several of them, with the loss of one (yet a gallant man), Dr. Hall,
a Clergyman, and a valiant active man in arms for that garrison, whose death
is very much lamented.' Several allusions in this poem (ll. 25-36, 49-58,
73-4) suggest that R. Hall was a clergyman, though the 'Gown' (l. 34) would
also fit a lawyer. I cannot trace any Hall of suitable age in Foster's or Venn's
Alumni, but this seems a better identification than with the Halls of High
Meadow in the Forest of Dean (Chambers, ii. 339), between whom and the
Vaughans no connexion has been established, except that they were in some
way related to the Wynters.

The two elegies and the poem 'Upon a Cloke lent him by
Mr. *J. Ridsley*[1] go far to justify Thomas Powell's description
of Henry Vaughan as 'a young Tyrtaeus',[2] like the bard who
heartened the Spartans by his war-songs in the Second
Mycenaean War. There were probably other war-poems in
Olor Iscanus as it was first projected,[3] but they were perhaps
omitted because of their pronounced royalism. There is,
then, clear evidence of Vaughan's ardent support of the
royal cause. The evidence is only less clear of his having
borne arms. It must surely be as an eyewitness and a
participator in the Rowton Heath battle of 24 September
1645 that he wrote of R. W.:

> O that day
> When like the *Fathers* in the *Fire* and *Cloud*
> I mist thy face! I might in ev'ry *Crowd*
> See Armes like thine, and men advance, but none
> So neer to lightning mov'd, nor so fell on. . . .
> But here I lost him. Whether the last turn
> Of thy few sands call'd on thy hastie urn,
> Or some fierce rapid fate (hid from the Eye)
> Hath hurl'd thee Pris'ner to some distant skye
> I cannot tell, but that I doe believe
> Thy Courage such as scorn'd a base Reprieve.[4]

There is even clearer evidence of Vaughan's military
service in the humorous poem to Ridsley on returning him
a voluminous cloak with 'stiffe, hollow pletes' and wire
supports, serviceable for a campaign but too fantastic for
civil wear. Vaughan tells how he had lain one night naked,
'Pure Adamite', wrapped in the cloak; its 'villanous, biting,
Wire-embraces' had by morning marked his body with
strange '*Characters* and *Hierogliphicks*'. His friend, he says,
would have laughed to see him in it as it served to protect
him on the stormy winter's day when the garrison of

---

[1] M 52.
[2] Commendatory verses prefixed to *Thalia Rediviva*, M 598.
[3] See below, pp. 73-5.
[4] M 50-1, ll. 50-5, 61-6. There was a Captain Vaughan among the
prisoners taken at Rowton Heath (J. R. Phillips, *The Civil War in Wales*, ii.
272; cf. Chambers, ii. xxxii), but this can hardly be the poet if he was in the
garrison of Beeston Castle six weeks after, nor is there any allusion extant to
his brother Thomas's having ever been a prisoner of war.

Beeston Castle surrendered after two months' siege, and were allowed to march out with drums beating and to cross the Dee on their way to Denbigh:

> Hadst thou been with me on that day, when wee
> Left craggie *Biston*, and the fatall *Dee*,
> When beaten with fresh storms, and late mishap
> It shar'd the office of a *Cloke*, and *Cap* . . .
> I know thou wouldst in spite of that day's fate
> Let loose thy mirth at my new shape and state.[1]

The cloak served him so well that day that he wished he had had it earlier:

> O that thou hadst it when this Jugling fate
> Of Soulderie first seiz'd me! at what rate
> Would I have bought it then, what was there but
> I would have giv'n for the *Compendious hutt*![2]

But now, at the time of writing, he has no further use for it; Ridsley, he suggests, should sell it to a pedlar to serve him with a roof to protect his wares on a fair-day when it rains 'Dogs and Cats', or to an ale-wife who might make it a tent for two.

The elegy on 'R. Hall, slain at Pontefract, 1648' does not suggest the poet's participation in that siege which ended two months after the king's execution, but he draws on memories of what he has seen elsewhere when he contrasts Hall's daring with the comparative security of soldiers in protected positions:

> Thou wert no *Wool-sack* souldier, nor of those
> Whose Courage lies in *winking* at their foes,
> That live at *loop-holes*, and consume their breath
> On *Match* or *Pipes*, and sometimes *peepe* at death.[3]

This reads like a campaigner's reminiscence.

It may then be safely inferred from the war-poems in *Olor Iscanus* that Henry Vaughan, like his brother Thomas, saw military service.[4] The poems show that, at any rate at the

---

[1] M 52, ll. 19–22 and 27–8.   [2] M 54, ll. 85–8.   [3] M 59, ll. 41–4.
[4] Miss Morgan had at one time sought to reconcile the evidence of the war-poems with 'Ad Posteros' by suggesting that Vaughan was present in the Chester campaign as a physician, but in a letter to Miss Guiney, dated

time of writing them, which is 1651 at the latest, he commended combatant service with a good conscience. After
the defeat at Naseby on 14 June 1645 the king came to
Wales in the hope of raising recruits. He met the gentlemen
of Monmouthshire at Usk on 25 July, and on the following
5 August he spent the night at Brecon Priory as the guest of
Colonel Herbert Price. The outlook depressed him and
from Brecon he wrote on that day to his son Charles,
advising him to go to France rather than fall into the
enemy's hands; he finds his 'affaires in extremitie'—'It is
very fit for me to prepare for the worst'. The citizens of
Brecon had pulled down their city walls in order to
become an open town. This act must have been as repugnant to Price, the governor of the castle, as it was to
Vaughan, who complains of it to his 'retired friend' on
inviting him to Brecknock:

> Thou'ldst swear (like *Rome*) her foule, polluted walls
> Were sackt by *Brennus*, and the salvage *Gaules*.[1]

If Henry Vaughan had not already enlisted, he might well
have been moved to do so when King Charles came to
Brecon. And it would be natural for him to serve under
Colonel Price. 'As a rule', says Sir Charles Firth, 'the regiments raised for his [the king's] service seem to have been
equipped at the expense of their officers, and they were
generally raised in the district where the colonel's estates
lay.'[2] 'As neither the regiments of horse or foot were distinguished by numbers, each was officially designated by the
name of the colonel, and was called Colonel So-and-so's
regiment.'[3] The only evidence of Vaughan's soldiering,
apart from the war-poems, is a 'List of officers claiming
to the Sixty Thousand Pounds granted by his Sacred
Majesty for the relief of his truly loyal and indigent party',
dated 4 February 1662/3.[4] In this list occur the following

---

28 Mar. 1910, she wrote: 'I have quite given up my theory that Vaughan was
present at Rowton Heath as a surgeon, for I am sure that he did not turn to
the study of medicine till some years later.'
[1] M 46, ll. 13–14.   [2] C. H. Firth, *Cromwell's Army*, 1902, p. 19.
[3] Ibid., p. 46.
[4] State Papers Domestic, Car. II, 1663, vol. 68, no. 19.

among other names: 'Price, Sir Herbert (company of) . . .
Brecon. Vaughan, Hen., L. to Capt. Barth. Price . . . Brecon.
Prees, Will, Lieut. to Cap. Tho. Vaughan.' It seems safe to
identify Lieutenant Henry Vaughan of Brecon with the poet
and Captain Thomas Vaughan with his brother, all the more
certainly because the king's forces at Chester on 23 September
1645 included 'Col. Herbert Price his horse'.[1] The maintenance of Chester was vital to the royal cause; if it were to give
in, the king's hold on north Wales would be imperilled. On
24 September, the day after he had entered the city, King
Charles viewed from the Phœnix Tower on the city walls
the battle of Rowton Heath fought about two miles to the
south-east of the Chester fortifications. On the day after the
fight, which had begun well but had ended disastrously with
heavy losses, the king left Chester and by 1 November was
back in Oxford.

The little garrison at Beeston Castle, about nine miles to
the south-east of Chester, held out only a little longer. A
contemporary describes the castle as standing 'very loftily
and proudly upon an exceeding steep and high rock'. It had
been besieged on and off for nearly a year. Prince Rupert
had relieved it on 11 March 1644/5,[2] but it was again heavily
invested in the autumn and was obliged to surrender on
16 November, when the garrison was allowed to march out,
as Vaughan has told in his poem.

Only a few days before the surrender of Beeston,
Vaughan's native county, which had hitherto escaped the
actualities of war, experienced them for the first time.
Major-General Laugharne, in his successful prosecution of
the Parliamentary arms, entered Breconshire and made his
way to Brecon, where he was well received. The Castle,
under a deputy governor in the absence of Colonel Price,
could hold out for a few days only, and by the middle of
November the whole county was reduced and ordered to
pay £120 a week to the Parliamentary cause. A week later
34 of the leading gentry of the county, including many who

[1] R. Symonds, *Diary of the Marchings of the Royal Army*, Camden Soc.,
1859, p. 242.
[2] S. R. Gardiner, *Hist. of the Great Civil War*, 1889, ii. 139.

had supported the royal cause, signed a declaration of loyalty
to the Parliament.[1]

It remains to consider whether Henry Vaughan had had
any experience of soldiering before the Chester campaign.
His allusion to 'this Jugling fate Of Soulderie' that 'first
seiz'd' him[2] makes it probable that he had been serving for
some little while before. He cannot have enlisted at the outbreak of the war as he became secretary to Judge Lloyd after
his return home from London. Moreover, in the earlier
years of the war Breconshire had escaped close contact with
the fighting, and no armies of either side passed up the vale
of Usk. The nobility and gentry of south Wales, with the
notable exception of the Earl of Pembroke, were of strongly
royalist sympathies, but the people were apathetic and the
recruiting efforts were disappointing. No pamphlets were
issued in Welsh on the issues between King and Parliament.[3]
South Wales was not exposed, as north Wales was, to the
excitement caused by the king's visits in 1642 to the Border
towns, Chester and Shrewsbury, and to Wrexham. Sir
Edward Stradling of Glamorganshire is said to have brought
a thousand men from north Wales to the battle of Edgehill
which was fought on 23 October 1642, but they were
miserably armed and were mostly killed or taken prisoners.
By 1644 Welsh ardour for the royal cause was beginning to
cool off; there was much resentment at the constant heavy
exactions of money, the royalist raids on cattle and other
goods, and the way in which Colonel Gerrard rode rough-
shod over Welshmen, refusing them high command in the
army. There was also considerable dread of the soldiers
whom Lord Herbert, the son of the old Earl of Worcester,
was bringing from Ireland. Before the end of the year the
Parliamentarians were fast making headway in the Principality, and many of the leading Welsh royalists were losing
heart and drifting towards neutrality.

At the battle of Naseby on 14 June 1645 the king's infantry, 'Welshmen for the most part', were poorly equipped

[1] Phillips, i. 338–9; ii. 284.
[2] 'Upon a Cloke lent him by Mr. J. Ridsley', ll. 85–6 (M 54).
[3] Phillips, i. 24, 32, 98.

and were killed or captured 'almost to a man', and the prisoners were taken to London to grace a triumph through the crowded streets. 'Most of these unfortunate men were of Welsh origin.'[1] Henry Vaughan is not likely to have served with the Welsh infantry at Edgehill or Naseby. It is, however, possible that he had served in Colonel Price's regiment of horse for some time before the autumn campaign of 1645. In the preface to her interesting historical novel, *The Swan of Usk* (1940), Miss Helen Ashton acknowledges the help she has derived from 'some of Miss Morgan's unpublished material', but she goes beyond the evidence in stating that Miss Morgan's discovery of the list of officers claiming compensation in 1663 shows that Henry Vaughan 'enlisted in Sir Herbert Price's Regiment at the outbreak of the Civil War and served throughout with this regiment'. There is no evidence in Miss Morgan's collection except the list. But, as there is considerable likelihood of Vaughan's having served with Price for some time, it is worth while to trace what can be discovered about Price's movements in these years.

Herbert Price, M.P. for Brecon, had been from the beginning of the Civil War the most active and continuously loyal supporter of the royal arms in the county of Brecon. His interests, however, were divided between Hereford and Brecon. Through his mother being a Coningsby of Hampton Court in Herefordshire he had estates and connexions in that county.[2] Hereford was an important royalist stronghold, but Chester was even more important, and the earliest reference to Price's activities perhaps belongs to the Chester area. Sir William Brereton, M.P. for the county, and commander-in-chief of the Parliamentary forces in Cheshire, came to the relief of Nantwich and took it on 28 January 1642/3 after a successful fight with Sir Thomas Aston, who had brought troops from Chester to meet him. Aston had with him 'a new troop of horse come in the day before,

---

[1] Gardiner, op. cit. ii. 215–16, 222.

[2] *Archaeologia Cambrensis*, series 2, vol. iv, 1853, p. 66. Price is styled Sir Herbert in the 1663 list and he is later described sometimes as knight, sometimes as baronet, but the date of his being honoured is not known.

raised and commanded by one Captaine Price', which 'did
very well' in the disastrous retreat.[1] The surname Price is
common in Wales, and no Christian name is given, so that
the troop commander cannot with certainty be identified
with Herbert Price of Brecon. The next allusion is, however,
certain. When the surrender of Hereford was demanded by
Sir William Waller on 25 April 1643, Colonel Herbert Price,
acting governor of the city, sought vainly to negotiate terms
with the Parliamentarian general, but he and four other
members of Parliament were taken prisoners,[2] though Price
contrived his escape.[3] At the time one company of Price's
regiment was at Hereford and two at Abergavenny.[4] In
April 1644 Price was in Brecon, whither he had gone to
raise troops at the instance of the royalists in Carmarthenshire and Cardiganshire who were in desperate need of
reinforcements to resist Colonel Laugharne's growing
pressure. They had appealed in vain to Prince Rupert, who
was engaged in the north. Price was in correspondence with
Prince Rupert, and when the prince commands him to with-
draw to Hereford he represents to him that his leaving
Wales will strain the loyalty of the king's supporters in
those parts and leave them a prey to the rebels.[5] We have
already seen that Price entertained King Charles at Brecon
Priory on 5 August 1645 and was with his regiment
at Chester on 23 September on the eve of the battle of
Rowton Heath. He was perhaps again at Hereford when
it was surprised by Colonel Morgan and Colonel Birch
on 18 December 1645; a 'Lieut. Col. Price' is in the list
of prisoners as well as Vaughan's former employer, Chief
Justice Lloyd.[6]

The first Civil War ended with the king putting himself

[1] Hist. MSS. Comm. 12th Report, Appendix, Part ix, p. 40.
[2] Phillips, i. 154; ii. 69–70 (list of prisoners).
[3] J. Webb, *Memorials of the Civil War in Herefordshire*, 1879, i. 273.
[4] Ibid. i. 274.
[5] Letters of Price to Prince Rupert, from Brecon, 12 and 13 April 1644,
summarized in *Arch. Cambr.*, 1853, p. 68.
[6] Phillips, i. 347; ii. 286. Phillips takes it to be 'most probably Herbert
Price of Brecon', but the identification is uncertain because in the list of
prisoners taken at Hereford in Apr. 1643 (Phillips, ii. 70) there is a Lieut.
Col. Thomas Price besides Col. Herbert Price, M.P.

into the hands of the Scottish army at Newark on 5 May 1646 and with the surrender of Oxford on the following Midsummer Day. Raglan Castle, however, held out till 19 August, when the full list of officers surrendering included a Colonel Price, and, among the non-combatant 'Esquires and other Gentlemen of quality', Thomas Powell, but there is no Vaughan. If we could be sure that the colonel was Herbert Price of Brecon, and if a Vaughan had been named among the officers, we might listen to the tempting suggestion that here we have the clue to Vaughan's poem 'To his Learned Friend and Loyal Fellow-Prisoner, Thomas Powel of Cant., Doctor of Divinity'.[1] The evicted rector of Cantref is more likely to have suffered imprisonment for ignoring his eviction than for being present in the siege of Raglan, of which there is no evidence. It is still more fatal to this view that those who surrendered at Raglan were not made prisoners but were allowed honourable departure. This view may, therefore, be dismissed. 'Fellow-Prisoner' does not necessarily involve Powell and Vaughan being in the same prison, but only that both men had, perhaps at different times, suffered detention for their obstinate loyalty. Vaughan's imprisonment, whenever it was, may have led him to translate the poem of Ovid, to which he adds the title 'To his friends (after his many sollicitations) refusing to petition *Caesar* for his releasement'.[2] So resolute a royalist as Vaughan would not easily bring himself to petition the enemies of Charles I for his release.

Another conjecture may also be considered here. It has been suggested that Vaughan joined the king's garrison at Oxford after leaving Beeston Castle. The only ground for this suggestion is that his poem 'The King Disguis'd', which treats of Charles's flight from Oxford in the guise of a gentleman's servant on 27 April 1646, begins 'A King and no King! Is he gone from us?'[3] The words 'from us' may

[1] M 603.

[2] M 66. Ovid, *Epist.* iii. vii. Ovid's heading is simply 'Amicis'.

[3] M 605. The heading describes the poem as 'Written about the same time that Mr. *John Cleveland* wrote his'. Thomason dated his copy of Cleveland's poem 21 Jan. 1647, but both poets probably wrote directly after the king's flight, as the swift passage of events would soon rob the theme of interest.

indicate that the poet was in Oxford at the time, but it is too slight a clue to rest much upon it.

After the first Civil War Vaughan was at home. He dates the dedication of *Olor Iscanus* from Newton on 17 December 1647, and he was at home when his brother William died on 14 July 1648. Meanwhile there were the smoulderings of the second Civil War within the Welsh borders, and Brecon became important as the headquarters of Colonel Horton, who was sent to deal with the danger to the Parliamentarian cause. Colonel John Poyer, governor of Pembroke Castle, which had for long been the most important Parliamentarian stronghold in south Wales, was exploiting the discontent of his soldiers, who resented their intended disbandment. He seized Tenby Castle and declared openly for the king.[1] The Earl of Lanark, brother and heir of the Duke of Richmond, waiting to invade England in the hope of co-ordinated risings, was reproached for his delay in letters, dated 11 April and 4 May, informing him of the successful collecting of men under arms in the Welsh counties, who were 'resolved to oppose all forces by what authority soever sent without the King's or the Prince's that comes into Wales'.[2]   Before Colonel Horton could make Brecon his headquarters he needed to send troops to deal with 'divers gentlemen of the county, Mr. Games and others', who 'had drawn in some to garrison this town for the King'.[3] The leaders were arrested, but the outlook was still precarious, and the writer who sends this account from Brecon on 29 April 1648 adds: 'Here is a great desire that some eminent Commander would come with additional strength, because Col. Horton hath his health very ill.' The eminent commander was soon forthcoming, as on 1 May the Council of War in London, hearing that all south Wales was in a state of revolt, directed Cromwell to go there with sufficient forces to crush any risings and to deal with what was considered to be a dangerous situation. Before Cromwell's arrival Colonel

---

[1] Gardiner, op. cit. iii. 357–8.

[2] *Hamilton Papers*, Camden Soc., 1880, pp. 181–2, 197.

[3] Anonymous letter to a 'Right Honourable' person, dated from Brecknock 29 Apr. 1648 (Phillips, ii. 355, citing King's Pamphlets 362, 2).

Horton had defeated the Welsh royalists, who were now led
by Laugharne, the former Parliamentarian commander, at
St. Fagan's near Llandaff on 8 May.[1] Cromwell completed
the suppression, Chepstow Castle surrendering on 25 May,
Tenby six days after, and Pembroke on 11 July. He could
now leave Wales to go north to meet the invading Scots
army. There is no evidence of Henry Vaughan's having
taken any active part in this renewal of the war in Wales.

[1] Gardiner, iii. 364, 373, 394.

VI

OLOR ISCANUS

ON 15 September 1646 George Badger entered at Stationers' Hall 'Poems with the Xth satyre of Juvenall Englished, by Henry Vaugham [sic], gent'. We have no means of knowing what reception was given to that unpretentious little volume, but its author was at any rate not discouraged from proceeding very soon after to make a further bid for recognition as a poet. Already before the end of the next year he had another book ready for the press: the dedication of *Olor Iscanus* is dated from '*Newton* by *Usk* this 17. of *Decemb*. 1647'.[1] The book was not registered by 'Master Mozley' till 28 April 1651, exactly thirteen months after Humphrey Blunden had registered *Silex Scintillans*. The probable reasons for this long postponement will be considered later, but first a difficulty about the dedication, which has been unnoticed by editors and biographers, should be faced, and its solution will corroborate the dates already suggested in this book for certain events in Vaughan's life.

Kildare Digby, to whom *Olor Iscanus* is dedicated, succeeded his father in 1642 as second Lord Digby of Geashill in King's County, Ireland. He was born, according to the *Complete Peerage*,[2] 'circa 1631', which would make him only sixteen when Vaughan dedicated the book to him. There are, however, reasons for thinking that his birth may have been earlier. His father married Sarah, second daughter of Richard Boyle, first Earl of Cork, on 15 December 1626, she being in her eighteenth year. If their son and heir Kildare was born within the first year of marriage, he would be twenty by December 1647. Even this older age makes Vaughan's description of his obligations to his junior remarkable; he alludes to 'those *numerous* favours, and *kind Influences* receiv'd from your Lordship', which even 'Absence and time' have not availed to 'wear out of memorie'.

[1] M 35.   [2] Vol. iv, 1916, p. 353.

OLOR ISCANUS

SELECT
Poems, and translations
by
Hen: Vaughan Silurist

Flumina amo Silvasq3 inglorius

Ro: Vaughan sculp:

ENGRAVED TITLE-PAGE OF *OLOR ISCANUS*
(1651)

In what ways could Vaughan, who was now twenty-six, have been under obligations of long standing to this young man? The Digbys, besides their Irish estates, had for several generations had an English home at Coleshill in Warwickshire, the village where Richard and Lucy Wise, the parents of Vaughan's wife, lived. This is another indication that Vaughan was already married or at least engaged before he went on the Chester campaign. It is also worth noting that another Lord Digby,[1] son of the Earl of Bristol, and a cousin of Kildare, was at Chester with the king as his secretary of state and was on 16 October 1645 to replace Prince Rupert as lieutenant-general of the king's forces north of the Tweed. It is likely enough that Kildare had commended Vaughan to the notice of his distinguished namesake. Vaughan's close connexion with the Midland families is noticeable. Besides the dedication of *Olor Iscanus* to Kildare, Lord Digby, there are the dedications of *The Mount of Olives* on 1 October 1651[2] and of *Flores Solitudinis* in 1653[3] to Sir Charles Egerton, brother of Mrs. Richard Wise.

The postponement of the publication of *Olor Iscanus* for about three years and a half after the dedication was written is almost certainly to be explained by the change of mind with which Vaughan had come to view his secular verse after he had turned his attention to writing almost exclusively sacred verse. As the secular verse belongs to the period before he composed *Silex Scintillans*, except for a few occasional poems which could not come under his condemnation as 'idle Poems',[4] it is proper to consider *Olor Iscanus* before coming to *Silex Scintillans*. There is reason to think that the contents of *Olor Iscanus* as it appeared in 1651 differed considerably from what was in the projected volume of 1647. Little indication of the contents of the earlier collection can be gathered from the dedication, in which the poet asks the young Lord Digby

---

[1] George Digby (1612–77) was called up to the House of Lords on 9 June 1641 in his father's barony of Digby and succeeded his father as second Earl of Bristol in 1653. The first earl was fourth son of Sir George Digby of Coleshill.
[2] M 138.　　　　　[3] M 213, 215.　　　　　[4] M 388.

to allow his name 'to own as the *Genius* to these *papers*'. It cannot safely be inferred from the phrase 'these *papers*' that the projected volume included the prose translations which appeared in the 1651 book. The use of the word *papers* does not rule out the possibility of the contents being entirely poetical. Thus, Humphrey Moseley, in his preface to Milton's *Poems*, 1645, writes of his soliciting the author's 'Papers' from him. Dryden, in the preface to his *Fables*, says: 'I have added some Original Papers of my own, which whether they are equal or inferiour to my other Poems, an Author is the most improper Judge.' In *Olor Iscanus* 'The Publisher to the Reader',[1] which was obviously not written before 1651, and the commendatory verses of 'T. Powell Oxoniensis', 'I. Rowlandson Oxoniensis' and 'Eugenius Philalethes Oxoniensis' (Henry Vaughan's twin-brother), mention poems only, but give no indication of the nature and subjects of the poems. It is otherwise with another commendatory poem of Powell, which was to appear in *Thalia Rediviva* (1678), but which may have been intended to introduce *Olor Iscanus*, as originally planned in 1647. Powell greets Vaughan as 'a young Tyrtaeus'

> whose sweet persuasive Song
> Can lead our *Spirits* any way, and move
> To all *Adventures*: either *War* or *Love*.[2]

Henry Vaughan was no young Tyrtaeus in 1678, nor are there any war-poems in the 1646 volume or in *Thalia Rediviva*. Nor indeed are there any love-poems in the eventual *Olor Iscanus* or any war-poems except the two elegies and the campaigning poem 'Upon a Cloke lent him by Mr. *J. Ridsley*'. These few war-poems hardly match the description of Vaughan in another commendatory poem in *Thalia Rediviva* which places him above Tyrtaeus:

> That *Dorian* Minstrel never did excite,
> Or raise for dying so much appetite.[3]

It is evident that there were war-poems ready in 1647 but excluded from the eventual *Olor Iscanus*, which was

---

[1] M 36. [2] M 598.
[3] Commendatory verses of '*I. W.* A.M. Oxon.' in *Thalia Rediviva* (M 601).

confessedly a selection. The volume of 1651 is described on the title-page as 'A Collection of some select Poems, and Translations, Formerly written by *Mr.* Henry Vaughan *Silurist.* Published by a Friend'.[1]

This friend is likely to have been Thomas Powell, as Professor W. R. Parker has convincingly argued.[2] He was a lifelong neighbour of the Vaughans. Born in 1608 at his father's rectory of Cantref, he was successively Scholar and Fellow of Jesus College, and, as has already been shown, was in residence as Fellow during a large part of 1638 when the Vaughans first went to Oxford. From 1635 he was rector of Cantref, and from 1638 also prebendary of Christ College, Brecon, until he was evicted from both preferments. The literary association of Powell and Henry Vaughan was very close, and it would seem that, except possibly for his old schoolmaster, the poet had no friend who did more to encourage his poetic ambitions. Vaughan, on his part, contributed to more than one of Powell's books. Powell's *Elementa Opticae* (1651) was, as Wood says, 'commended to the world by the copies of verses of Olor Iscanus and Eugenius Philalethes his brother'.[3] In Powell's posthumous *Humane Industry* (1661) there are English versions of lines by Juvenal, Grotius, and Thomas Campion, 'Translated by *H. V.*', and an epigram of Martial 'with the Translation of M. *Hen. Vaughan Silurist,* whose excellent Poems are publique'.[4] Manuscripts of three unprinted works by Powell were in Vaughan's custody in 1673, as he tells Aubrey.[5]

The clearest indication of Powell's connexion with the publishing of *Olor Iscanus* is, as Professor Parker points out, that Moseley entered at Stationers' Hall on the same day, 28 April 1651, *Olor Iscanus* and, immediately below it, Powell's *Stoa Triumphans.* It seems an inescapable inference that Powell, the older and more experienced author, was the friend who selected the contents of Vaughan's 1651 volume and arranged for its publication.

---

[1] M 33.
[2] W. R. Parker, 'Henry Vaughan and his Publishers', Transactions of the Bibliographical Society, *The Library*, 4th series, vol. xx, 1940.
[3] *Ath. Oxon.* iii. 508.   [4] M 661–4.   [5] M 670.

Powell is possibly the writer of 'The Publisher to the Reader', though it is more likely to be Moseley's. If it is Moseley's, it may be compared with 'The Stationer to the Reader', signed 'Humph. Moseley', prefixed to *Poems of Mr. John Milton*, 1645: 'The Author's more peculiar excellency in these studies was too well known to conceal his Papers, or to keep me from attempting to sollicit them from him.' Dr. Tillyard comments on Moseley's words:

There is no need to see in the preface of Moseley, the publisher, a proof that but for his solicitations Milton would not have published at all: the preface is no more than the conventional Renaissance apology for going into print. The edition was arranged and supervised by Milton with great care.[1]

Slightly in favour of Moseley being the writer of the preface to *Olor Iscanus* is the sentence: 'I have not the Author's *Approbation* to the *Fact,* but I have *Law* on my *Side,* though never a *Sword.*' If the reference to law is to be taken seriously, it may mean that the publisher covenanted with the author in 1647 for the production of a volume of verse, and advanced him money on that account, and that later, for reasons which will be discussed, Vaughan desired to withhold his secular verse from publication, although Moseley had this claim on him. The jocose style of the preface is like that which Moseley used in the preface to William Cartwright's *Poems,* published in the same year as *Olor Iscanus.* He prided himself, not without justification, on his success in bringing to light poetical works of merit by little-known writers.

Whether the preface is Powell's or Moseley's, it deserves to be read with attention, as throwing some light on Vaughan's new attitude towards his secular verse, long before his severe condemnation of them in the preface which he dated 30 September 1654 for the enlarged edition of *Silex Scintillans.* Already in 1651 the writer of the preface to *Olor Iscanus* can say: 'The *Author* had long agoe condemn'd these *Poems* to *Obscuritie.* . . . Here is a *Flame* hath been sometimes *extinguished.*' That the editor or publisher had not 'the Author's *Approbation*' need not mean that the

[1] E. M. W. Tillyard, *Milton*, 1930, p. 169.

poems 'were in the end published contrary to his desire',[1] as Vaughan's first editor in the nineteenth century argued. Nor does the preface explicitly state that Vaughan destined his secular poems to the flames, as Virgil did; in fact he preserved many secular poems of those years and eventually found a place for them in the late garnering of *Thalia Rediviva*. It would appear probable that Powell overcame Vaughan's reluctance so far as to allow him to make a selection from his work in verse and prose and be responsible for the publication. No one but Vaughan can have given him access to his manuscripts, and probably there was some discussion between Vaughan and his editor as to what should be included in the volume of 1651. As a proof of his new-found religious ardour, Vaughan must seek to reduce any sense of inconsistency between the tone of *Olor Iscanus* and that of *Silex Scintillans* already published in the previous year. This might be best effected by describing the poems on the title-page as 'Formerly written' and 'Published by a Friend', which, together with the preface, would reduce the author's responsibility for publishing his secular verse.

In actual fact, 'Formerly written' would apply to the larger number of the poems. There are in all seventeen English poems and five Latin original poems, making little more than one-quarter of *Olor Iscanus*; almost exactly of the same length are the verse-translations from Ovid, Ausonius, Boëthius, and Casimir; the remainder of the volume is occupied by four prose translations.

The description 'Silurist' after the author's name on the title-page of *Olor Iscanus* had already been used the year before in *Silex Scintillans*, and it keeps its place in *The Mount of Olives* and *Flores Solitudinis*, but is absent from *Hermetical Physick*, where it would be less appropriate; there is no author's name on the title-page of *Thalia Rediviva*, but three of the commendatory poems are addressed to 'Mr. *Henry Vaughan* the Silurist'. This self-chosen description would

---

[1] Lyte, p. xxvi. Lyte believed that Henry Vaughan's brother Thomas was responsible for publishing *Olor Iscanus* and that the 'apologetic advertisement' was his.

not only distinguish Henry Vaughan from other Henry
Vaughans but would mark his love of that part of south-east
Wales which, according to Tacitus,[1] was inhabited by a
British tribe to whom he gives the name *Silures*. The motto
from the Georgics on the title-page, 'Flumina amo, Sylvas-
que Inglorius', and its continuation on the verso

> O quis me gelidis in vallibus ISCÆ
> Sistat, & Ingenti ramorum protegat umbrâ![2]

express Vaughan's devotion to his native stream and wood-
land and his willingness to make his permanent home there,
'lost to fame', rather than in the literary environment of
London that had attracted him in early years. There is,
perhaps, also a nostalgic note, as if he had chosen the motto
while away from home on military service. The motto
leads the reader to expect more poems about the Breconshire
country than the book contains. Even in the opening poem
'To the River *Isca*' and in the Latin poem on the same theme
he shows more concern to ensure that the Usk should have
its *vates,* as Thames and Severn, Avon and Tay, already had,
than that he should write any lines specially distinctive of
his own river; the English poem has far more of literary
allusions than of descriptive detail. It is his theme that
poets, like angels, 'hallow' the places they have visited, so
that it may be said, 'That there their Genii live.'

> Hence th' *Auncients* say, That, from this *sickly aire*
> They passe to *Regions* more *refin'd* and *faire*,
> To *Meadows* strow'd with *Lillies* and the *Rose*,
> And *shades* whose *youthfull green* no *old age* knowes,
> Where all in *white* they walk, discourse, and Sing
> Like Bees *soft murmurs*, or a *Chiding Spring*.[3]

There is more of his native country in *Silex Scintillans* than
in all his secular verse.

---

[1] Tac. *Ann.* xii. 32–3 and *Agric.* 11, 17. The Silures offered a strenuous
resistance to the Romans.

[2] Virg. *Geo.* ii. 486, 488–9. Virgil wrote *amem* and *O qui*. Vaughan has
substituted *Iscae* for *Haemi*. Virgil had prayed that the Muses might teach
him the secrets of the universe, as Lucretius had known them; but, if that
high knowledge be denied him, let him be content to celebrate in song the
beauties of the country.   [3] M 39.

Of the seventeen English poems in *Olor Iscanus* all of the first ten except 'An Invitation to Brecknock' were, either demonstrably or almost certainly, written by 1647.[1] 'The Charnel-house' reads like an early imitation of Donne. 'Monsieur Gombauld'[2] was occasioned by the appearance of Richard Hurst's translation of Gombauld's prose romance *Endymion* in 1639 while Vaughan was still at Oxford. Vaughan's final couplet

> And while there is a *People*, or a *Sunne*,
> *Endymions* storie with the *Moon* shall runne

is an evident versifying of Hurst's sentence: 'As long as there shall be any speech of the Moone as she shall shine in the heavens, thy name shall remaine in the mouths and memory of man.' 'In Amicum foeneratorem' and 'To his friend ———'[3] deal with Vaughan's experiences in London. The elegy to R. W. and the Cloke poem refer to his soldiering in 1645–6, though the elegy was not written until his friend's death had been to him 'A full years griefe'.[4] 'Upon Mr. *Fletchers* Playes, published, 1647'[5] refers to the first collected edition in that year of the *Comedies and Tragedies written by Francis Beaumont and John Fletcher*. Vaughan's tribute was not among the many prefixed to that volume, and in his opening lines he expresses his unworthiness to have his poem 'in some *Suburb-page* (scandal to thine) Like *Lent* before a *Christmasse*'.[6] He begins 'I knew thee not', just as George Daniel of Beswick begins his poem 'To the Memorie of Mr. Fra: Beaumont and Mr. Jo: Fletcher':

> I knew thee not. Therefore what I may say
> Is free from passion.[7]

Vaughan was only 4 years old, and Daniel 9, when Fletcher died in 1625, and it is interesting that these poets pay their

---

[1] This agrees closely with H. R. Walley's reckoning in his article, 'The Strange Case of *Olor Iscanus*', *Review of Engl. Studies*, Jan. 1942, though I give reasons (p. 83, below) for assigning a later date than he does to 'An Invitation to Brecknock'.

[2] M 48.   [3] M 43 and 44.   [4] M 49, l. 3.   [5] M 54.

[6] Advent was early known as Quadragesima Sancti Martini, a Lent before Christmas.

[7] *The Poems of George Daniel*, ed. Grosart, 1878, i. 209.

tribute to a poet of the previous generation. Vaughan
counts Fletcher happy to have died before 'the Kirk' and
'the Eares' (a cant name for the close-cropped Puritans)
had silenced the stage.

The place of the discarded or postponed poems on possibly dangerous themes was supplied by poems written
after 1647. They include the vigorous and attractive elegy
on R. Hall, 'slain at *Pontefract,* 1648'[1] and 'An Epitaph upon
the Lady *Elizabeth,* Second Daughter to his late Majestie'.[2]
These offer more promising themes for poetry than the
literary exercises which constitute so many of the poems in
this collection. The Princess Elizabeth, a sickly but studious
child, spent eight of the fifteen years of her life in captivity,
and is said never to have recovered from the shock of her
father's execution. By order of the Council of State she
was moved from Penshurst to Carisbrooke, the sad scene
of her father's imprisonment, on 17 August 1650, and there
died of fever on the following 8 September. She was buried
in St. Thomas's Church, Newport, without funeral rites and
with no memorial except the initials 'E. S.' (Elizabeth Stuart)
cut in the wall. Vaughan's epitaph faithfully presents her
troubled short life with tenderness and beauty. It is interesting to note that, with his new devotion to Herbert, there
are in this short poem phrases from three of *The Temple*
poems, besides two lines taken almost verbatim from a
poem of Francis Beaumont from which he had previously
borrowed. Vaughan's loyalty to the royal house, his tender
feeling for the young, and his growing sense of the unseen
find scope in this little elegy. It includes the lines:

> Thou seem'st a *Rose-bud* born in *Snow,*
> A flowre of purpose sprung to bow
> To headless[3] tempests, and the rage
> Of an Incensed, stormie Age.
> Others, e're their afflictions grow,
> Are tim'd, and season'd for the blow,
> But thine, as *Rhumes* the tend'rest part,
> Fell on a *young* and *harmless* heart.

[1] M 58. See above, p. 61.   [2] M 63.
[3] The epithet *headless,* if not a variant spelling of *heedless,* may mean 'senseless, stupid' (*O.E.D.* s.v. Headless, sense 3b).

The occasional nature of so many poems in *Olor Iscanus* perhaps accounts for their limited interest and their undistinguished quality. Vaughan's compliment to Powell on his translation of Virgilio Malvezzi's *Christian Politician* was unlikely to elicit a striking poem, though it would give an opportunity for contrasting the 'true States-men' with the Puritan rulers.[1] A happier example is his verse-invitation to his neighbour, Thomas Lewes, rector of Llanfigan, to a friendly meeting made the more possible by the freezing of the Usk, which lay between their homes.[2] Of more literary interest, because it deals with a contemporary author and a notable play, is the poem 'To Sir *William D'avenant,* upon his *Gondibert*'.[3] This play was published in 1651 when its author was in the Tower, 'mur'd in solitarie stones'. Vaughan handsomely hails Davenant as 'The Prince of *Poets* and of *Lovers* too'. The allusion to 'thy aged *Sire*' is more likely to be to Jonson, among whose 'sons' Davenant was reckoned, than to the gossip which made him a natural child of Shakespeare.[4]

There is literary rather than poetical interest in the poem 'To the most Excellently accomplish'd, Mrs. *K. Philips*'.[5] It is not improbable that the epithalamium 'To the best, and most accomplish'd Couple ——'[6] celebrates the marriage of Katherine Fowler in August 1648 at St. Gabriel's, Fenchurch, to James Philips, of the Priory, Cardigan.[7] Vaughan was already, in 1651, familiar with the poems of Orinda thirteen years before they appeared in print. The extravagance of his praise is, no doubt, what was expected of a contemporary, and it is unconvincing about her achievements, though it reveals his own humility:

> These Raptures when I first did see
> New miracles in Poetrie,

[1] M 60. Powell's translation was forestalled by another translator in 1647, and his own translation remained, unprinted, in Vaughan's keeping (M 670).

[2] M 61. Two lines are taken straight from Herbert's 'The Discharge'.

[3] M 64. Miss Guiney would like to read the opening line 'Will, wee are rescued!' instead of 'Well, wee are rescued!'

[4] M 64, l. 28. Cf. H. F. B. Brett-Smith, 'Vaughan and D'avenant', *Modern Language Review*, Jan. 1916.   [5] M 61.   [6] M 57.

[7] The date of the marriage, wrongly given as 1647 in the *D.N.B.*, is found in Col. J. L. Chester, *London Marriage Licences*, 1887, col. 1054.

And by a hand, their God would misse
His *Bayes* and *Fountaines* but to kisse,
My weaker *Genius* (crosse to fashion)
Slept in a silent admiration, . . .
It was your light shew'd me the way.[1]

Orinda returned the compliment, if her poem did not
precede Vaughan's, in verses 'upon these and his former
Poems', which found a place in the preliminary pages of
Thalia Rediviva,[2] after having made an earlier appearance in
the authorized edition of her poems published three years
after her death. In his later poem 'To the Editor of the
matchless *Orinda*',[3] Vaughan greeted the publication, in
1667, of her poems under the editorship of Sir Charles
Cotterel, M.P. for Cardigan; he calls it 'a fruitful year'
that sees this publication in an age when poetry is 'at so
low an Ebbe', but he says nothing very intimate about her
personality or distinctive about her poetry. A recent writer
has questioned the common assumption that Vaughan and
Orinda enjoyed a close friendship.[4] The exchange of com-
pliments in verse did not go for much in that age. There
is no allusion to Vaughan in *Letters from Orinda to Poliarchus,*
nor any fancy name in it which suggests him.[5] Orinda's
husband, a colonel in the Parliamentary army, a member of
the Barebones as well as of the Long Parliament, who
acquired many sequestrated estates of royalists and stripped
the lead off St. Davids Cathedral to build his own house
at Cardigan, would have been little to the mind of Henry
Vaughan. Orinda sometimes visited the Aubreys at Llantrithyd in Glamorganshire, where Vaughan may have met
her, but there is no evidence of their having ever met or
of his having been at the Aubreys' house.

The most lively poem in *Olor Iscanus* is 'To his retired
friend, an Invitation to *Brecknock*'.[6] It can be dated with

---

[1] M 62, ll. 15–20, 30.
[2] M 597. The *D.N.B.*, s.v. Katherine Philips, is wrong in stating that her
poem appeared in *Olor Iscanus*.   [3] M 621.
[4] P. W. Souers, *The Matchless Orinda*, 1931, pp. 71–3.
[5] Miss Guiney suggested that Orinda's fancy name for Vaughan was
Timander (M 623) or Silvester (as Wood once writes of him), and Amoret
for his wife (M. 597); but these names do not occur in *Letters from Orinda*.
[6] M 46.

some degree of certainty. It is 'since *Charles* his raign', and as 'the slow Isicle hangs At the stiffe thatch', it cannot refer to a September meeting of the Great Sessions but to the March meeting in 1648/9, two months after the king's execution. The former secretary of Sir Marmaduke Lloyd, once Chief Justice of the Brecon circuit, resents the 'new fine *Worships*' who have replaced 'the old cast *teame* Of Justices vext with the *Cough*, and *flegme*'. The latter can be identified as Walter Rumsey, formerly Puisne Justice of the circuit, Sir Marmaduke's colleague, who was troubled with phlegm in the throat and invented the provang, a whalebone instrument with a sponge fixed at the end.[1] Eltonhead, who replaced Lloyd, was a Lancashire man with a Yorkshire mother, and is probably the 'old *Saxon Fox*' at whose expense Vaughan makes merry.

Mr. E. L. Marilla has recently objected[2] that Vaughan's secular has been unduly overshadowed by his sacred verse, and that this has been partly because so many of his editors and critics, from Lyte to Grosart and Beeching, have been clergymen. But the lay anthologists—Palgrave, Churton Collins, Quiller-Couch, Grierson, Massingham, Norman Ault—have shown a similar preference, selecting almost solely from *Silex Scintillans*. Sir Herbert Grierson, both in *Metaphysical Lyrics and Poems* and in the *Oxford Book of Seventeenth Century Verse*, goes outside *Silex* for a single item from *Poems*, 'To Amoret gone from him',[3] and, in the latter anthology, he includes also two poems from the 'Pious thoughts' of *Thalia Rediviva*.[4] Mr. Ault in *A Treasury of Unfamiliar Lyrics*, 1933, has 'A Song to *Amoret*'[5] besides poems from *Silex*. None of these anthologists has chosen

---

[1] Rumsey published an account of his provang in *Organon Salutis*, 1657.
[2] E. L. Marilla, 'The Significance of Henry Vaughan's Literary Reputation', *Modern Language Quarterly*, June 1944. It should be remembered with reference to the earlier anthologists that, though Lyte published Vaughan's sacred verse in 1847, the secular verse was not available except in the rare seventeenth-century editions until Grosart included it in his edition of the complete works in 1870–1. George Ellis in the second edition (1801) of his *Specimens of the Early English Poets* was the first modern anthologist to print any secular verse of Vaughan, and he gave only the first, second, and fourth stanzas of 'To the best and most accomplish'd Couple' (M 57).   [3] M 8.
[4] 'The Shower' (M 641) and 'The Revival' (M 643).   [5] M 8.

anything from *Olor Iscanus* or from the secular part of
Thalia Rediviva. There is, then, some general agreement that
no poems in *Olor Iscanus* reach the standard of the best
poems in *Silex Scintillans*.

The small collection of original poems, English and
Latin, needed some supplement to make a sizeable volume.
Besides the four prose treatises, which will be discussed
later,[1] *Olor Iscanus* included verse-translations which occupy
as much space as the original poems. There are versions of
four poems of Ovid, one of Ausonius, thirteen of the Metra
of Boëthius, and six odes of Casimir and his 'The Praise of a
Religious Life'. Similarly in later years Vaughan would add to
Thalia Rediviva five more of the Metra of Boëthius and three
poems of Claudian. As all the verse-translations appearing
in *Thalia Rediviva* were probably written by 1651, they can
be considered here together with those in *Olor Iscanus*.

Vaughan had a good grounding in Latin, and at all times
in his life read freely in Latin verse and prose. Like other
scholars of his day, his command of Greek was very much
less, and when he wished to make an English translation of
treatises of Plutarch he wisely made it from a Latin version.[2]
His fondness for the Latin poets is evident in his quotations
and in his borrowing Virgilian phrases for his original
Latin poems. He has, indeed, left no translation of his
favourite Virgil, 'that inimitable *Prince* and *Patriarch* of
Poets', except for thirteen lines from the fourth Georgic,
which he puts in *The Mount of Olives*.[3] He shared the attraction which the Elizabethans and his own generation had
for Ovid. As in all his translations in verse or prose, he
feels himself free to expand, or to omit what does not serve
his purpose, and to make the matter topical by contemporary and English references. Thus, he translates the voca-
tive *Bacche* as 'blith god of *Sack*',[4] and *Vos quoque, consortes
studii, pia turba, poetae* becomes 'And you my trusty friends

---

[1] See Chapter X.
[2] It may be only printers' errors or careless proof-reading, but Greek
words are wrongly spelt, and accents and breathing-marks are in impossible
positions. The few German words he quotes are also wrongly spelt, but his
Latin is generally correct, if not always forcible or clear.
[3] M 184.   [4] M 65, ll. 1 and 47–8.

(the Jollie Crew Of careless *Poets!*)', which recalls the tone
of 'A Rhapsodis'. If there are some felicitous renderings,
there are others that are infelicitous, as when he translates
tenerorum lusor amorum 'the soft-soul'd Lecturer of Love'.[1]
The habit of borrowing from other writers is illustrated in
his translations as abundantly as in his original poems. In
a translation of Ovid he adopts, almost without change, six
lines from Felltham's *Resolves*, a book from which he often
borrowed, early and late.[2] The famous poem of Ausonius,
'Cupido cruci affixus', was translated by Vaughan's contemporary, Thomas Stanley, in 1647.[3] Vaughan's rendering
of this poem is freer than his versions of Ovid and Boëthius,
and, except for a line and a half from one of Donne's
Elegies, it is his own work.

The *Philosophiae Consolatio* of Boëthius has attracted English translators in many ages, from King Alfred and Chaucer
to the Elizabethans and Queen Elizabeth herself, and the
Metra or verse-interludes were translated again and again
in the seventeenth century, for instance by Sir Richard Fan-
shawe. Dr. Johnson was one of the last great English men of
letters to translate them. One can understand why the Metra,
with their beauty as well as their serene and religious temper,
attracted Vaughan in evil times. Some of his interpolations
we recognize as characteristic of the author of *Silex Scintillans*;
for instance, when he introduces his favourite word *white* in
translating *Felix nimium prior aetas*, 'Happy that first white
age!'[4] At times he is obscure and at times flatly prosaic:

And (which of all things is most sad)
The good man suffers by the bad.[5]

Even the lovely theme of Orpheus and Eurydice fails to
inspire him to write a memorable poem, though there are
a few happy passages in his rendering.[6]

[1] M 72, l. 76.
[2] *Epist.* IV. iii, ll. 53–8 (M 69). Cf. Jean Robertson, 'The Use made of
Owen Felltham's *Resolves*: a study in plagiarism', *Mod. Language Review*, Apr.
1944. Martin (p. 682) had already drawn attention to Vaughan's copious
borrowings from Felltham.
[3] T. Stanley, *Poems and Translations*. Printed for the Author, and his
friends. 1647. The translations were published by themselves in 1649.
[4] M 83, l. 1.   [5] M 79, ll. 37–8.   [6] Boëthius, III. xii (M 628).

Mr. Walley maintains that the order of translations in
Olor Iscanus probably represents the order of their composition.[1] A cording to this view, Vaughan's passing from
Ovid and Ausonius to Boëthius marks the growing seriousness of his mind, and next he leaves the pagan consolation
of Boëthius for the Christian faith of Casimir. This contention seems justified, although Casimir's lyrics are Horatian
rather than explicitly Christian. Mathias Casimir Sarbiewski
(Sarbievius) produced his *Lyricorum libri IV* in 1632, and
the book quickly won popularity in England as well as on
the Continent. An English translation appeared in 1646
and Sir Edward Sherburne produced versions of Casimir's
poetry in the same year as *Olor Iscanus* appeared. Mrs. Lucy
Hutchinson, after grappling with Lucretius and his 'foppish
casual dance of atoms', Puritan though she was, tried her
hand at translating the fashionable Polish Jesuit.[2] Vaughan
would appreciate Casimir's praise of simple country life
and 'wholsome mornings':

> But he, whose *Constancie* makes sure
> His *mind* and *mansion*, lives secure
> From such *vain tasks*, can *dine* and *sup*
> Where his *old parents* bred him up.
> *Content* (no doubt!) most times doth dwell
> In *Countrey-shades*, or to some *Cell*
> Confines it selfe, and can alone
> Make simple *straw*, a Royall *Throne*.[3]

There are some of Vaughan's usual interpolations: when
Casimir mentions a usurer, without naming his race,
Vaughan, perhaps with some unhappy experience of his
own in mind, alludes to his '*Jewish Crueltie*'.[4]

The versions of three poems of Claudian, which appeared
in *Thalia Rediviva*, were probably written at least as early
as the versions of Boëthius, and may be considered here.
They represent an earlier interest of Vaughan. He was in
good company in translating 'The Old Man of Verona', as
Randolph and Cowley translated this poem; indeed, in his

---

[1] 'The Strange Case of *Olor Iscanus*', *R.E.S.*, Jan. 1942, p. 32.
[2] In a manuscript volume of hers which the present writer has inherited.
[3] *Lyr.* iv. 15, ll. 27–34 (M 88).   [4] M 92, l. 116.

disconcerting way, Vaughan borrowed profusely from Randolph's versions of this poem and of 'The Sphere of *Archimedes*'.[1] He translates also 'The Phoenix',[2] and it may be noted that he made more poetical use of the legend, with its customary Christian reference to the general resurrection, in his poem 'Resurrection and Immortality' in *Silex Scintillans*.[3]

The original poems in *Thalia Rediviva* which were written during the time that *Olor Iscanus* was being composed, and some of which might have found a place in the volume projected in 1647, may be mentioned here. 'The Eagle',[4] confessedly a product of his 'unfledg'd witt', is a playful and daring experiment that nearly succeeds; more and better poems of this kind he might have accomplished had he pursued this vein. If it is generally thought a failure, Palgrave's high praise of it as an illustration of Vaughan's 'strange visionary power' should be noted.[5] The poem on the *Zodiacus Vitae* of Petro Angelo Manzoli (Marcellus Palingenius), full of the technical terms of astrology, reflects an early interest of Vaughan, from which he would retreat later.[6] The attractive poem 'On Sir Thomas Bodley's Library'[7] is early. 'The King Disguis'd',[8] commenting on Charles I's escape in disguise from Oxford on 27 April 1646, was probably excluded from *Olor Iscanus* because its royalism might have exposed its author to political trouble. For the same reason the poem to Thomas Powell 'his Learned Friend and Loyal Fellow-Prisoner'[9] might have been withheld, especially if Powell edited the volume of 1651. The Etesia poems belong to the days of courtship and are parallel to the Amoret poems in the volume of 1646,[10] and are as 'innoxious'[11] as they are. Charming as some of them are, they are seldom, if ever, as felicitous as the love-poems of Vaughan's contemporaries such as Carew, Suckling, Lovelace, and Waller. It is not by these poems that Vaughan is chiefly remembered.

[1] M 635. [2] M 636. [3] M 401, ll. 28–34.
[4] M 606. [5] *Y Cymmrodor*, vol. xi, part 2, p. 203.
[6] M 611. [7] M 613.
[8] M 605. See above, pp. 69–70. [9] M 603. See above, p. 69.
[10] See above, pp. 51–2. [11] M 390.

Vaughan's severe condemnation of 'idle verse' may have
led him to withhold from the earlier collections 'Fida: Or
The Country-beauty; to Lysimachus'.[1] It is the only one
of his printed poems that could be thought to consort ill
with *Silex Scintillans*. It appears to be a reporting to Lysimachus—whether he be his brother Thomas or a friend—
of the physical charms of the country beauty, and ends by
asking Lysimachus, if he could but see her as the poet has
now seen her, 'Would'st thou not swear she is a witch?'
The poem is prettily composed and, partly because the poet
allows himself more freedom, it is much more alive than
his other love-poems, which mostly follow in the wake of
Habington's *Castara* with their rather frigid tone. The
contrast is evident in such lines as these:

> Her *Skin*, like heav'n when calm and bright,
> Shews a rich *azure* under *white*,
> With *touch* more soft than heart supposes,
> And *Breath* as sweet as new blown *Roses*.
> Betwixt this *Head-land* and the *Main*,
> Which is a rich and flowry *Plain*:
> Lyes her fair *Neck*, so fine and slender
> That (gently) how you please, 'twill bend her.
> This leads you to her *Heart*, which ta'ne
> Pants under *Sheets* of whitest *Lawn*,
> And at the first seems much distrest,
> But nobly treated, lyes at rest.
> Here like two *Balls* of new fall'n snow,
> Her *Breasts*, Loves native *pillows* grow;
> And out of each a *Rose-bud* Peeps
> Which *Infant* beauty sucking, sleeps.[2]

The poem which follows, 'Fida forsaken',[3] is cryptic and
unattractive. The clue to its meaning is lost; Fida appears
to have been undone by some scoundrel, who, the poet
suggests, may best be left to his fate. A few poems only in
Thalia Rediviva belong to later years and will be considered
in the context of Vaughan's subsequent history. He would
write very little poetry after finishing the second part of
Silex Scintillans at the age of thirty-four.

[1] M 618.　　　　　　　[2] M 620, ll. 51–66.　　　　　　　[3] M 620.

VII

AT HOME

HENRY VAUGHAN'S home throughout life, except for the four years at Oxford and London, and a probably short period of soldiering, was until the end of his days, so far as we know, in his native village. The dedication of *Olor Iscanus* on 17 December 1647 was from Newton by Usk, and Vaughan was at home at the time of his brother William's death in July 1648. His poem inviting a friend to join him at the Brecon Assizes of March 1648/9 need not imply his being a regular resident of Brecon; the friends are to forgather at an inn. Even after marriage Henry Vaughan may have continued to live in the family home to which he was the heir.

Of his mother, Denise Vaughan, strictly nothing is known beyond her name and family and her outliving her husband, except for the poet's allusion to 'the pattern of his chaste and faithful mother' (*Castae fidaeque . . . more parentis*), and even these words are taken by some to refer to Mother Church.[1] Of his father a good deal has come to light through the records of the law-courts, since he was involved in litigation throughout his life. As has been already shown,[2] he was repeatedly engaged in lawsuits about his wife's property for the first sixteen years of their married life. In the years 1649 and 1650, when Henry Vaughan was composing the first part of *Silex Scintillans*, Thomas Vaughan was prosecuted twice.

One Roger Thomas of Merthyr in the county of Brecon, sued 'Thomas Vaughan of Llansantfred gent., late under sheriff to Roger Vaughan high sheriff of Brecon' for improper discharge of his office as under-sheriff, and contempt of

---

[1] 'Ad Posteros', l. 23 (M 32). Vaughan calls the Church 'Mother' in *The Mount of Olives* (M 186, l. 15) and in his poem 'The Constellation' (M 470, l. 39). Herbert does the same in 'The British Church', ll. 1, 25, and 'Lent', l. 5. Cowley also alludes to 'my Mother Church' ('On the Death of Mr. Crashaw', l. 47).

[2] See above, pp. 11–12.

court was also alleged against him.[1] A far more serious charge was brought against him about the same time closely involving his honesty. A Commission was set up for Breconshire on 4 July 1649 under the Elizabethan Act of 1601 'to redresse the Misemployment of Landes, Goodes and stockes of money heretofore given to charitable uses'. Among other alleged abuses of charitable funds brought before the Commissioners, one concerned a legacy for the provision of a Free School at Llansantffraed. The jurors, who included Leoline Jenkins, the future Principal of Jesus College, reported to the Commissioners as follows:

Wee find that one John Powell late of Llansanfread in the county of Brecon yeoman, deceased, by his will and testament did give devise and bequeath all his landes and Tenementes scituate lyinge and beinge in the parish of Llangasty Tallylin . . . and the rentes yssues and profittes thereof for and towardes the maintenance of a Freeschoole in the said parish of Llansanfread forever And for the bringinge upp of poore fatherlesse Children of the said parish of Llansanfread beinge of the cleere yearely value of Tenne poundes per Annum And now in the possession and occupation of one Thomas Vaughan, gentleman and his undertenantes, And that the said Thomas Vaughan hath for the space of fourteene years last past before the date of this Inquisition entered uppon the said landes, and the rentes yssues and profittes . . . hath converted to his owne use whereby the said pious use hath beene frustrated for the tyme aforesaid.[2]

At an Inquisition held at Brecon on 14 June 1650 the five Commissioners received the above findings on oath of the jury, and, after considering 'other Evidences and testimonies', required Thomas Vaughan to render up possession of the property to certain new trustees chosen by the parishioners 'to be their feoffees and trustees', and to pay the arrears for the fourteen years, amounting to £140.[3] It should be borne in mind that the Inquisition was held at a time of bitter political and religious animosity, and that the Commissioners included, besides Thomas Vaughan's fellow

[1] Exch. Q.R. Depositions, 24 Car. I, Hilary. Brecon, no. 9. 23 Jan. [1649/50] at Builth.
[2] Chancery Petty Bag. Charity Inquisitions, &c., co. Brecon: Bundle 20, no. 17, and Depositions, 13. 16. [3] Ibid.

magistrates, a personal enemy in Jenkin Jones, the fiery
Puritan leader. Thomas Vaughan in the following January
sued the Commissioners and brought witnesses to establish
his title to the lands. His son Henry, 'aged about xxvii
yeares', deposed upon oath that he was present when his
father received an acquittance upon his having paid all debts
and demands in respect of the Llangasty lands. It is, however, clear that the purposes of the Free School trust were
neglected for fourteen years until the matter was brought
before the Commissioners. The whole incident must have
made an unhappy impression and caused distress to a man
of such integrity as Henry Vaughan. His father's unreliabi-
lity in money matters seems also to receive some corroboration from a punning remark of Aubrey about his cousin
that he was 'a coxcombe and no honester then he should be
—he cosened me of 50s. once'.[1]

Thomas Vaughan the elder was for many years personally
concerned with the tithes of Llansantffraed. In a Chancery
suit in Michaelmas term 1649, brought by Thomas Vaughan
the younger, rector of Llansantffraed, against certain persons
for trespass on 'Little Island', which lay on the farther bank
of the Usk in the parish of Llanfigan, his father is described
as 'fformer [i.e. farmer] of the said Rectorie of Llansantffread
under the plaintiff his son'.[2] The witnesses in his favour
include Charles Walbeoffe, high sheriff, who spoke of the
elder Thomas Vaughan as a Justice of the Peace. After his
son's eviction the father continued to be a farmer of the
tithes, and as late as 1656 his use of them was called in
question and brought him into conflict with the Parliamentary authorities.[3]

Henry Vaughan's association with his brother Thomas
during the years down to 1650 was less continuous than might
have been deduced from the fact of Thomas being rector.
Henry's account in a letter to Aubrey is that his brother
'was ordayned minister by bishop Mainwaringe & presented
to the Rectorie of St. Brigets by his kinsman Sr George

---

[1] *Brief Lives*, ii. 268.
[2] Exch. Q.R. Depositions. Mich. 1649. Brecon, no. 13.
[3] See below, pp. 199–200.

Vaughan'.[1] It is not known how the advowson for this
turn came to Sir George Vaughan, and his heir's title to
the patronage was disputed in 1662.[2] Sir George Vaughan
of Fallerston in the county of Wiltshire was a very distant
kinsman of young Thomas Vaughan; their common ancestor was the Roger Vaughan who was said to have died at
Agincourt, Sir George being seventh in descent in one line
and Thomas eighth in descent in another line, but, as has
been frequently illustrated in these pages, cousinship had a
wide extension in contemporary Wales. Sir George had a
link with Llansantffraed, as his sister Bridget was married
to Edward Games of Newton.[3] The living appears to
have been worth £60 a year, as that is the figure given
in the account of the collector of sequestrated tithes in
the county of Brecon for 1652, and the 'fifths' allowed
to the extruded incumbent was at the rate of £12 a year.[4]
The rectory house was near the church, and in 1655
the sum of £30 was allowed by the sequestrators for its
repair.[5]

Theophilus Jones, the historian of Breconshire,[6] and
others have given 1640 as the year of Thomas Vaughan's
appointment to the rectory, but this seems too early; he
was then only 19 and in his third year at Oxford, where he
continued to reside at least as late as midsummer 1642.[7]
Indeed, Henry states that his brother 'continued there for
ten or 12 years'.[8] Thomas Vaughan would not have been
of canonical age for ordination as deacon till 1644 and as
priest till 1645. He may, of course, have been admitted to
holy orders at an earlier age by dispensation of the archbishop, but in any case an Act of 1571 ruled 'that no person
shall hereafter be admitted to any benefice with cure, except
he then be of the age of three and twenty years at the

---

[1] M 668.   [2] See below, p. 203.
[3] Edward Games was high sheriff in 1623; in a lawsuit of 1649 his age is
given as 60. Miss Morgan distinguishes his home as Upper Newton, nearer
Brecon than the Vaughans' Newton.
[4] Lambeth: Sequestered Livings, 1650–62. No. 36.   [5] Ibid.
[6] Op. cit. iii. 216. Similarly Bodl. Gough MS. Wales 6, p. 7, 'about 1640',
and the D.N.B.
[7] The Buttery Books of Jesus College are missing from July 1642 till 1647.
[8] M 667.

least'.[1] Some support for his not being appointed rector before 1644 is that one Johan Parry, giving evidence at the trespass suit in 1649, states that five or six years ago she was at the time the wife of 'the late incumbent, Mr. Watkins, then being Rector of Llansantffread'.[2] It would seem from this testimony that Thomas Vaughan's predecessor, Andrew Watkins, appointed in 1631, was still rector in 1643 or 1644. If Thomas Vaughan 'continued' at Oxford for ten or twelve years, as Henry states with his characteristic vagueness (but he cannot mean 'four or five'), he can have given only scant attention to the duties of his cure, from which he was also absent during his time of military service, unless that service was only for the period preceding his appointment to the rectory.

Thomas Vaughan was apparently successful in his appeal to the Barons of the Exchequer, according to the rules laid down by the Act of July 1643, against a sequestration order of the Brecon County Committee for Sequestrations, as he survived to be evicted by the Propagators in 1650.[3] The Vaughans' friend, Thomas Powell of Cantref, had failed in a similar appeal. The 'Act for better Propagation and Preaching the Gospel in Wales, Ejecting Ministers and Schoolmasters, and Redresse of Grievances', passed on 22 February 1649/50, removed many incumbents who had survived the activities of the county committees. The *gravamina* against Thomas Vaughan were more serious than against any other Breconshire incumbent.[4] The document from which John Walker obtained his information about this case for his use in *The Sufferings of the Clergy* reads thus:

Tho: Vaughan out of Lansantfread for being a comõn drunkard, a common swearer, no preacher, a whoremast[r], & in armes personally against the Parliament.[5]

---

[1] 13 Eliz. cap. xii. 3 (Prothero, *Statutes and Constitutional Documents*, pp. 64–5).
[2] Exch. Q.R. Depositions. Mich. 1649. Brecon, no. 13.
[3] T. Richards, *Hist. of Puritan Movement in Wales*, pp. 50–2, citing S.P.D., Interreg. B 8, ff. 293–4.
[4] T. Richards, *Religious Developments in Wales, 1654–1662*, p. 490.
[5] Bodl. MS. Walker e. 7, f. 213b. Walker (*Sufferings of the Clergy*, 1714, ii. 389), in his ignorance of Welsh names, makes two parishes of St. Bridget's and Llansantffraed, and judges 'Thomas Vaughan, A.M. Llansantfread, R.'

Walker duly incorporates these charges of the propagators in his book, but comments: 'What was in their Opinion worse than All, for having been in *Arms* for the *King*: And perhaps *this last Article*, was the only *Proof* and *Evidence* of *all the rest*. His Cure lay Vacant Eight Years after. the *Sequestration*.' No doubt, bearing arms on the royalist side was the most fatal charge and was sufficient, without other charges, to ensure eviction. And there is no question of its truth, as we have it on Thomas Vaughan's own testimony. In a money suit which he brought while living in the parish of St. Giles in the Fields, on 18 May 1661, when it would be in his favour to testify to his royalism, he deposes: 'Your orator tooke up arms for the King'.[1] It is, of course, possible that he entered the army before taking orders,[2] but it is more likely that he was soldiering at the same time as his brother Henry, both of them in Colonel Price's regiment of horse.[3]

to have been 'a Person different from' the Thomas Vaughan, Rector of St. Bridget's, because, he says, Wood in his account of the latter 'is wholly Silent, as to anything of this Living [i.e. Llansantffraed], or of his bearing Arms for the King'. But Wood named St. Bridget's because his source is Henry Vaughan's letter (M 667–9), which names St. Bridget's twice, but not Llansantffraed, nor does the letter mention military service.

[1] Chanc. Pro., Hamilton 354. 45. *Vaughan* v. *Bolnest*.

[2] This is the sequence of events described in Wood's account of Thomas Vaughan: 'prorumpente autem nupero civili Collegio & Academiae valedixit, Artium, ut opinor, Baccalaureatu decoratus. Sacris postmodum ordinibus per *Manwaringum*, Episcopum *Menevensem*, initiatus, Parochiae natalis Rectoriam consequebatur' (*Hist. et Antiq.*, ii. 320). In the St. Davids Bishops' Registers, vol. iii, 1636–1705, 'there are no entries for the years 1638 to 1660' (J. Conway Davies, 'The Records of the Church in Wales', *The National Library of Wales Journal*, vol. iv, summer 1945, p. 6).

[3] Thomas Wogan (Bodl. MS. Tanner 57, f. 67) reported to Speaker Lenthall on 18 May 1648 a list of those officers 'who drew from Laugharne with their Troopes & faithfully serve yᵉ Parliament under Colonell Horton', and recommends that they be paid out of the delinquents' estates. After naming Captain Richard Jones who 'came in with a full Troope of Horse, & fought gallantly at the last Battle fought uppon the 8th of May against Laugharne' (the general under whom Jones had hitherto served), Wogan continues: 'Capt. Tho. Vaughan came likewise with his troope of horse, and did as aforesayde.' But the names Thomas and Vaughan were common in Wales, and it is unlikely that a member of the resolutely loyal Llansantffraed family was a turncoat. It will be noticed, however, that the 'Cap. Tho. Vaughan' mentioned in the list of officers claiming relief at the Restoration is not given as making a claim for himself (see above, p. 65).

Unhappily there is some support for one of the moral charges brought against Thomas Vaughan by the propagators. In his notebook Thomas Vaughan tells of a dream which he had on 9 April 1659, near the date of the first anniversary of his wife's death:

I dreamed I was in some obscure, large house, where there was a tumultuous, raging people, amongst whom I knew not any but my brother H. My dear wife was there with me, but having conceived some discomfort at their disorder, I quitted the place, and went out, leaving my dear wife behind me.[1]

In his dream he 'called to mind some small, at least seeming, unkindnesses I had used towards my dear wife in her lifetime', and he continues:

These were my thoughts, whereupon I turned in, and taking her along with me, there followed us a certain person, with whom I had in former times revelled away many years in drinking.

It is possible that 'a certain person' was 'my cousin J. Walbeoffe', about whom he had had an evil dream on the previous 17 July.[2] John Walbeoffe in 1666 succeeded his first cousin Charles, son of Henry Vaughan's old friend, in the Llanhamlach estate, and 'being of a gay and extravagant turn, left the estate very much encumbered, to his son Charles'.[3] The 'many years' of Thomas Vaughan's revelling habits belong to 'former times', and in the last paragraph of his notebook he speaks of his life, 'I bless God for it, being much amended.'[4]

One of the most striking features of the first part of *Silex Scintillans* is the series of elegies, with no title but each headed with a pilcrow or paragraph-mark. They commemorate the premature death of a younger brother; 'this Primrose' he is called in the first elegy, and in the same poem the words 'for one *Twenty*' may indicate that that was his age, seven years junior to the twins.[5] His Christian name and the date of his death have become known through Miss

---

[1] B.M. MS. Sloane 1741 (Waite, p. 450).
[2] Waite, p. 446. Waite misprints the name as 'J. Wakebross'.
[3] Theo. Jones, iv. 20.   [4] Waite, p. 452.
[5] 'Thou that know'st for whom I mourne', ll. 10, 27 (M 416).

Morgan's discovery of litigation about the purchase of materials for a shroud ordered by Thomas Vaughan senior on 14 July 1648 for his son William. This account had not been settled, and just before it would lapse by seven years' delay in settlement John Lewis, a Brecon mercer, finding Thomas Vaughan in the town, caused him to be arrested for the unpaid account and secured a judgement in Lewis's favour in the Brecon town court. Thomas Vaughan proceeded to institute an action against Lewis and others for wrongful arrest. Henry Vaughan was among those who deposed on oath. He stated that the letter ordering the shroud was not in his father's handwriting and that he was unable to say whether the signature was his father's though he 'doth acknowledg that it hath some likeness and assimilation' to it. The letter was taken to Lewis by Thomas Vaughan's son-in-law, William Parry, of whom we know nothing further. The result of the action is not known.[1]

Further light is thrown on William Vaughan, strangely enough, in the literary war of coarse personalities waged between his brother Thomas and Henry More, the Cambridge Platonist. In his earliest published work, *Anthroposophia Theomagica* (the preface is dated 1648), Eugenius Philalethes asks his readers' indulgence because 'this *Piece* was compos'd in *Haste*, and in my *Dayes* of *Mourning*, on the *sad Occurrence* of a *Brother's Death*'.[2] Henry More, provoked by Vaughan's onslaught on Aristotle, replied in the following September under the pen-name Alazonomastix Philalethes in *Observations upon Anthroposophia Theomagica*, and included in it this callous comment:

Of a brothers death. Some young man certainly that killed himselfe by unmercifull studying of *Aristotle*. And Philalethes writ this booke to revenge his Death.[3]

Within a few weeks Thomas Vaughan returned to the charge in *The Man-Mouse taken in a Trap, and tortur'd to death*

[1] Exch. Court, Commonwealth. Hilary, 1655. Brecon, no. 22; and Exch. Depositions by Commission. Mich. 1656. Brecon, no. 7.
[2] Op. cit., p. 65 (Waite, p. 60).   [3] H. More, op. cit., p. 38.

for Gnawing the Margins of Eugenius Philalethes, and in it he
again refers to his dead brother:

Some young man certainly, &c. Here Mr. *Mastix*, you tell me,
and adde withall *it is certain, I had a Brother who kill'd himself by
studying of Aristotel.* Who told thee so, thou *Negro*, thou *Mouse*,
thou *Moore*? He did *not kill himself*, and his *death* came not by
studying of *Aristotel*, but by a *far more glorious imployment*.[1] ... Sure
Alas [i.e. Alazonomastix], I shoud deal gently with thee, thou
hast an affection to be thought my *Brother*. Content thy self, thou
canst not be, there was never a *FOOL* of *my Fathers house*. . . .
'Tis a Relation, *Mastix*, I can no way allow of: my *Brothers* were
all *White Boyes*, there was not a *Moore* amongst them.[2]

Thomas Vaughan's allusion to his brother's dying 'by a
far more glorious imployment' suggests that William died,
though at home, as a result of wounds or sickness incurred
in the Civil War. If this inference is allowed, it adds point
to a phrase in Henry Vaughan's final prayer in *The Mount of
Olives* in which he complains that his enemies 'have washed
their hands in the blood of my friends, my dearest and
nearest relatives'.[3] We know of friends like R. W. and R.
Hall, but of no near relation, who died in the war.

There must have been much in Henry Vaughan's home
circumstances, as well as in the public events of the time,
political and religious, to sober him and turn his mind to
the graver issues which brought him to write *Silex Scintillans*. From the close of the first Civil War in 1646 the
Puritan régime had established itself almost universally in
south Wales and bore hardly on the uncompromisingly
royalist families. Vaughan's father had perhaps received
hard measure at the hands of his brother magistrates and
had suffered in reputation. Henry Vaughan had lost his
employment under Sir Marmaduke Lloyd, and, although
he was the heir to Newton, the estate was encumbered by
his father's financial mismanagement and by the exactions
of the Parliamentary Government. The execution of Strafford and Laud had been followed by that of the king on
30 January 1648/9 which profoundly shocked more than half

[1] *The Man-Mouse taken*, pp. 84–5.   [2] Ibid., pp. 9–10.
[3] M 167.

the nation. The fortunes of the Church sank lower and lower and it was threatened with a total eclipse from which there might be no recovery. Already before the Propagation Act came into operation in 1650 Vaughan's friends, the rectors of Cantref and Llanfigan, had been evicted. In this seemingly hopeless condition of Church and State, as Henry Vaughan viewed them, he might have yielded to despair if he had not come to fix his hopes upon the eternal verities and the unseen world.

VIII

CONVERSION

I saw Eternity the other night
Like a great *Ring* of pure and endless light,
   All calm, as it was bright,
And round beneath it, Time in hours, days, years
   Driv'n by the spheres
Like a vast shadow mov'd, In which the world
And all her train were hurl'd.[1]

HERE is authentic poetry of such arresting quality as had not been apparent in the *Poems* of 1646 or would be found in the *Olor Iscanus* of 1651. There was nothing in the secular verse to prepare the reader for this heightened feeling and majestic utterance. Nor did 'The World' stand alone; there were many other poems, such as 'The Retreate', 'The Dawning', 'Peace', and 'Joy of my life!', in the first issue of *Silex Scintillans*, which revealed a true poet who was moved to noble expression by the thoughts that had come to possess him. Henry Vaughan had now something distinctive to communicate, and the new depth and intensity of his thought and feeling gave him utterance. The author of *Silex Scintillans* was a changed man, and this change is of the highest importance in the consideration of him as poet. Unlike the miscellaneous collections of *Poems* and *Olor Iscanus*, *Silex Scintillans*, from the first poem 'Regeneration' to the last, is profoundly religious and mystical, not only in phrase but in temper; it is as purely religious as *The Temple*. We need to ask what has given this new direction to his thoughts and caused him to produce poems so immediately different, in tone and subject and achievement, from anything he had written before.[2]

We must look first at his own account. In the dedication

---

[1] *Silex Scintillans*, 1650: 'The World', ll. 1–7 (M 466).
[2] A different view is expressed by E. L. Marilla, 'The Religious Conversion of Henry Vaughan', *R.E.S.*, Jan. 1945. He believes himself to find more likeness in the two volumes of secular verse to *Silex Scintillans* than I do.

of the first issue of *Silex Scintillans* 'To my most merciful, my most loving, and dearly loved Redeemer, the ever blessed, the onely Holy and Just One, Jesus Christ, The Son of the living God, And the sacred Virgin Mary', he writes:

> My God! thou that didst dye for me,
> These thy deaths fruits I offer thee;
> Death that to me was life and light,
> But dark and deep pangs to thy sight.
> Some drops of thy all-quickning blood
> Fell on my heart; those made it bud
> And put forth thus, though Lord, before
> The ground was curst, and void of store.
> Indeed I had some here to hire
> Which long resisted thy desire,
> That ston'd thy servants, and did move
> To have thee murthred for thy love;
> But Lord, I have expell'd them, and so bent,
> Beg, thou wouldst take thy Tenants Rent.[1]

We have next to look at the fuller account which he gave in the preface, dated 30 September 1654, to the re-issue of *Silex Scintillans* with its second part, though we shall do well to bear in mind that his reflections in 1654 may represent an austerer view of his previous life and writings than he had held when he published the first part in 1650. In this preface, after lamenting the widespread 'malady' of 'idle verse' which had long prevailed, and the recent vogue of translations of 'lascivious fictions', he speaks of himself and his earlier compositions with the most disconcerting disparagement:

And here, because I would prevent a just *censure* by my free *confession*, I must remember, that I my self have for many years together, languished of this very *sickness*; and it is no long time since I have recovered. But (blessed be God for it!) I have by his saving assistance supprest my *greatest follies*, and those which escaped from me, are (I think) as innoxious, as most of that *vein* use to be; besides, they are interlined with many virtuous, and some

---

[1] M 394. In l. 12 I have for clearness altered the spelling *the* to *thee*. In the last six lines Vaughan alludes to Mark xii. 1–9 and to Herbert's poem 'Redemption' (*Works*, p. 40).

pious mixtures. What I speak of them, is truth; but let no man
mistake it for an *extenuation* of faults, as if I intended an *Apology*
for *them*, or my *self*, who am conscious of so much *guilt* in *both*, as
can never be expiated without *special sorrows*, and that cleansing
and pretious *effusion* of my Almighty Redeemer: and if the world
will be so charitable, as to grant my request, I do here most
humbly and earnestly beg that none would read them.[1]

Milton, too, had condemned 'libidinous poetasters' and the
'vulgar amorist', but had never wished any published poems
of his to go unread.[2] Vaughan looks for reform, less to 'the
power of the Magistrate' than to example:

The first, that with any effectual success attempted a *diversion* of
this foul and overflowing *stream*, was the blessed man, Mr. *George
Herbert*, whose holy *life* and *verse* gained many pious *Converts*, (of
whom I am the least) and gave the first check to a most flourishing
and admired *wit* of his time.[3]

Just as Milton in 1642 had realized 'that he who would not
be frustrate of his hope to write well hereafter in laudable
things, ought himself to be a true poem',[4] so Vaughan
writes:

he that desires to excel in this kinde of *Hagiography*, or holy writing,
must strive (by all means) for *perfection* and true *holyness*, that a
door may be opened to him in heaven, and then he will be able to write
(with *Hierotheus* and holy *Herbert*) A *true Hymn*.[5]

There is a further intimation of Vaughan's discipleship
to Herbert. In his poem 'Obedience' Herbert would symbo-

---

[1] M 390.

[2] *The Reason of Church Government* (*Milton's Prose Works*, Bohn's edn., ii.
480–1).

[3] M 391. Chambers (i. 297) suggests diffidently that the 'admired wit' is
Donne, but Herbert was only 22 when Donne took orders, though Vaughan
may have mistakenly supposed that the younger poet was responsible for
Donne's changing from secular to sacred verse. Martin (p. 694) suggests
Andrew Melville, but there was nothing 'foul' in his writings, and Herbert,
although justifiably taking exception to Melville's harsh words about the
Anglican liturgy, recognized that he was a sincere and religious man. Miss
Guiney thought that no particular person was intended, but that Vaughan
means 'the sort of intellectuality then admired'.

[4] *An Apology for Smectymnuus*, Bohn iii. 118.

[5] M 392. Vaughan alludes to Herbert's poem 'A true Hymne', *Works*,
p. 168.

lize the entire devotion of his poetic gift to his Master's service by conveying it as his 'special Deed', just as a man might convey a lordship:

> He that will passe his land,
> As I have mine, may set his hand
> And heart unto this Deed, when he hath read;
> And make the purchase spread
> To both our goods, if he to it will stand.
>
> How happie were my part,
> If some kinde man would thrust his heart
> Into these lines; till in heav'ns Court of Rolls
> They were by winged souls
> Entred for both, farre above their desert![1]

Vaughan comes forward and accepts the challenge in 'The Match'. It will be noticed how close the opening lines are to the words just quoted from the preface of 1654, and how recent was his change of mind when he wrote 'The Match' which first appeared in 1650:

> Dear friend! whose holy, ever-living lines
> Have done much good
> To many, and have checkt my blood,
> My fierce, wild blood that still heaves, and inclines,
> But is still tam'd
> By those bright fires which thee inflam'd;
> Here I joyn hands, and thrust my stubborn heart
> Into thy *Deed*,
> There from no *Duties* to be freed,
> And if hereafter *youth*, or *folly* thwart
> And claim their share,
> Here I renounce the pois'nous ware.[2]

Already in the first part of *Silex Scintillans* Vaughan's obligation to Herbert is everywhere apparent. From *The Temple* he borrows or imitates not only subjects and titles but phrases and whole lines at a time; he uses Herbert's words as freely as if they were Holy Writ without needing other acknowledgement than is found in the preface. There is no example in English literature of one poet borrowing so

---

[1] *The Temple:* 'Obedience', ll. 36–45, *Works*, p. 105.   [2] M 434.

extensively from another. Sometimes, no doubt, the close imitation is infelicitous. It was more natural for the parish priest to celebrate the events of the Christian year and their specific doctrines than for the layman, though Vaughan achieves a measure of success in his poems for Passiontide, Easter, and Ascensiontide. Yet his greater triumphs are won when he essays the remote themes that were congenial to him, such as eternity and the unseen world and the 'commerce' between earth and heaven, but even in these more original poems there are frequent echoes of *The Temple*.

Before he published his preface of 1654, Vaughan had repeatedly expressed his debt to Herbert. In *The Mount of Olives* (1652), before quoting in full 'The Posie', by 'Mr. *George Herbert* of blessed memory', he introduces it thus:

We have had many blessed Patterns of a holy life in the *Brittish Church*, though now trodden under foot, and branded with the title of *Antichristian*. I shall propose but one to you, the most obedient *Son* that ever his *Mother* had, and yet a most glorious true *Saint* and a *Seer*.[1]

There are five other quotations from *The Temple* in this short treatise, without the author's being named. Eight lines are quoted from Herbert's 'Content' in *Flores Solitudinis* (1654),[2] again without naming the author. In *The Life of Paulinus* 'Master *Herbert*' is named when Vaughan refers to 'The Forerunners',[3] and in another context there is an allusion to the mind and practice of 'blessed Mr. *Herbert*'.[4]

It would seem that Miss Morgan seriously understated Vaughan's indebtedness to Herbert when she wrote, in describing his conversion, that his reference in the preface to Herbert's influence 'only means that he had abandoned secular verse for religious poetry'.[5] If it were that only, the debt would be immeasurable, because it was the making of him as a poet, but the debt was both literary and spiritual. Not only did *The Temple* profoundly affect *Silex Scintillans*, but also Vaughan was moved by what he had heard or had inferred from *The Temple* of Herbert's character and holy

[1] M 186.   [2] M 216.
[3] M 379. *The Temple:* 'The Forerunners', *Works*, p. 176.
[4] M 377.   [5] Letter to *The Times Literary Supplement*, 3 Nov. 1932.

living.[1] This is evident from his many references to Herbert's manner of life, and, though Herbert and his poetry were not the sole cause of Vaughan's conversion, it is the only one which he names himself; he gives no other clue, and we must reckon with it.

There were, no doubt, other causes. Principal among them was the death of his brother William in July 1648. Of the nine poems in the *Silex Scintillans* of 1650 with a paragraph-mark only for heading, five at least are elegies for his brother.[2] This series of elegiac poems appears to be continued throughout the year that followed William's death; in one of them[3] he counts 'Twelve hundred hours' since that event, and in the last elegy, the last poem but one in the book, he ends with the words: 'Thus all the year I mourn.'[4] The first of the elegies, 'Thou that know'st for whom I mourne', is curiously self-centred; it echoes the Psalmist's words, 'Lord, make me to know mine end'; 'serious thoughts begin to tame The wise-mans-madnes *Laughter*', and he takes his brother's death as a warning, and even as a judgement upon his own mis-spent years:

> But 'twas my sinne that forc'd thy hand
>   To cull this *Prim-rose* out,
> That by thy early choice forewarn'd
>   My soule might looke about . . .
> Then make my soule white as his owne,
>   My faith as pure, and steddy,
> And deck me, Lord, with the same Crowne
>   Thou hast crownd him already![5]

It can hardly have been Vaughan's first sight of the death of the young, as he is likely to have seen men killed when he was soldiering, though he did not witness the deaths of his friends R. W. and R. Hall, but William Vaughan died at home, as the lawsuit about the shroud proves. In a later

---

[1] Vaughan would have read Nicholas Ferrar's preface to *The Temple*. Barnabas Oley's 'A Prefatory View of the Authour' was included in *Herbert's Remains*, 1652. Walton's *Life* did not appear till 1670.

[2] Some readers think that 'Joy of my life!' (M 422) must refer to his wife rather than to a brother, but see below, p. 195.

[3] 'Silence, and stealth of dayes!', l. 3 (M 425).

[4] 'I walkt the other day', l. 63 (M 479).   [5] M 417, ll. 9–12 and 61–4.

poem, 'The Garland',[1] describing his 'youthfull, sinfull age' when he 'played with fire' and 'never thought that fire would burn', he tells of his being arrested in his pursuit of pleasure when 'at the height of this Careire I met with a dead man'; the reference is obscure, but it indicates that an unexpected confrontation with death had exercised a sobering effect upon him. The word 'forewarn'd' suggests that William's death began Henry Vaughan's change of heart rather than completed it, and the first poem in *Silex Scintillans*, 'Regeneration',[2] describes him as 'A Ward, and still in bonds', as if the process of conversion was begun only.

Miss Morgan attributed Vaughan's religious conversion 'primarily to his careful study of the Bible, followed by the unexpected death of his youngest dearly loved brother'.[3] The only support she gives for this view is the penultimate poem in the second part of *Silex Scintillans*, 'To the Holy Bible'.[4] In that poem, written when he believed himself to be 'nigh unto death', as he explains in the preface,[5] he tells how the Bible was the first book 'put in my hand, When yet I could not understand', and how he had long neglected it and struggled against its influence, until, like a child who quits his nurse till he is 'either hurt or sick', he returned to it and found at last what his restless soul had failed to find elsewhere:

> By this milde art of love at length
> Thou overcam'st my sinful strength,
> And having brought me home, didst there
> Shew me that pearl I sought elsewhere. . . .
> Living, thou wert my souls sure ease,
> And dying mak'st me go in peace.[6]

The expression is paralleled in the elegy written 'Twelve hundred houres' after his brother's death, which ends:

> Yet I have one *Pearle* by whose light
>   All things I see,
> And in the heart of Earth, and night
>   Find Heaven, and thee.[7]

It is probable, in the case of one who became so diligent

---

[1] M 492.   [2] M 397.   [3] Letter of 3 Nov. 1932, as above.
[4] M 540.   [5] M 392.   [6] M 541, ll. 23–6, 33–4.
[7] 'Silence, and stealth of dayes!', ll. 29–32 (M 426).

and devout a reader of the Bible, that it played some part
in his change of mind, but I find it difficult to accept Miss
Morgan's view that it was the primary cause. There is no
evidence that his conversion preceded his brother's death,
and many poems in *Olor Iscanus* which were written shortly
before that event have an unregenerate tone. It seems to
me more probable that the shock of his brother's death or
some other cause that made him 'either hurt or sick' brought
him to a renewed study of the Bible rather than that this
intense study preceded William's death. There must, I
think, have been a cause which drove him back to the
Bible, rather than that the Bible had 'found' him (in
Coleridge's phrase) when he was not in such conscious need
of comfort and guidance. If about the same time he made
acquaintance with *The Temple*, its author's conspicuous love
of the Bible, from which he sought to 'suck ev'ry letter, and
a hony gain', would help to lead Vaughan back to the
spiritual source of Herbert's life and poetry.

It has often been held that a grave and prolonged illness,
threatening to be fatal, caused or precipitated Vaughan's
conversion.[1] But the only certain references to illness
belong to the period between the publication of the first and
second parts of *Silex Scintillans*. It is, indeed, possible that the
'Emblem' prefixed to the 1650 issue of *Silex* alludes to sickness, where Vaughan says that God tried the gentle way of
love without success, and then, changing His way of dealing,
used force, so that the poet can say *'Moriendo, revixi'*.[2] This
interpretation receives some support from a prayer for use in
sickness, included in *The Mount of Olives* (1652): he thanks
God 'for this thy present visitation', and continues:

Thou gavest me health, and I took no notice of thy *gift*. . . . For
what end soever thou hast sent this present *sicknesse*, whether for
my *dissolution*, or for a temporal *correction* of my sinful life, grant I
beseech thee, that both may be for thy *glory*, and the salvation of
my poore soule.[3]

---

[1] Lyte (p. xxx) started this idea: 'He was at this time visited by a severe
and lingering sickness, . . . and while he was in this condition, more deep
and solemn religious views and feelings appear to have broken in upon his
soul than any he had before harboured.'

[2] M 386, l. 15.   [3] M 188–9.

But it is, I think, assuming too much to take these expressions to be both autobiographical and retrospective, referring to an illness which preceded the publication of the first part of *Silex Scintillans*. The certain references to illness are all later. The dedication, dated 1 October 1651, and the undated preface of *The Mount of Olives* (1652) make no allusion to sickness, but the Epistle Dedicatory, dated 1653, of *Flores Solitudinis. Collected in his Sicknesse and Retirement* (1654) refers to 'the incertainty of life, and a peevish, inconstant state of health' which 'would not suffer me to stay for greater performances, or a better season'.[1] Still more explicitly, in the preface, dated 30 September 1654, to the completed *Silex Scintillans* (1655), Vaughan warns his readers that they will misunderstand 'the last *Poems* in the book' and 'would judge all to be *fatherless*, and the *Edition* posthume', if he did not tell them how near he had been to death, but '*the God of the spirits of all flesh* hath granted me a further use of *mine*, then I did look for in the *body*; and when I expected, and had (by his assistance) prepared for a *message* of *death*, then did he *answer* me with *life*'.[2] Vaughan introduces in his *Life of Paulinus* (1654) a sentence, which is not in his source, that seems to reflect his own mind and recent experience, though he is telling of Paulinus: 'This sicknesse was a pure stratagem of love, God visited him with it for this very purpose, that he himselfe might be his Cordial.'[3] Vaughan's nearness to death in or about 1653 would doubtless have deepened his piety, but there is no sufficient evidence of his having had a similar sickness before writing the first part of *Silex Scintillans*.

There is one other influence in his life which may have played some part in his conversion. If, as is probable, the poem 'Fair and yong light!' commemorates the death of his wife Catherine while he was engaged in writing the second part of *Silex Scintillans*, its opening words deserve some attention:

> Fair and yong light! my guide to holy
> Grief and soul-curing melancholy;

[1] M 215.   [2] M 392.   [3] M 356.

> Whom living here I did still shun
> As sullen night-ravens do the Sun,
> And lead by my own foolish fire
> Wandred through darkness, dens and mire.
> How am I now in love with all
> That I term'd then meer bonds and thrall,
> And to thy name, which still I keep,
> Like the surviving turtle, weep![1]

A possible explanation of these lines is that Vaughan resisted for long the gentle pressure of his 'yong light' and 'guide', and went his own way, until other and more potent causes brought him to another mind. Now that he has lost his wife, he recognizes more fully in retrospect that, if he had been less self-centred and more open to her influence, he might sooner have reached peace of mind. Her influence was telling on him all the while subconsciously, but it was not sufficient of itself to effect her husband's conversion, which was caused by other and more arresting experiences. There is no other evidence of his wife's influence, and it is precarious to rest much upon this hint, but it deserves consideration. The broken fortunes of Church and State, as they affected Vaughan's personal life and peace of mind, would also deepen his sense of spiritual need, but they were not the primary causes of his conversion. For instance, the execution of King Charles on 30 January 1648/9 took place after Vaughan had already written several of the elegies on his brother, with their deeply religious tone.[2]

[1] M 513. The turtle-dove's proverbial affection for its mate seems decisive of this poem's commemorating Vaughan's wife, not his brother. The *O.E.D.* s.v. Turtle, sense 2 *fig.*, gives several early examples of this use. Another good example, nearer Vaughan's time, is Quarles's description of 'the widow'd turtle' in the third stanza of *Emblems*, IV. xii.

[2] An explanation may be diffidently offered of a puzzling reference to 'twenty years' in the poem 'The Call' (M 416), in which he bids his heart awake: ''Tis now, since you have laine thus dead Some twenty years.' It was not unusual for religious writers to date the dawn of reason, the beginning of the power to discern between right and wrong, at about seven years of age. The poet would regard the years of infancy as innocent, followed by some twenty years of careless living. This would date his conversion at the age of 27 in 1648, the year of William's death. He could still speak of himself as young ('Idle Verse', M 446, l. 5, and 'The Match', M 435, l. 10).

IX

THE PURITAN RÉGIME

WE shall be in a better position for understanding the mind and feeling of the author of *Silex Scintillans* if we consider the workings of the Puritan régime during the years in which that book was being written, and show how closely the changes affected Henry Vaughan and his family and his nearest friends. His strong feeling leads him to intrude constant allusions to the times in his writings. We can admire his loyalty to his ideals in Church and State, and yet regret that the calm and remote air of his divine poems and devotional pieces should so often be ruffled by these political and ecclesiastical outbursts. As Miss Guiney has faithfully and sorrowfully recorded: 'To-day, one can but be disturbed with extraneous echoes here, with stains of old trouble, which really have no place in ethics or in art, inasmuch as they are not eternal.'[1] Yet it is necessary to see the background of those years and to understand why he was so deeply stirred.

The Puritan régime established itself in south Wales so soon as the first Civil War ended in victory for the Parliamentarian cause in 1646. Till then much of the legislation had not taken effect in a remote part of the island in which royalist feeling was predominant, especially among the ruling classes. For instance, the Ordinance of 4 January 1644/5 prohibiting the use of the Book of Common Prayer could be ignored with impunity for a while, and indeed the continued use of the Prayer Book was a common charge alleged for evicting ministers in 1650. But long before the Propagation Act of that year came into force, several of Henry Vaughan's friends had been sequestered by the County Sequestration Committee. His old schoolmaster, Matthew Herbert, was displaced by a new rector of Llangattock in August 1646, soon after the royalist defeat. It was

---

[1] From the preface to Miss Guiney's edition of *The Mount of Olives*, 1902, p. x.

maintained after the Restoration that he had been 'sequestered contrary even to the orders of the then Parliament,
before any charge was exhibited against him'.[1] Like others
of Vaughan's clerical friends, Matthew Herbert was uncompromising and continued to serve his parishioners. According to a witness in 1664, who came from Llanelly, one of
the chapelries attached to Llangattock, Herbert preached in
that parish until he was stopped in 1655. In that year he
had even dared to sue some of the parishioners for not
paying tithes to him 'as rector', but was obliged to give a
guarantee not to molest them further under a penalty of
£200. In April of the following year he was committed to
Brecon jail for seventeen weeks. He was threatened with
banishment, but was saved from this fate by his neighbours,
among them a local Parliamentarian leader, interceding on
his behalf.[2]

Vaughan's nearer neighbours, Thomas Powell, rector of
Cantref, and Thomas Lewes, rector of Llanfigan, were also
sequestered by the Brecon Sequestration Committee before
the passing of the Propagation Act. Their fortunes were
strangely parallel throughout life. From Breconshire homes
they went to Oxford at the age of eighteen and were
matriculated from Jesus College on the same day. In the
same year, 1635, at the age of 25 they were appointed to
their Breconshire livings, and both suffered sequestration,
followed by eviction in 1650 under the Act. Powell had
appealed against his sequestration by the Brecon Committee, but, unlike Thomas Vaughan, without success.[3] The
sufficient charges for evicting Powell were 'Adhering to
the King, and Reading Common Prayer'; it would have
been difficult to bring graver charges against a man who
was reputed to be 'a Learned and Orthodox Man, of a
Godly Life and Conversation, and a Constant Preacher in
Welch and *English*'.[4] Both Powell and Lewes for a few more
years continued to serve their parishioners more or less,
especially as no 'settled' ministers replaced them. There

---

[1] Lambeth MS. 1027 f. 30, cited in Richards, i. 53. For Matthew Herbert's
later fortunes, see below, pp. 201–2.   [2] Richards, ii. 283, 315.
[3] Richards, i. 52.   [4] Walker, *Sufferings of the Clergy*, ii. 337.

was considerable sympathy for them, and they were able, while remaining in the district, to organize resistance, as will be shown later.

The Act for the Propagation of the Gospel in Wales, passed on 22 February 1649/50, initiated a far more vigorous purgation of the royalist clergy than the County Committee with their local knowledge of the clergy and natural sympathy with many of them had exercised. The Act named 71 persons as commissioners. The first named was Colonel, afterwards Major-General, Thomas Harrison, a regicide, but as he was appointed in the following June to the chief military command during Cromwell's absence in Ireland, the leadership of the commission in Wales passed to Colonel Philip Jones. The other commissioners were substantial middle-class men—country squires, lawyers, soldiers—who had shown steady support of the Parliament; there were no peers and few of the larger landowners.[1] Any five of the commissioners were empowered to summon Welsh incumbents, to hear evidence and eject them if they considered the charges proved. They could also appoint in their stead ministers who 'shall be recommended and approved of' by five or more of the approvers, who were named in the Act. The approvers were all themselves 'Ministers of the Gospel'. The most powerful of them throughout Wales was Vavasor Powell, who was called by his opponents 'that great Clero-Mastix'.[2] In Breconshire the most active approver was Jenkin Jones of Llandetty, who showed as much ardour in military service as in preaching the Gospel. On the nomination of Major-General Harrison 'Capt. Jenkin Jones' was granted by the Council of State on 12 September 1650 a militia commission over a troop of horse,[3] and in May of the following year, shortly before Charles II invaded England from Scotland, he was ordered to join Harrison in the north with his hundred troopers.[4]

The Propagation Act was to run from Lady Day 1650 for three years 'and no longer'. The commissioners and approvers began their work at once and most of their evictions

[1] Richards, i. 93–4.   [2] *Strena Vavasoriensis*, 1654, p. 12.
[3] Cal. S.P.D., 1650, pp. 280, 511.   [4] Ibid. 1651, pp. 175, 187–8.

were effected in the first twelvemonth. Thomas Vaughan
was now extruded from Llansantffraed.

There was considerable disaffection in Breconshire,
though there was also support for the Commonwealth
régime, and Parliament and its committees were besieged
by petitions from both sides.[1] John Gunter of Tredomen
and William Thomas of Brecon, commissioners for sequestration in the county of Brecon, wrote to the Parliamentary
Committee for Compounding on 25 October 1651 as
follows:

> The Commissioners named in an Act of 22 February 1650 . . .
> have for the last two years ousted most of the ministers in So.
> Wales and Co. Brecon, which has 73 parishes, & have not supplied
> others; there are only two at present preaching; nevertheless,
> they have disposed of all the rectories, vicarages, . . . tithes,
> impropriations, glebe lands & all ecclesiastical livings whatso-
> ever, the revenues whereof in Co. Brecon alone amount to 4000 l.,
> or 5000 l. a year; whereas the Act gives them power only to dis-
> pose of the profits for propagation of the Gospel.[2]

They also complain that there are 'vast sums' still unac-
counted for in the hands of the commissioners and others
'that managed sequestrations from the beginning of the
wars to 20 April 1650' (i.e. until the propagators took over
from the former officials). The London Committee in
answer state that they are 'much aggrieved at the sadness of
your relation about rectories, etc.': 'We have told Major-
Gen. Harrison and the Army Committee, who will make it
known to Parliament. You are to force the late Committee
to bring you their accounts from December 1649.' The
Brecon Committee reports on 14 May 1652 that three of the
late commissioners, including Henry Vaughan's friend
Charles Walbeoffe, 'are so refractory that, without some
special course is taken with them, no satisfactory result will
be obtained'.[3] Walbeoffe was, in consequence, fined £20.

The evidence of Gunter and Thomas is not to be taken

---

[1] Petitions from south Wales in support of the Act were sent on 20 and
28 June 1650 (Richards, i. 250).

[2] Record Office: Cal. of Cttee. for Compounding 1643–60, part i, p. 495.

[3] Ibid., p. 578.

without qualifications. There was, indeed, some justification for the widespread belief that the funds of the Welsh
livings were not used to provide 'settled' or even 'itinerant'
ministers to supply the place of the evicted incumbents, but
when, after much pressure, commissioners were appointed
by an Ordinance of 31 August 1654 to audit the accounts,
they satisfied themselves that the moneys were not being
improperly used, though there were serious arrears.[1] We
need not concern ourselves here with the vexed question of
the use made of church revenues, either by the former
committees or by the propagators, but we must note that
the spiritual destitution, which was very general in the
county, is proved in the case of the parishes of Llanfigan,
Cantref, and Llansantffraed. Llanfigan was unserved until
1658, when the Triers appointed a youth of 21, who was
seldom resident.[2] The living of Cantref was also left
unfilled. The Petty Constables of Llansantffraed, giving
evidence on oath at Crickhowell on 21 August 1662, stated
that the commissioners for propagation 'have nott put anie
Minister or curate to officiate in Llansanfred since Thomas
Vaughan Rector weare eiected out of his Lievinge, nor
anie other Itinerant Minister'.[3] This is not quite correct,
as after nearly eight years' vacancy Meredith Penry was
admitted rector on 12 December 1657 on the presentation
of the Lord Protector.[4]

Although many churches were unserved and closed,
tithes were still due to be paid to the sequestrators, but
there was a natural unwillingness to continue paying when
there was no visible return of service. It is in the light of
such facts that we understand how Henry Vaughan could
write:

The wayes of *Zion* do mourne, our beautiful gates are shut up,
and the Comforter that should relieve our souls is gone far from
us. Thy Service and thy Sabbaths, thy own sacred Institutions and
the pledges of thy love are denied unto us; Thy Ministers are
trodden down, and the basest of the people are set up in thy holy

[1] Cal. S.P. Dom. 1654, pp. 337, 348. [2] Richards, ii. 21, 138–40.
[3] Lambeth: Sequestered Livings, 1650–2. MS. 1027, no. 36a.
[4] Lambeth Augmentation Book 998, p. 150.

place. O Lord holy and just! . . . return and restore us, that joy
and gladnesse may be heard in our dwellings, and the voyce of the
Turtle in all our land.[1]

Further evidence of the common belief that the propagators were failing to use the church revenues 'for the propagation of the Gospel' is afforded in 'The Petition of the
Six Counties of South Wales. Presented to the Parliament
of the Common-wealth of England. For a supply of
Ministers in lieu of those that have been Ejected.'[2] The
petition was presented at the Bar of the Commons on
10 March 1651/2 by Colonel Freeman, M.P. for Hereford
and Attorney-General for south Wales, with 15,000 signatures. Freeman was assisted by John Gunter as solicitor
for the petition. The petitioners profess to be 'well-affected
to the Parliament' and state that they 'rejoiced when we
heard of your care in passing the Act'. The Rump was not
likely to take these protestations at their face value. The
record of the promoters of the petition was against them;
their sympathies were royalist, though they had ostensibly
conformed to the new government and some of them had
even taken office. Freeman, formerly 'domestic of the late
King's son', had been a prisoner in the Fleet until the
Council of State discharged him on 31 December 1651 on
his taking the Engagement and giving a security of £500
'never to act anything prejudicial to the Comonwealth'.[3]
Gunter and Thomas, although they had been reappointed
sequestration commissioners for Breconshire as recently as
25 November 1651, were displaced on the following 16
December. Gunter's activities about the petition aroused
the suspicion of the Council of State so seriously that an
Order was made on 3 August 1652 for his being committed
to the Sergeant-at-arms 'in order to his further examination',
and on the same day it was ordered that Freeman was 'to
be brought in safe custody to Council'.[4] Freeman was

---

[1] M 166. Vaughan is quoting from Lamentations i. 4 and the Song of
Songs, ii. 12.

[2] Printed in 1652 without publisher's or printer's name. Alexander
Griffith, ejected vicar of Glasbury, Breconshire, probably edited this pamph-
let, as he certainly edited *Strena Vavasoriensis*, 1654.

[3] Cal. S.P. Dom. 1651–2, pp. 85, 93.   [4] Ibid., pp. 354, 380, 381.

discharged after examination on 26 October, but on 18 June 1653 he was deprived of the office of Attorney-General.[1] Although its manifest *parti pris* must be discounted, the petition expresses the genuine concern of very many in south Wales at the neglect of spiritual provision:

> Your Petitioners indure a Famine of the Word of God; Children are not bred up in the instruction and information of the Lord; the vast Revenue of the outed Ministers are set out at extraordinary undervalues; the Churches are in most places shut up, and the Fabric thereof ready to fall to the ground for want of repair.

Again, we cannot be surprised at the intensity of Vaughan's feeling as he gives vent to it in the last paragraph of the preface, dated 17 April 1652, to *Flores Solitudinis:*

> All that may be objected is, that I write unto thee out of a land of darkenesse, out of that unfortunate region, where the Inhabitants sit in the shadow of death : where destruction passeth for propagation.[2]

There is a still harsher reference to the propagators in his *Life of Paulinus:*

> Some dispositions love to stand in raine, and affect wind and showers beyond Musick. *Paulinus* sure was of this temper; he preferred the indignation and hatred of the multitude to their love, he would not buy their friendship with the losse of Heaven, nor call those Saints and propagators, who were Devills and destroyers.[3]

A turn of the tide at the close of 1653 raised new hopes in the breasts of those who, often too boldly for their own security, had pleaded for a more tolerant church policy. On 20 April 1653 Cromwell had expelled the Long Parliament, and the Assembly of Nominees, known as the Saints' Parliament, lasted only from 4 July to December, when its ecclesiastical policy became plainly repugnant to Cromwell's more liberal mind. It was not unreasonable to hope that better times would come when the Saints had resigned their power into Cromwell's hands. In this emergency the council of officers drew up the Instrument of Government, and, in accordance with its provisions, Oliver Cromwell was installed as Lord Protector on 16 December 1653. But, if new hopes were raised in one camp, new antagonisms arose

---

[1] Ibid., p. 456; 1652–3, p. 423.   [2] M 217.   [3] M 346.

in another. There were those who thought the Protector's
rule no good substitute for the rule of the Saints. Prominent among them, and the first to give bold utterance to
this opposition, was the Welsh evangelist, Vavasor Powell.
Immediately after Cromwell's installation, Powell denounced
the Protectorate in a sermon at Blackfriars. For this act he
was taken before the Council of State and kept in custody
for some days, but on his release he repeated his offence.
Then, returning to Wales, he organized resistance. This
gave a handle to his enemies, who were quick to take
advantage of it. Jenkin Jones was associated with Vavasor
Powell in this new development, and it soon involved
Henry Vaughan's friends and his own father, as the following series of letters will show.

On 31 January 1653/4 Jenkin Jones wrote to the evicted
rector of Llanfigan this warning or threatening letter:

Mr. Lewis.

I am like to be comanded (with pte of my troop) to wait upon
your cock-fight, but if you and others doe forbear, you will spare
some trouble to yourselfe and to

Sr. Your frend
JEN: JONES

Your plaine and positive answer I expect & by to-morrow.

The next letter shows that the cock-fight was a cloak for
illegal drilling in order to be prepared for Jones's threat of
bringing his troopers, or at any rate a meeting for considering how to meet the danger. Jones's opponents saw in his
letter a precious opportunity of discrediting him with 'his
Highness' by revealing that he was assembling armed force
without authority.[1] Thomas Vaughan was evidently in
communication with Lewes, and received from him Jones's
letter. On 8 February he forwarded Jones's letter, with a
covering letter of his own, to Charles Roberts, who had succeeded Gunter as solicitor for the petition and who would

[1] Similarly Alexander Griffith communicated to the Protector on 17 March
1653/4 news of 'seditious' utterances of Vavasor Powell and Jenkin Jones,
and letters of theirs 'which shew that they have listed troopes, which they
keep on foote to the terror of the inhabitants, though (as I am informed)
they are not of the established army, raised by command from your highness'
(*Thurloe State Papers*, ii. 174).

know the best use that could be made of the incriminating letter. Thomas Vaughan has been commonly taken to be the evicted rector, but there is no other evidence of his returning to Llansantffraed, and Thomas Vaughan of Newton is more likely to be his father, who was a most uncompromising royalist. This is the letter of 8 February 1653/4:

Cosin Roberts,

By the Inclosed from Capt. Jenkin John Howell to Mr. Lewes of Llanvigan, you may see, that he threatens the Countrey with his troope; Mr. Morgan of Therw & diverse others of the best in the County were att this Cock-fight, which was kept noe other-wise, than according to the custome of all other Schooles. We conceived that there was noe troope in our County, nor under his command, butt it appears by this his owne letter, that he hath them still listed, and keeps them up privately, for though he came not to the Cock-fight according to his menaces, yet he had that morning att his house above thirty horse with Sadles & Pistolls, which did much trouble and terrifie the countrey people. I pray learn, if his Highness hath lately granted him a Commission, otherwise I know noe reason, butt these actions should be taken notice of.

Our Justices of the peace still slight the Lord Protectour's authority & have now issued forth their warrants for the Con-tribution, some in the name of the keepers of the liberty by authority of Parliament, others without any name att all, and diverse gentlemen have been served with them, butt refused to execute them. I wonder att these proceedings, and more att those that suffer them. Ile assure you the people by reason of this public & persevering contempt will not believe that there is a Lord Protectour, & doe butt laugh att such relations.

I could wish, that those whome it concerns, would looke to it, lest their too much clemency prove hurtfull to them. I pray lett me heare from you with the first conveniency, & how the busines goes betwixt me & Mr. Games. Farewell.

Your friend &
affectionate kinsman
THOMAS VAUGHAN.

Newton, Ashwednesday, 1653.
For my respected kinsman Mr. Ch. Roberts
att his Chamber in Grayes Inne, London. This.[1]

[1] The originals of this letter and of Jenkin Jones's are in Bodl. MS.

It is hard to believe that Thomas Vaughan (whether it is the father or the son) was sincere in professing solicitude about the Protector's authority in Wales, but there would be no chance of a hearing if this were not assumed. Nor is it to be overlooked that there was a reasonable hope of the Protector's introducing a more generous ecclesiastical policy than that of the unpopular propagators.

While Thomas Vaughan was communicating with the solicitor of the petitioners, Henry Vaughan's friends, Thomas Powell and Thomas Lewes, and another Breconshire evicted clergyman, Griffith Hatley of Abereskir, were engaged in a correspondence with Jenkin Jones. As two of these three were friends of Henry Vaughan, it is worth while to give the letters. Dr. Thomas Richards says of these evicted men that 'they were bent on testing the new tolerance of the Protectorate'.[1] Their first letter was dated two days before Thomas Vaughan's letter:

Mr. Jones, we desire to be resolved by you, whether the ejected Ministers of this Country, who have been silenced & suspended (now this long time) ab officio & beneficio may at last have the door of utterance opened, and be permitted to preach the Gospel freely among those that do much want it, & do as earnestly call for it, as the parched Earth after the dew and Raine of Heaven. The reason why we put this business to the question is: because about the last spring, some of our fellow Ministers, taking the boldnes to preach the word of God, (were some of them) sent prisoners to Chepsto Garrison, others pull'd out of the Pulpit, and all the rest were threatened to have the same measure meted out to them, if they should make the same attempts; and therefore wee desire to know whether we are under the same restraint still, or are at liberty: wee doubt not but that you can resolve us herein, as well as any other in this County, and we hope you will be pleased to satisfie our civill request herein, and vouchsafe a

Rawlinson A. xi. ff. 334–5. They are printed, with some mistakes, in *Thurloe State Papers*, ii. 120. T. Vaughan's letter is given inaccurately in Waite, p. xi. Charles Roberts was a Brecon man; his epitaph in the Priory Church ran: 'Here lyeth the body of Charles the sonne of Thomas Roberts, Gent. He died the 22 day of 7ber Anno Domini 1673' (MS. Harl. 6831). The nature of his kinship to the Vaughans I have not discovered.

[1] Richards, ii. 285.

line of answer, which you may direct to either of the subscribers,
who are

Sir

Your friends, as far as you are a
friend to Christ, and his wayes

THO. LEWIS, THO. POWELL, GRIFFITH HATLEY.

Feb. 6, 1653 [i.e. 1653/4].[1]

It was more than three weeks before Jones received the
above letter, to which he replied on the following day:

Gentlemen, Your Letter dated Feb. 6. 1653. I received the first of
March. And in answer to what you propose therein, I shall onely
put you in minde that you are still, and (more) than like to be in
the same condition with those in the last Spring; And tell you that
you are to expect the same measure from the present Power
(whose connivance you seem (at least) to fancie to your selves)
as your brethren had the last Spring from the (then) powers;
And also that you need not pretend your being pressed as from
pitty to water the parched earth, there being more Sermons
Preached (now) in one moneth, then were formerly in twelve, and
with very much (though I dare not say with a greater) blessing;
consider the restraint-fearing Spirit that's in you.

Your friend, and servant,

JEN. JONES.

March 2, 1653 [i.e. 1653/4].[2]

Four days later the three evicted incumbents sent this
answer:

Mr. Jones, wee thank you for your Letter: wherein you have
fully resolved us, what we must expect, if we Preach the Gospell
in this poor Countrey; nothing but bonds and imprisonment, if
you divine aright, abide us. If we be silent, and do not Preach,
we are reproached, and if we do Preach we are menaced. A hard
dilemma, Sir, notwithstanding your paines in preaching (which
nevertheless is much abated of what it was, since you have caught
the fish that you looked for), there are many dry and thirsty soules
in this Country, that are very seldom refreshed with the dew
of Heavenly Doctrine, and for want thereof do daily relapse to
Popery, and that in no small number; we could name above 20
Parish churches in this County, in many whereof there have not

---

[1] *A True and Perfect Relation of the Petition of the Six Counties*, 1654, p. 50.
[2] Ibid, p. 51.

been above two Sermons this 12 moneth, and in most of them none at all; yet the Inhabitants pay their Tithes still as formerly. Their complaints have fill'd the ears of men long since, and have (no doubt e're this) ascended up to the eares of the Lord of Saboth. We shall therefore (in compassion to these poor soules) adventure to bestow our paines among them, and put our selves upon the candor and clemency of our present Governour, from whom we do expect (and doubt not to find) better measure then you forbad us; or then our fellow Ministers received (the last Spring) when other powers swayed, to wit, your own.

That there are more Sermons preached (now) in a month then was formerly in 12 will hardly find credit, with any that knowes this Country, and is such a story that men will admire to have proceeded from your Pen: since that we do not know of above two Itinerant Preachers, resident in the Country (and one of the two hardly worth the name of a Preacher), whereas formerly there was a preaching Minister almost in every parish (some Impropriations except) and most of them graduated in the Universities, and able and painfull men in their callings. Consider better of that passage of your Letter, and consider what spirit you are of: for the Spirit of God is a spirit of truth, *Nec mendax est, nec mordax.*

> Your loving friends
> THO. LEWIS, THO. POW., GR. HATLY.

March 6, 1653 [i.e. 1653/4].[1]

This last letter was defiant, and perhaps it was for some illegal act of preaching that Powell suffered imprisonment, before he 'went beyond the Seas'.[2] His going abroad deprived Henry Vaughan of the advice and literary encouragement of his best friend, whom he had addressed in a Latin poem as *Eximio viro et amicorum longè optimo*.[3]

The Protector's church policy was in fact more liberal than that of the propagators. The Rump in the last weeks before its expulsion had not renewed the Propagation Act, which therefore lapsed on Lady Day 1653. Cromwell, soon after becoming Protector, instituted by Ordinance on 20 March 1653/4 a Board of Triers to examine the fitness of

---

[1] *A True and Perfect Relation*, &c., pp. 51–2.

[2] J. Walker, *Sufferings of the Clergy*, ii. 337. A less probable alternative view of the occasion of Powell's imprisonment is given above, p. 69.

[3] Heading of the Latin poem in Powell's *Elementa Opticae*, 1651; this heading is absent from the same poem when it reappears in *Olor Iscanus* (M 93).

ministers nominated to livings by the patrons, whose rights
to present were respected if they were not 'delinquents'.
Yet Llansantffraed, Llanfigan, and Cantref continued to be
unserved.

The allusions to contemporary events are constant in
Silex Scintillans and are often violent. Such outbursts do
not make for great poetry and they mar some of Vaughan's
best poems. The fine theme of 'The World' is sadly lowered
when its splendid opening is immediately followed by the
caustic description of the 'darksome States-man'.[1] With
his aristocratic disdain for popular government Vaughan
is especially bitter against those who had newly risen to
power, and who, in his opinion, sought 'self-ends'; their
'thriving vice' is specially offensive to him.[2] The cant word
zeal rouses him to fury:

> But here Commission'd by a black self-wil
>   The sons the father kil,
> The Children Chase the mother, and would heal
>   The wounds they give, by crying, zeale.[3]

Charles I is the father they kill, and the Church of England
is the mother they harry. With his devotion to the older
conception of saintliness, and his knowledge of the lives
of the primitive saints, Vaughan resents the name of saints
being given by themselves or their adherents to the Puritan
leaders—'they who assume to themselves the glorious stile
of Saints'.[4] He shares the common Cavalier view that his
opponents are pretenders to a piety which is not genuine;
'who Saint themselves, they are no Saints'.[5] He contrasts
this reputed saintliness with 'the patience of the Saints'.[6]

---

[1] M 466. Miss Guiney was minded to identify the 'darksome States-man'
with Cromwell, but in 1650, when this poem was published, he was not in
full power. I do not myself think that his policy, patent to the world, at all
resembles the digging of the mole 'Who workt under ground', or that his
conscience was tortured by self-reproaches. For Miss Guiney's view and a
criticism of it by Sir E. K. Chambers, see *Athenaeum*, 29 Mar. 1902.

[2] M 511, ll. 37–40 and 517, ll. 9–16.

[3] 'The Constellation', ll. 37–40 (M 470). There is another allusion to zeal
and self-ends in 'The Agreement', ll. 29–30 (M 529).

[4] M 140, ll. 6–7.   [5] M 509, l. 72.

[6] M 516, ll. 5–8. Cf. the scornful allusions to 'new lights' (M 485, l. 9)
and 'green heads' (M 404, l. 25).

Even when he is translating Nieremberg's grave treatise
Of Life and Death there is a long interpolation in which he
gives vent to his angry feeling; he pictures what a just man
would make of the human scene if God opened his eyes to
show him the faithful being 'plundered, tortured, mur-
thered, and martyred', and

> their murtherers in the mean time pretending Religion, Piety, and
> the Glory of God: And after all this outward *Scene*, should so
> enlighten his eyes, that he might discover another inward one, I
> meane their secret thoughts, and close devices, their tyranny,
> covetousnesse, & sacriledge varnished outwardly with godly
> pretences, dissembled purity, and the stale shift of liberty of Con-
> science.[1]

And in telling the story of St. Paulinus he turns aside to
introduce a topical reference:

> It was not the Custome, but the nature (if I may so say) of those
> Primitive times to love holy and peacefull men. But some *great
> ones* in this later age, did nothing else but countenance *Schismaticks*
> and *seditious raylers, the despisers of dignities*, that covered their
> *abominable villanies* with a pretence of *transcendent holinesse*, and a
> certain *Sanctimonious excellencie* above the Sons of men.[2]

In his poem 'Religion' Vaughan laments the decline of
English piety, which has become 'a tainted sink', but he
redeems this ugly phrase with a beautiful couplet to end
the poem:

> Look downe great Master of the feast; O shine,
> And turn once more our *Water* into *Wine!*[3]

In 'The Brittish Church' he laments that 'The Souldiers
here' have dared to divide and stain Christ's 'seamlesse
coat', and at the end of the poem he quotes or invents a
sentence framed from the Song of Songs: *O Rosa Campi!
O lilium Convallium! quomodò nunc facta es pabulum Aprorum!*[4]

---

[1] M 278.   [2] M 371.   [3] M 405, ll. 51-2.
[4] M 410. Cf. 'L'Envoy', M 542, l. 30: 'Thy seamless coat is grown a rag.'
He returns to the symbol of the flower and the wild beast three times: *The
Mount of Olives* (M 161, ll. 9-12), *Life of Paulinus* (M 354, l. 11), and 'The
Holy Communion' (M 458, ll. 49-50). He takes *Rosa* from Tremellius's
Latin Bible, whereas the Vulgate has *flos*, just as he quotes from Beza's New
Testament (M 432) instead of drawing from the Vulgate. With the same
freedom he quotes at will from the Geneva Bible as well as from the Autho-
rized Version or even fuses them.

As one who loves the old observances of the Church feasts
and fasts, he resents the prohibition of the keeping of
Christmas and Good Friday:

> Shal he that did come down from thence,
>   And here for us was slain,
> Shal he be now cast off? no sense
>   Of all his woes remain?
> Can neither Love, nor suff'rings bind?
>   Are we all stone, and Earth?
> Neither his bloudy passions mind,
>   Nor one day blesse his birth?
> Alas, my God! Thy birth now here
> Must not be numbred in the year.[1]

His sense of reverence is distressed by the Puritan innova-
tion of sitting to receive Communion:

> Give me, my God! thy grace,
> The beams, and brightnes of thy face,
>   That never like a beast
>   I take thy sacred feast,
> Or the dread mysteries of thy blest bloud
> Use, with like Custome, as my Kitchin food.
>   Some sit to thee, and eat
> Thy body as their Common meat,
>   O let not me do so!
>   Poor dust should ly still low,
> Then kneel my soul, and body; kneel, and bow;
> If *Saints*, and *Angels* fal down, much more thou.[2]

In 'Jacobs Pillow, and Pillar' Vaughan sees the Church
of England reduced to a 'litle *Goshen*, in the midst of night',
'a Pillar . . . conceal'd from men'.[3] But he encourages the
'peaceful, humble, and pious' reader of *The Mount of Olives*
to believe that its supporters, though for the moment
driven into silence and obscurity, are more numerous and
more faithful than appears:

Onely I shall adde this short Exhortation: That thou wouldest
not be discouraged in this way, because very many are gone out of

[1] 'Christs Nativity' (M 443). Cf. 'The Nativity' (M 645), 'The true Christmas' (M 646), and 'Life of Paulinus' (M 379, ll. 29–39).
[2] 'Dressing', M 456. Cf. 'The Throne', ll. 5–6 (M 533), and 'The Feast',
l. 59 (M 535).   [3] M 527.

it. Think not that thou art alone upon this Hill, there is an innumerable company both before and behinde thee. Those with
their Palms in their hands, and these expecting them. . . . Look
not upon transitorie, visible things, but upon him that is eternal,
and invisible.[1]

In the concluding words of *Silex Scintillans* he tells how he
longs for the turning of 'our sad captivity' when the persecution of the Church shall be over.[2]

There was one practical issue of the times which appears
to have exercised Vaughan's mind. With the establishment
of the Puritan régime in Breconshire after the royalist
defeat in the first Civil War, it would have been difficult in
a county where the landed gentry and magistrates had been
overwhelmingly royalist to provide the *personnel* of the
many committees and administrations required for local
government. It was not unnatural that many with royalist
sympathies, recognizing that the old order was gone, at
least for some time to come, believed they could best serve
the locality according to the traditional service which their
class had rendered, and save the new enactments from bearing too hardly upon their friends, by themselves taking
office. A good example of these 'collaborationists', as they
would be called to-day, was Vaughan's cousin, Charles
Walbeoffe, of an ancient family long settled at Llanhamlach,
and himself married to a daughter of Sir Thomas Aubrey of
Llantrithyd. Perhaps he could not easily have refused office,
when the Parliament in February 1647/8 made him one of
the county commissioners 'for raising Threescore Pounds',
and similarly when on 27 June 1649 he was 'added to the
Committee for assessment of the Ninety Thousand Pounds
per mensem in the county of Brecon'. He also served on
the County Committee for Sequestrations, and was high
sheriff for 1648. Yet, when in that year the Civil War
again smouldered in Wales, he became a Commissioner of
Array and Association for the king, and, as was afterwards
charged against him, 'sat as Justice of the peace in the court
at Brecon when the friends of Parliament were prosecuted'.[3]

---

[1] M 141.   [2] 'L'Envoy', l. 62 (M 543).
[3] *Journal of H. of Commons*, v. 466, 17 Feb. 1647; vi. 244, 27 June 1649;

Again he became reconciled to the new order, as has been already stated,[1] but proved himself 'refractory' and was fined, and in 1652 he was removed from the Commission of the Peace for his support of the Six Counties' Petition.

Henry Vaughan claims to have been 'privy' to Walbeoffe's heart, 'Mans secret region', and when his friend died on 13 September 1653 wrote one of the most attractive of his occasional poems. In it he commends Walbeoffe's public-spirited service, his freedom from self-interest, and his refusing the common temptation of improving his fortunes by sacrilege and pillage. So far from condemning his accepting office under the Commonwealth, Vaughan praises him for it:

> As poisons by
> Corrections are made Antidotes, so thy
> Just Soul did turn ev'n hurtful things to Good;
> Us'd bad Laws so, they drew not Tears, nor Blood.
> Heav'n was thy Aime, and thy great rare Design
> Was not to Lord it here, but there to shine.
> Earth nothing had, could tempt thee. All that e're
> Thou pray'dst for here, was *Peace*; and *Glory* there.[2]

Yet, if Vaughan commended his friend for accepting office, there are allusions to his having himself refused tempting offers of place, at a time, too, when his broken fortunes needed support. This seems to be the interpretation of 'The Proffer'. His strict conscience and uncompromising spirit cause him to refuse:

> No, No; I am not he,
> Go seek elsewhere.
> I skill not your fine tinsel, and false hair,
> Your Sorcery
> And smooth seducements; I'le not stuff my story
> With your Commonwealth and glory.[3]

There are similar allusions in 'The Men of War' in which he desires to 'hold fast and slight the *Lure*', that may only

Committee for Compounding, 14 May 1652; *Mercurius Cambro-Brit.*, 1652, p. 17; Chambers, ii. 345.
[1] See above, p. 112.   [2] M 610, ll. 41–8.   [3] M 487, ll. 31–6.

serve 'a temporal self-end';[1] and in 'The Ass', the poem
which follows, he writes:

> If the world offers to me ought,
> That by thy book must not be sought,
> Or though it should be lawful, may
> Prove not expedient for thy way;
> To shun that peril, let thy grace
> Prevail with me to shun the place.[2]

'His sole asylum, since he was thus cut off from the recon-
structing Commonwealth which he abhorred, was in the
interior life.'[3]

---

[1] M 517, ll. 15, 40.   [2] M 519, ll. 37–42.
[3] L. I. Guiney, preface to her edition of *The Mount of Olives*, p. vi.

X
THE PROSE TREATISES

THE mind of the author of *Silex Scintillans* will become clearer to us if we take stock of the books which he was reading, translating, and writing in the years when he was engaged upon his sacred poems. Of his bookish habits we learn from his poems 'On Sir Thomas Bodley's Library' and 'To his Books'.[1] Books were his 'consolations' in 'sad times', and they survived to keep him company when other companions were lost to him:

> Burning and shining *Thoughts*; man's posthume *day*:
> The *track* of fled souls, and their *Milkie-way*.
> The dead *alive* and *busie*, the still *voice*
> Of inlarg'd Spirits, kind heav'ns white *Decoys*.

Before his conversion we are made aware of his interest in contemporary poetry and of his considerable intimacy with the Latin classics. From 1648 to 1655, except for some allusions to contemporary poetry in *Olor Iscanus*, there is a marked diversion of his literary interest to works of piety, primitive, medieval, and of his own day. Together they show a remarkable width of reading for one who was still in the early thirties. One wonders, too, how he had access in a remote Welsh village to books of some rarity. Either he must have bought freely in London or he was lent books by some older friend like Thomas Powell. 'Man in Darkness', one of Vaughan's few original prose works, is very full of quotations and references for so short a treatise. Besides the classical authors, the Fathers are cited—Chrysostom, Cyprian, Ambrose, Gregory the Great, Jerome, Anselm. There are also citations from writers so little known as Marcellus Empiricus, a physician of the fifth Christian century, and Alanus de Insulis. Vaughan quotes repeatedly from treatises of Petrarch and Drexelius, though he does not name the latter. His acquaintance with the Hermetic writers will be discussed in

[1] M 613, 639.

the next chapter when the influence of his brother Thomas is estimated.

Even clearer light on the way in which Vaughan's mind was working in these years may be obtained from considering the books which he elected to translate. The choice was almost certainly his own, as it is hard to suppose that any publisher proposed to him works so little likely to find purchasers. They did not, in fact, sell well, as no second editions were called for. Vaughan's translations were not publishers' hack-work, but works which the translator believed to be for the edification of such readers as he could find. There were in all nine translated treatises which he printed in these years—four short pieces in *Olor Iscanus*, a short piece attributed to St. Anselm in *The Mount of Olives*, three more in *Flores Solitudinis*, and the only long one, Nolle's Treatise on *Hermetical Physick*, printed separately a little before the enlarged *Silex Scintillans*.[1]

The four brief discourses which fill out *Olor Iscanus* to make it a volume of any size are perhaps the least significant of Vaughan's mind. The two discourses of Plutarch and the one by Maximus of Tyre, a Greek sophist of the second Christian century, he translated from the Latin versions in a posthumous edition of 1613 by Dr. John Reynolds, President of Corpus Christi College, Oxford. The first discourse, 'Of the Benefit we may get from our Enemies', may have appealed to him as the treatment of a practical question in troubled times, though Plutarch probably had private rather than public enemies in mind. 'To forbeare revenge upon an Enemie, when wee opportunely may, is the highest glory in all humanity'[2]—this is a sentiment which the times needed. Vaughan was well aware that the sufferings and deprivations caused to himself and his friends by the Civil War and the subsequent Puritan régime were likely enough to stir feelings of revenge and, at times also, to excite hopes of a war of retaliation. However much such feelings may have rankled in the breasts of his associates, Vaughan strove to repress them in himself. Many of

[1] In 1655 or a year or two later came Henry Vaughan's translation of another work of Nolle: see below, p. 183.   [2] M 105.

his sacred poems show how he shrank from any idea of a renewal of civil war:

> Give me humility and peace,
> Contented thoughts, innoxious ease,
> A sweet, revengeless, quiet minde,
> And to my greatest haters kinde.[1]

With his intense feeling about 'this iron age' and 'exil'd Religion', it was only his sense of the duty of maintaining a Christian temper that could be proof against what Plutarch called 'obtrectation, malevolence, with an Implacable and endles resentment of Injuries'.[2]

The second discourse of Plutarch, 'Of the Diseases of the Mind and the Body', and the companion piece of the 'Plato-nick Philosopher', Maximus Tirius, with the same title, may show Vaughan's growing interest in medicine, though there is little in them about physical treatment. Plutarch's is a pleasant little essay, maintaining that diseases of the mind, because unperceived by the patient, are more danger-ous than those of the body which force themselves on the patient's attention and oblige him to have resort to the physician. Maximus Tirius also finds the diseases of the mind more pernicious: 'The disease of the body hath never yet occasion'd wars, but that of the mind hath occasion'd many.'[3] The sufferer from bodily ills is made 'desirous of health' and therefore 'fitter for cure', but the mind, once infected and bewitched, 'will not somuch as heare of health'.[4]

Olor Iscanus ends with Vaughan's translation from a Latin version of 'The Praise and Happinesse of the Countrie-Life; Written Originally in *Spanish* by *Don Antonio de Guevara*, Bishop of Carthagena, and Counsellour of Estate to Charls the Fifth Emperour of Germany'. The bishop's gentle moralizing is obvious enough and presents a romantic and unreal picture of rural innocence, but it may have attracted the Silurist who had early turned his back on the attractions of the town and elected to spend the rest of life in his native village. In his poem 'Retirement' he professes to

[1] 'The Men of War', ll. 41-4 (M 517).
[2] M 106. [3] M 119. [4] Ibid.

understand why Abraham left to Lot 'the Cities of the plain' which were 'the Thrones of Ill', and for himself 'Did love to be a Country liver'.[1]

To the original prose writings which form the first two sections of *The Mount of Olives* Vaughan added, as a companion piece to his own 'Man in Darkness', for the comfort of the reader 'after thou hast past through that *Golgotha*',[2] a discourse of the blessed state of the saints in the New Jerusalem, entitled 'Man in Glory'. The Latin original had been printed for the first time in 1639 in Paris, 'where', says Vaughan, 'it took so well, that it was presently translated into French'.[3] Its Jesuit editor took it to be a work of St. Anselm, transcribed by Eadmer, a canon regular of Canterbury, Anselm's chaplain and biographer. 'Some brokages and disorderly parcels of it'[3] were already to be found in the *De Similitudine*, also attributed to Anselm. Neither work is now believed to be Anselm's, and 'Man in Glory' will not add to his credit or to Vaughan's judgement in choosing it. It includes a terrible passage[4] in which the writer attempts to describe the eternal pains of hell. The most original passage is that in which it is represented that no one need fear shame when his secret sins are made known in heaven, as the sins and failings of St. Peter and 'that blessed Convert *Mary Magdalen*' are already known there and only redound to the glory of God. The saints 'will have no such thoughts of thee, as thou at present dost suspect', for 'when they see that God hath freely and fully forgiven thee, they will not so much as have a thought of abhorring, or judging thee in the smallest matter', but rather 'have in greater admiration the infinite mercy of God both towards thee, and towards themselves'.[5] A strange attraction of heaven is that the blessed will be rendered 'equall for swiftnesse to the very Angels'; their 'velocity' is likened to 'the beams of the Sunne, which as soone as ever the body of that Planet appears above the earth in the East, passe in a moment to the utmost West'.[6] It is a little surprising that these rather childish fancies

---

[1] M 642.   [2] M 140.   [3] M 192.
[4] M 200, ll. 20–31.   [5] M 202.   [6] M 195–6.

should please Vaughan or that he should expect them to please readers in his generation. He prefixes a poem of his own on St. Anselm, which probably has a hidden allusion to the execution of Laud; Anselm had fled from the persecution of William II, but, were he to return and see the present plight of the Church, he would declare that, in comparison with the persecution to-day, '*Rufus* was a Saint'.[1] Such a judgement does more credit to Vaughan's heart than to his head.

Of more significance in illustrating Vaughan's mind at this time are the 'rare and elegant pieces' which make up his next book, *Flores Solitudinis*. In the dedication to his wife's uncle, Sir Charles Egerton, he tells him that these pieces 'Collected in his Sicknesse and Retirement' will lead him 'from the *noyse* and *pompe* of this world into a silent and solitary *Hermitage*'.[2] And in the preface, dated 17 April 1652, he tells the reader that he sends the book abroad 'to bee a companion of those wise *Hermits*, who have withdrawne from the present generation, to confirme them in their solitude, and to make that rigid *necessity* their pleasant *Choyse*'.[3] It is evident that Vaughan, in his continued ill health and in his abhorrence of the reigning powers, was well content to escape into his 'private grove' where he could pursue his meditations undisturbed. Such poems as 'The Retreate', 'The Dawning', and 'Rules and Lessons' in the first part of *Silex Scintillans* show how he had come to value retirement and solitude like an eremite. For him, when he was almost despairing of outward things, 'the contempt of the world', which he tells Egerton is the theme of his book, is not difficult, but congenial.

All the contents of *Flores Solitudinis* are of Jesuit origin. Johannes Eusebius Nierembergius, in spite of his German name, was a Spanish Jesuit, who was born and died at Madrid. For the Epistle of Eucherius and the Life of Paulinus Vaughan was indebted to Jesuit editors. In his obscurity he could afford to ignore the prejudices of the day, find his spiritual nourishment where he would, and commend it to the few who read his books.

[1] M 193.   [2] M 213.   [3] M 216.

Nieremberg's *De Arte Voluntatis* (1631), from which Vaughan selected two long sections for translation, was a work intended to give the pith (*medulla*) of Platonic, Stoic, and Christian ethic, and is therefore more plentifully illustrated from pagan writers—Plato and the Platonists, Seneca and Epictetus—than from Christian. The section, 'Of Temperance and Patience', may well have appealed to Vaughan with its emphasis upon indifference to worldly possessions and upon the patience that is needed to endure troublous times, and, after his manner, he interpolates many allusions to his own times. The discourse, if sometimes ponderous, has its occasional brilliant passages, as when virtue is likened to music[1] or when it is said of the Creator:

God made not man by a *Fiat*, as he did the rest of the Creatures, but fell to work himself, and like the *Potter* that first tempers, then fashions the Clay, he made him by makeing, not by speaking.[2]

It is just as the sculptor at the north portal of Chartres Cathedral has represented the creation of man. Again, the comparison of man's life to an actor's is familiar, but Nieremberg handles the theme well, and Vaughan translates him well:

The *World* is a meer *Stage*; the *Master* of the *Revels* is *God*; the *Actors* are *Men*; the Ornaments and flourishes of the *Scenes* are honour, power and pomp; the transitory and painted *Streams* of Mortality, which passe along with the *current* of time, and like *flowers*, do but onely appeare, when they stay longest. . . .

The *Actors* care not how the *Scenes* varie: they know, that when the *Play* is ended, the *Conquerour* must put off his *Crown* in the same *Ward-robe* where the *Fool* puts off his *Cap*. . . .

The *stageplayer* is not commended, because he *acts* the *part* of a *Prince*, but because hee *acts* it well, and like a *Prince*. It is more commendable to *act* a foole, a begger, or a mourner to the life; then to *act* a King, or a Philosopher foolishly.[3]

Vaughan's second choice from Nieremberg's book is an eloquent meditation on the theme, *Memento mori*, 'a very humane and elegant *Philosophy*, which taught men to season, and redeeme all the daies of their lives, with the memory

[1] M 262.   [2] M 245.
[3] M 273, ll. 30–5; 275, ll. 25–8; 276, ll. 3–7.

of the one day of their death'.[1] At the time when Vaughan
was translating this discourse he was hardly expecting his
long sickness to issue otherwise than in death. But for this
fact its pietism might seem exaggerated: '*Philosophie*, or
humane Knowledge is nothing else but a Contemplation of
death;... for the fruit of Philosophy is Virtue, and Virtue is
nothing else but an imitation of death, or the Art of dying
well, by beginning to dye while we are alive.'[2] Even this
sentiment had been already expressed in *Silex Scintillans*:

> Thy Accounts thus made, spend in the grave one houre
> Before thy time; Be not a stranger there
> Where thou may'st sleep whole ages; Lifes poor flowr
> Lasts not a night sometimes. Bad spirits fear
> This Conversation; But the good man lyes
> Intombed many days before he dyes.[3]

The third item in *Flores Solitudinis* is 'The World Con-
temned, in a Parenetical Epistle written by the Reverend
Father Eucherius, Bishop of *Lyons*, to his kinsman Valerianus'. Eucherius is a conspicuous example of *contemptus
mundi*. As Vaughan states in his preface, Eucherius shows
to his kinsman 'the *vanity*, and the *iniquity* of *riches* and
honours', which Vaughan calls 'the two grand inticements
of *popular spirits*'.[4] With a characteristic glance at the times,
Vaughan adds that 'the Age we live in hath made all his
Arguments, *Demonstrations*'. Eucherius was persuaded that
his age was witnessing the 'convulsions of the dying world';
'for certain it cannot last very long'.[5] Vaughan enlarges
upon his original, and in the same volume, in his preface to
the *Life of Paulinus*, he expresses his own belief that the end
of this world 'truely draws near, if it be not *at the door*'.[6]
Eucherius turned his back on the worldly distinction which
had begun to open before him, entered the recently established abbey of Lerins in A.D. 432, and twelve years later
was obliged to yield to the public opinion which demanded
that he should be bishop of Lyons.

---

[1] M 296.   [2] M 292.
[3] 'Rules and Lessons', ll. 121–6 (M 439).   [4] M 312.
[5] M 330. Cf. Vaughan's own statement in 'Man in Darkness', M 171, l. 13:
'the dissolution of the whole is not far off.'   [6] M 338.

In his Epistle to Valerianus Eucherius instanced Paulinus, 'the great Ornament and light of France', as one of those who had given up great place to enter the religious life, and Héribert Rosweyde, the Jesuit editor of Eucherius, appended a Life of Paulinus, 'collected out of his own Works and ancient records of him' by another Jesuit writer, Francesco Sacchini.[1] It was, therefore, natural for Vaughan, who translated the Epistle of Eucherius from Rosweyde's edition, to add a Life of Paulinus under the title, 'Primitive Holiness, Set forth in the Life of blessed Paulinus. Collected out of his own Works, and other Primitive Authors by *Henry Vaughan*, Silurist.' This description might be taken by the reader to mean that Vaughan compiled his Life from the Works of Paulinus 'and other Primitive Authors', but the words only reproduce what is found in Sacchini's title of his *Vita Paulini*, 'Ex scriptis eius, & veterum de eo Elogiis concinnata.' The larger part of Vaughan's 'Primitive Holiness' is a free translation and adaptation of the *Vita Paulini*, so that it is very much more his work than the translations hitherto discussed.

A further reason for Vaughan's choosing to write this Life is that Paulinus not only turned to the religious life but also devoted himself to the composition of sacred poetry. What Dr. Raby says of Paulinus is hardly less true of Vaughan himself:

But for his conversion, he would have employed his poetical gifts upon trifling subjects and rhetorical themes; now that he had devoted himself to religion, he used his talent to express those ideas and emotions which had really mastered his life. In short, he became a true poet.[2]

---

[1] *D. Eucherii De Contemptu Mundi. Accedit Vita D. Paulini*, Antwerp, 1621. Rosweyde, after editing this book, proceeded next year, with another Jesuit, Fronton Le Duc (Ducanus), to edit the *Opera* of Paulinus, including a reprint of Sacchini's *Vita Paulini*. Vaughan had access to both editions.

[2] F. J. E. Raby, *A History of Christian-Latin Poetry*, 1927, p. 104. Charles Bigg (*Wayside Sketches in Eccles. Biogr.*, 1906, p. 35) makes a direct comparison of Paulinus to Vaughan: 'Paulinus was not a man of action. He was neither scholar nor theologian. He had not the commanding personality of Ambrose or Basil. He was just a Christian poet of the same stamp as Prudentius, a crystal soul with a slender but genuine gift of song. Child-like simplicity, tender affection, high-bred courtesy not without a sly vein of humour, sincere

Paulinus was born in or near Bordeaux, where his father had an estate, besides other patrimonies in Italy 'more becomming a Prince then a private man'.[1] He was educated by Ausonius; this in itself would interest Vaughan, who, in the opening poem of *Olor Iscanus*, alludes to Ausonius's famous poem on the Moselle, and, later in that book, gives an English version of his idyll, 'Cupido cruci affixus'.[2] When Paulinus embraced the Christian faith under the influence of Ambrose at the age of 38 and decided to relinquish his high position in the imperial service, Ausonius sought to dissuade him from 'changing thy Ivorie-chair for a dark Cell',[3] and hinted that his wife Therasia, with her ardent Spanish temperament, was a 'Tanaquil, the Imperatrix of her Husband'.[4] Paulinus replied in a poem, which Vaughan translates, 'I am not he, whom you knew then'; serious thoughts now engage his soul, and he must 'leave false honours, and that share Which fell to mee of this fraile world'.[5] After his wife's death Paulinus became bishop of Nola in 410 and laboured there till his death in 431.

Vaughan is much freer in telling the life of Paulinus than in translating Nieremberg and Eucherius, and the narrative is attractively written. The poems introduced from the *Carmina* of Paulinus and from other writers give him an opportunity of exercising his gift of verse-translation. He is also freer than ever to make topical allusions. He accompanies a passage from the *Vita Paulini* about the evil of bringing 'unseason'd persons into the Ministry' with his own comment: 'Wee need no examples: Wee have lived to see all this our selves.'[6] When he tells of Hadrian's desecration of Bethlehem and Calvary, he proceeds:

Some men amongst us have done the like: Two *Seasons* in the year were consecrated by the *Church* to the memory of our *Saviour*: The *Feast* of his *Nativity* and *Circumcision*, and the *Feast* of his

devotion, absolute self-denial—these are his endowments. . . . The sweet shade-loving violet is his counterpart, and Henry Vaughan, the Silurist, who retired into Wales, and from that peaceful retreat looked out on the horrid confusion of the Civil Wars, is his spiritual brother.' Dr. Bigg overlooks the evidence of Vaughan's taking part in the war.

[1] M 341.   [2] M 39, l. 7, and M 72.   [3] M 348, l. 34.
[4] M 343, l. 40.   [5] M 349, ll. 46-7.   [6] M 354, l. 14.

Passion and *Resurrection*. These two they have utterly taken away:
endeavouring (in my opinion) to extinguish the *memory* of his
Incarnation and *Passion*, and to race his blessed name out of those
bright columnes of light, which the *Scripture* calls *daies*. They will not
allow him two daies in the year, who made the dayes and the
nights.[1]

Vaughan's comparison of Puritan prohibitions with the
Emperor's iconoclasm shows grievous lack of proportion,
but it reveals the depth of his feeling.

Two prose works remain to be discussed that are wholly
his own composition: 'Solitary Devotions' and 'Man in
Darkness, or A Discourse of Death', which are the first
two items in *The Mount of Olives*. He must have been
engaged upon this book very soon after he had published
the first part of *Silex Scintillans*, as his dedication to Sir
Charles Egerton is dated 'this first of October. 1651', and
the book was entered at Stationers' Hall on the following
16 December.[2] His purpose in publishing 'these weake
productions' is made clear in the dedication and preface as
well as in the text of the book. In this time of spiritual
destitution, as he regards it, when the parish churches are
'now vilified and shut up'[3] and when 'Thy Service and thy
Sabbaths, thy own sacred Institutions and the pledges of
thy love are denied unto us',[4] he would encourage his
readers to maintain the private exercise of their religion in
regular prayer and meditation, lest the good seed 'wither
away in these times of persecution and triall'.[5] His choice
of the title and sub-title of the book answers to this emphasis
upon the value of 'Solitary Devotions':

The *Sonne* of *God* himselfe (when *he* was *here*,) had no place to
put his head in; And his *Servants* must not think the *present
measure* too hard, seeing their *Master* himself took up his *nights-
lodging* in the cold *Mount* of *Olives*.[6]

That a young layman of thirty years of age should publish
a book of devotions is remarkable, but there were precedents for the spiritual life of the Church being promoted by

[1] M 379.   [2] A copy was in Thomason's hands on 16 Feb. 1651/2.
[3] M 147, l. 29.   [4] M 166, ll. 12–13.
[5] M 149, l. 31.   [6] M 138.

the writings of laymen: for instance, Sir Richard Baker printed several volumes of *Meditations* on the Lord's Prayer and the Psalms, and, among Welshmen, Rowland Vaughan of Caer Gai translated into Welsh Bishop Bayly's *Practice of Piety* (1630) and other devotional books.

Vaughan's 'Solitary Devotions' are original, though he draws freely from the Bible and the Book of Common Prayer. They come from one who accepts whole-heartedly the theology and religious practices of an Anglican churchman. There is the full orthodox belief in the Divinity of Christ 'very God, and very man',[1] the Trinity, the Redemption, and the Atonement; 'the great design and end of thine Incarnation was to save sinners.'[2] He loves the observance of the Church feasts and 'that more strict and holy season, called Lent', for 'Such was in our Church . . . and such still are the preparation-dayes before this glorious Sabbath in all true Churches'.[3] It is noticeable that nearly half of the 'Devotions' is concerned with preparation for receiving the Holy Communion and with prayers to use privately at 'this glorious Sacrament', 'this soveraigne Sacrament', 'this great and solemne Feast, this Feast of mercy and miracles'. The ample provision of devotions at the Sacrament suggests that Vaughan, like John Evelyn, contrived to receive it from time to time at the hands of priests who continued to minister after their eviction and after the prohibition of the Prayer Book. Vaughan's explicit and devoted churchmanship, so fully evinced in *The Mount of Olives*, makes it clear that his celebration of the great Christian doctrines and of the Church's year in *Silex Scintillans* is no mere imitation of George Herbert but expresses his own mind, while it is also true that, with an elevation above Herbert's, he ascends in his greater poems to the remote spaces of eternity. It is characteristic of the author of *Silex Scintillans* that he should also in *The Mount of Olives* dwell so often on the thought of the departed and the eternal order.

There are many echoes in *The Mount of Olives* of the poems in the first part, and anticipations of those yet to be published in the second part, of *Silex Scintillans*. In the opening

[1] M 165, l. 6.   [2] M 161, ll. 28–9.   [3] M 156, ll. 29–31.

paragraph of *The Mount of Olives* he bids the reader 'be up before the Sun-rising'; 'When all the world is asleep, thou shouldst watch.'[1] The same counsel is offered in stanzas of great beauty in 'Rules and Lessons'[2] and appears again in 'The Dawning' and 'The Night'. It corresponds with Vaughan's own spiritual experience of the value of solitude in the night and before the world is astir. It is the same voice that speaks to us in the meditations and prayers as in the meditative poems; we understand the poems all the better for being familiar with *The Mount of Olives*.

'Man in Darkness', 'a short and plaine Discourse of Death', pursues a theme which was congenial to that age. A fine example of this kind of writing is *Contemplatio Mortis et Immortalitatis*, put out anonymously in 1631 by Henry Montagu, Earl of Manchester, and better known in its later editions as *Manchester al Mondo*. Of greater and more enduring fame is Jeremy Taylor's *The Rule and Exercises of Holy Dying*, published a few months before *The Mount of Olives*, while its author was serving as chaplain to Richard Vaughan, Earl of Carbery, at Golden Grove in Carmarthenshire. The tone of 'Man in Darkness' is devout and humble, sombre, and even macabre, as in a passage on hell which he takes from Drexelius.[3] He translates long passages from Petrarch's *De Contemptu Mundi* and *De Otio Religiosorum*.[4] Other patristic and medieval writers are quoted, and it is characteristic of Vaughan's mind at this time for him to appeal to primitive Christianity: 'let us but have recourse to the ages that are past, let us aske the *Fathers*.'[5] The little treatise as a whole has a medieval cast, ascetic and severely orthodox. Like the medieval writers, he accepts many edifying but pre-scientific notions—the hyena's tears, the torpedo-fish which kills the fisherman with its eye (he had already used this illustration in 'The Charnel-house'),[6] and the turtle-dove that 'hath no gall'. He cites as 'a *Symboll* of the resurrection' Cornelius Agrippa's professed discovery

---

[1] M 143, ll. 9, 20.　　　　　　[2] M 436.　　　　　　[3] M 178.
[4] e.g. M 172-3, 187. The only selection from Vaughan in *The Oxford Book of English Prose* (no. 180) is largely a paraphrase of Petrarch; it would have been better to choose a more original passage.
[5] M 171, ll. 31-3.　　　　　　　　　　　　　'M 41, ll. 11-12.

of indications of life in the severed members of creatures
when cast 'into a pot of seething water'.[1] The phrase, 'a
deaths-head crownd with *roses*', is verbally repeated in his
poem 'Joy'.[2] But if there is an unmistakable sternness in the
theme, there is also considerable beauty in the writing.
Flowers move him by their loveliness as well as by their
fragility: 'let us looke alwayes upon this *Day-Lilie* of life,
as if the *Sun* were already *set*.'[3] His delight in the singing of
birds, a natural music 'to which all *arted strains* are but
discord',[4] is more than once expressed, and any mention of
the stars makes him eloquent:

> When thou also seest those *various, numberles, and beautiful
> luminaries* of the night to move on in their *watches*, and some of
> them to *vanish* and *set*, while all the rest do *follow after*, consider
> that *thou* art carried on with *them* in the *same motion*, and that there
> is no hope of subsisting for thee, but in *him who never moves, and
> never sets*.[5]

His allusion to Christ's passing the night in prayer 'when
the birds of the aire lay warme in their nests' reminds us of
his poem 'The Bird', in which the bird pillows its head in
its 'own warm wing' through the stormy night.[6] The ass
on Palm Sunday 'made infinitely happy by so glorious a
rider' anticipates the thought in his poem 'The Ass'.[7]

Vaughan's prose, whether original or in translating, has
a quiet beauty and an epigrammatic force: 'Vanity is often-
times a bubble that swims upon the face of Virtue';[8] 'Death
is the *Inne* where we take up, that we may with more chear-
fullnesse set forwards, and be enabled to overtake, and to
keep company with eternity';[9] 'Mutuall Consolations are a
double banquet, they are the Churches *Eulogiae*, which we
both give and take.'[10] A longer passage will better illustrate
the fineness of the thought and its concise expression:

> Charity is a relique of Paradise, and pitty is a strong argument
> that we are all descended from one man: He that carries this rare

---

[1] M 176.   [2] M 185, l. 38 and 491, l. 6.   [3] M 186, ll. 4–6.
[4] M 177, l. 27.   [5] M 187, ll. 22–7.   [6] M 162 and 496.
[7] M 162 and 518.   [8] M 334, l. 42.   [9] M 285, ll. 11–13.
[10] M 374. *O.E.D.* s.v. Eulogia, defines it as bread 'blessed and distributed
as symbols of mutual love'.

Jewell about him, will every where meete with some kindred. He
is quickly acquainted with distressed persons, and their first sight
warmes his blood. I could believe, that the word *stranger* is a
notion received from the posterity of *Cain*, who killed *Abel*.[1]

As in his poems, Vaughan makes much use of alliteration:
'All is gone, all is dust, deformity, and desolation';[2] and less
often he uses assonance: 'Keep me . . . from the hours and
the powers of darknesse.'[3] Like Sir Thomas Browne, he
takes pleasure in unusual words of Latin origin: ejulation,
presension, velitation, manuduction (instruction), relucen-
cies, contristation, delirations of philosophers, revertency,
the great Archiplast, luctual, lusorie, uberous, extrarious,
irremisse, dejicient, assimilant, concrescent, salutiferous.[4]
The use of such words seldom leaves the reader in any
doubt of their meaning, and the strangeness adds a touch of
distinction. Vaughan is another example of a poet who can
write graceful and effective prose.

[1] M 352.   [2] M 173, l. 3.   [3] M 152, l. 32.
[4] All the above words are found in the *O.E.D.* except Archiplast, dejicient,
extrarious (Vaughan is translating Lat. *extrarius*), irremisse, revertency.

XI

THOMAS VAUGHAN AND OCCULT PHILOSOPHY

THOMAS Powell of Cantref, who had good opportunities of knowing the Vaughan brothers, says of 'this
bright *Gemini*' in the introductory poem which he contributed to *Olor Iscanus*:

> What *Planet* rul'd your *birth*? what *wittie star*?
> That you so like in *Souls* as *Bodies* are! . . .
> Not only your *faces*, but your *wits* are *Twins*.[1]

There are so many parallels in the writings of the brothers
that it is evident that they shared their thoughts and interests
to a considerable degree, and for a full understanding of
Silex Scintillans it becomes necessary to pay some attention
to the career and writings of the younger brother.

Up to their twentieth year the twins were together: at
home, under Matthew Herbert at Llangattock Rectory, and
at Oxford, until Henry left to study law in London. Probably it was two years or more after Henry's return to
Newton that his brother was appointed rector of Llansantffraed,[2] but Thomas's continued residence at Oxford for
several more years after taking his degree[3] must have meant
that there were fewer opportunities of the brothers' associat-
ing than if he was continuously resident on his cure. The
brothers may have been together in military service, if, as
is probable, they both enlisted in Colonel Price's regiment
of horse.[4] After eviction from his benefice in 1650, Thomas
Vaughan, according to Wood, 'retired to *Oxon*, and in a
sedate repose prosecuted his medicinal genie, (in a manner
natural to him) and at length became eminent in the chymi-
cal part thereof at *Oxon*, and afterwards at *London* under the
protection and patronage of that noted Chymist Sir *Rob.
Murrey* or *Moray* Kt, Secretary of State for the Kingdom of

---

[1] M 36.   [2] See above, pp. 91–3.
[3] Letter to Aubrey, 15 June 1673 (M 667): 'My brother continued there
for ten or 12 years.'   [4] See above, p. 65.

Scotland.[1] Henry's account of his brother in his letters of
1673 to Aubrey does not mention his going to Oxford after
his eviction, but says only: 'My brothers imploym[t] was in
physic & Chymistrie.'[2] Henry also mentions his brother's
connexion with Sir Robert Moray, which was not until
the Restoration. Thomas was not long at Oxford, as by
1651 he was already in London,[3] engaged in experimental
work. Our chief evidence of his activities and also of the
events of his personal life is a small quarto notebook in
the Sloane collection at the British Museum. It bears
the title 'Aqua Vitae, non Vitis' and consists chiefly of
chemical formulae and records of experiments in alchemy
and medicine, but there are as well memoranda about
himself and his wife with pious remembrances of his wife
after her death.[4]

From the notebook we learn that on 28 September 1651
Thomas Vaughan married Rebecca, whose surname is not
given, and who perhaps came from Mappersall, Bedford-
shire.[5] His wife assisted him in his experiments, and he
repeatedly expresses his debt to her; their combined initials
are often written in the book. He tells of finding 'two
secrets' in the preparation of nitre 'whiles wee lodged att
M[r] Coalmans in Holborn before wee came to live att the
Pinner of Wakefield'.[6] He speaks also of 'a great glass full

---

[1] *Ath. Oxon.*, 1692, ii. 253. In his earlier account (*Hist. et Antiq.* ii. 320)
Wood states that after his eviction Thomas 'ad Medicinae studium sese
convertebat', but does not mention his return to Oxford to study chemistry
there before going to work in London.

[2] M 667–8.

[3] It may save others from pursuing a false track if it is stated that the
warrant issued on 25 Dec. 1651 by Dr. Zouche, assessor of the Chancellor's
Court, at the suit of the Principal and Fellows of Jesus College, to attach one
Thomas Vaughan for a debt of £14. 0s. 8d., on the rumour that he was
'likely to leave the towne', probably does not refer to the poet's brother.
In consequence of this suit, payment of the sum was duly made by 'Tho.
Vaughan fellow Comn[r]' (Bodl. MS. Eng. Hist. c. 5). Our Thomas Vaughan,
who had graduated in 1642, was not likely to be a Fellow-Commoner in
1651, and the debtor is almost certainly the Thomas Vaughan, gent., who
matriculated from Jesus College on 20 Mar. 1650/1.

[4] MS. Sloane 1741. The personal memoranda in this MS. are mostly
reproduced in Waite, pp. 445–52.

[5] Waite, p. 446.

[6] MS. Sloane 1741, f. 105[v]. For the Pinder of Wakefield see note on p. 196.

of eye-water, made at the Pinner of Wakefield, by my dear
wife and my sister Vaughan, who are both now with God'.[1]
The Vaughans are not known to have had any sister except
Mrs. William Parry, and 'my sister Vaughan' is likely to
have been Henry Vaughan's first wife, Catherine. Rebecca
Vaughan died on 17 April 1658 and was buried on the 26th
at Mappersall.[2] Her husband observed the first and later
anniversaries of her death by entering expressions of his love
in the notebook. He had lived with her seven years, and
'I guess I shall not live so long after her, as I have lived with
her'.[3] Actually he survived her seven years and a half.
There is no mention of any children.

Until the Restoration Thomas Vaughan appears to have
experimented entirely on his own account, 'nor had I any
to instruct me.'[4] At the Restoration he might have claimed
reinstatement in his rectory, but we should expect him to
have wholly deserted ministerial life for chemical research.
There is, however, a perplexing entry in the returns of
William Lucy, Bishop of St. Davids, in answer to the
interrogatories issued by Archbishop Sheldon to the provin-
cial bishops on 7 July 1665. To the sixth article of inquiry
'concerning Non-Conformist Ministers', the bishop returns
eight names, including 'Thomas Vaughan clerke M.A. was
Ejected out of the Rectory of Llansanffread in the County of
Brecon for Non Subscripc̄on and left the Dioecesse'.[5] The
others similarly described were Puritans who were unable
to subscribe to the provisions of the Act of Uniformity of
1662. The introduction of Thomas Vaughan's name in this
return may be a merely mistaken record of his eviction in

[1] Waite, p. 449.
[2] Waite, p. 446. The *D.N.B.* wrongly gives 16 Apr. for the day of her
death, and says that she died at Mappersall, but the nine days' interval
between death and burial suggests that she died in London.
[3] Waite, p. 451.   [4] Preface to *Euphrates*, A 5ᵛ (Waite, p. 386).
[5] Lambeth, MS. Tenison 639, f. 337. G. Lyon Turner, *Original Records
of Nonconformity*, 1911, i. 183; at ii. 1210 Turner includes 'Thomas Vaughan,
M.A.' among 'Congregational or Independent' ministers in the county of
Brecon, but he notes that Calamy does not give this name. Richards (ii.
491), in his transcription of the Lambeth record about Thomas Vaughan,
by a slip reads 'non-submission', but it should be 'Non-Subscription' as of
the other seven in the bishop's return.

1650 and of his omitting to claim reinstatement at the Restoration under Clause IV of the Act of September 1660.[1] In any case he may have preferred the opportunity which presented itself now for regular employment under the Crown in the researches to which he had given himself for many years without assistance. Sir Robert Moray,[2] who enjoyed the confidence of Charles II, had long devoted what leisure he could find from soldiering and diplomacy to chemical pursuits. He was the 'soul', so Huygens reports, of the Royal Society and presided over its meetings from March 1661 to July 1662, and he was assigned a pavilion in the gardens of Whitehall in charge of the king's laboratory. Vaughan may have owed his introduction to Moray to Dr. Thomas Williams, formerly of Trebishwn, who later became the King's Chemist and was made a baronet; when Aubrey visited Moray on 4 July 1673 he noted a Dr. Williams being there.[3] Here at last was Vaughan's opportunity. In a suit which he brought on 18 May 1661 he described himself: 'Your Orator has made a study of natural philosophy and chemical physick.'[4] For the remaining five years of his life he was in the employment of the Crown.

In September 1665 Charles II and his court removed to Oxford because of the plague, and remained there till the following January. Thomas Vaughan accompanied Moray to Oxford and found lodging at the rectory of Albury, of which Samuel Kem, a veritable Vicar of Bray, remained rector for forty years. Albury is near Rycote, separated from it by the river Thame, and is distant from Oxford by road about ten miles. Vaughan did not return to London when the court left Oxford, but died in Kem's house on 27 February 1665/6, and was buried in the church on 1 March at the expense of Sir Robert Moray, whom Henry Vaughan calls his brother's 'great friend'.[5] Henry, in his letters to Aubrey seven years after, was unable to name the

[1] Actually the bishop instituted Thomas Lewes (see below, p. 203) to the rectory of Llansantffraed on 15 Sept. 1660, within a few days of the passing of the Act of Sept. 1660.
[2] For Moray see Sir H. Lyons, *The Royal Society*, 1944, and his Life by Alex. Robertson, 1922.　　　　　　　　　　　　　　　　[3] See below, p. 145.
[4] Chanc. Pro., Hamilton 354. 45. *Vaughan* v. *Bolnest*.　　　　　　[5] M 667.

village, and wrongly places it on the Thames and 'within 5 or 6 miles of Oxford'.[1] Aubrey, in forwarding Henry Vaughan's former letter of 15 June 1673 to Wood, scrawled on it, with the date 8 July:

Yesterday morning I wayted on my ever to be honoured friend Sir Robert Moray & spent 3 houres discussing w[h] him in his chambers, when also came in Dr. Grew, Mr. Gregory, and Dr. W[ms]. As to my cosen Tho: Vaughan he told me he buryed him at Albury neer Ricot within three miles of Oxon. he dyed at Mr. (Sam) Kem's house, the Minister.[2]

Aubrey was only just in time to get this information, as he tells Wood in the same letter that, though Sir Robert 'was then, to my thinking, as well as wont to be', yet 'at 8 last night was suddenly taken w[h] an acrid flegme, and dyed in halfe an houre'.

It will be noticed that Henry Vaughan says nothing of the cause of his brother's death, nor does Aubrey, nor Wood either in his Latin history of Oxford or in the 1692 edition of his *Athenae Oxonienses*, but in his annotated copy of that edition, full of corrections and additions for the next edition, there is a slip in Wood's hand adding: 'Eugenius Philalethes died as twere suddenly w[n] he was operating strong mercurie, some of w[ch] by chance getting up into his nose marched him off. So Harris of Jesus Coll.'[3] This sentence, except that it ends 'killed him' (instead of the colloquial 'marched him off') and that it does not mention

[1] M 667, 671, letters of 15 June and 7 July, 1673. Henry Vaughan may confuse the rivers Thames and Thame, but 'upon the Thames side' (M 671) cannot mean 'the Thame's side', as in 'Daphnis', his elegy on his brother, he says

For though the *Isis* and the prouder *Thames*
Can shew his reliques lodg'd hard by their streames.

The Thames, known in its Oxford reaches as the Isis, is not near Albury, but the Thame flows half a mile from the church and eventually joins the Thames at the Oxfordshire Dorchester.

[2] Bodl. MS. Wood F. 39, f. 216. 'Sam' is inserted by Wood. Moray died on 4 July 'in his pavilion in the gardens of Whitehall' (*D.N.B.*). Probably Aubrey should have dated his letter 5 July. Wood has testily noted on the letter: 'I pd 3d for yt.'

[3] Bodl. MS. Top. Oxf. b. 9. I cannot identify Harris, unless it is one Daniel Harris who matriculated from Jesus College in the same year as Thomas Vaughan.

4795   L

Harris as his authority, appeared in the 1721 edition of *Athenae Oxonienses*.

Henry Vaughan told Aubrey that his brother 'gave all his bookes & manuscripts'[1] to Sir Robert Moray, but nothing is known of them. Henry included twenty-four of his brother's Latin verses in *Thalia Rediviva*, and placed a note at the end: 'Desiderantur Alcippus et Jacintha (Poema heroicum absolutissimum), cum multis aliis Oxonii ab Authore relictis.'[2] This heroic poem appears to be no longer extant. Henry Vaughan precedes his brother's poems in *Thalia Rediviva* with his own 'Daphnis. An Elegiac *Eclogue*', commemorating Thomas Vaughan.[3]

There is no record of Thomas Vaughan's revisiting Llansantffraed after his eviction if the Ash Wednesday letter of 1653/4 is not his, but his father's.[4] There is, however, nothing improbable in his having gone home during the lifetime of his father and mother, or in his brother Henry's visiting him in London. But, as for his thoughts and writings having influenced Henry while he was writing *Silex Scintillans*, it should be noticed that this was also the period of Thomas's most active literary output. In the year 1650, when he was evicted and when the first part of *Silex* was published, Thomas Vaughan published no less than four books, and the dedication of the first book is dated 'Oxonii 48',[5] so that he must for some years before 1650 have been turning his mind towards the subjects of those books. He gives a description of himself in 1650, which need not be taken too seriously; in his acrimonious controversy with Henry More he remarks: 'You tell me I am *a very unnaturall son to my mother Oxford*. Do not thou *prophane* her *name* with thy rude, illiterate *Chops*. I am thou know'st *Mastix* a *notable wag* and a *saucy Boy*, whom she hath

---

[1] M 667. The *D.N.B.*, s.v. Thomas Vaughan, is wrong in assigning the will at Somerset House (53 Mico) to our Thomas Vaughan: it is that of Thomas Vaughan, vicar of Cropredy, Oxon., whose son, the sole executor, matriculated at Oxford in 1631, aged 18.

[2] *Thalia Rediviva*, 1678, p. 93.

[3] M 656. For a discussion of this difficult poem see below, pp. 220–2.

[4] See above, p. 117.

[5] *Anthroposophia Theomagica*, 1650, at end of the dedication.

sometimes *dandl'd* on her *Knees*.'[1] This kind of schoolboy-like flippancy runs through his polemics with More.[2] A more dignified and serious tone pervades his treatises on occult philosophy. Their scope is indicated by their titles. In 1650 appeared in quick succession the following three volumes: *Anthroposophia Theomagica* 'Or a Discourse of the Nature of Man and his state after Death; Grounded on his Creator's Proto-Chemistry and verifi'd by a practicall Examination of Principles in the Great World'; *Anima Magica Abscondita* 'Or a Discourse of the universall Spirit of Nature'; *Magia Adamica* 'Or the Antiquitie of Magic. . . . Whereunto is added a perfect, and full *Discoverie* of the True *Coelum Terrae* or the *Magician's* Heavenly *Chaos*, and *first Matter* of all Things'. All these were given as 'By Eugenius Philalethes'. The next year came *Lumen de Lumine*, to which was appended a second reply to More under the title *The Second Wash: Or The Moore Scour'd once more*. In 1652 appeared *Aula Lucis*, 'By S.N., a Modern Speculator', S.N. being the final letters of Thomas Vaughan's names.[3] The last of the short treatises, *Euphrates*, was published in 1655. It will be seen that Thomas Vaughan's period of writing exactly corresponded with his brother's: all of Henry Vaughan's nine books, except *Poems* of 1646 and *Thalia Rediviva* of 1678, appeared between 1650 and 1655.[4]

While Thomas Vaughan develops his own theories and draws upon his own experiments in alchemy, he quotes freely from the writings attributed to Hermes Trismegistus and Dionysius the Areopagite and from Raymond Lully, and cites also Paracelsus and Robert Fludd, but he expresses his special discipleship of Cornelius

---

[1] *The Man-Mouse taken*, 1650, p. 81.

[2] Elias Ashmole has copied out (Bodl. MS. Rawl. D. 864) the notes signed 'T. V.' which he found in a copy of his *Theatrum Chemicum*, including such marginal comments as 'Away, Animal, thou liest', 'Ha, ha, hee!' Thomas Vaughan ejaculates 'Ha! ha! he!' six times in *The Man-Mouse taken*. It is known that he disapproved of Ashmole's writings.

[3] Henry Vaughan names *Aula Lucis* in his list of his brother's books (M 668).

[4] There is uncertainty about the date of *The Chymists Key*; see below, note on p. 183.

Agrippa.[1] His first book has a portrait of Agrippa and a poem to 'Glorious Agrippa', who is hailed as 'Natures *Apostle* and her Choice *High Priest*';[2] 'He indeed is my Author, and next to God I owe all that I have unto him.'[3] He contributed 'An Encomium on the Three Books of Cornelius Agrippa, Knight' to an English translation of Agrippa's *Occult Philosophy* in 1651. Henry Vaughan in introducing a quotation from that work in *The Mount of Olives*, published in the next year, without naming the author styles him 'A great *Philosopher* and *Secretary* to *nature*'.[4] We have no means of knowing whether Henry was further acquainted with Agrippa's works. The brothers shared an interest in another German writer, Heinrich Nolle, but this interest will be better discussed in the chapter on Henry Vaughan as doctor.[5]

Thomas Vaughan employs many of the terms used by the alchemical writers and researchers, but is anxious to dissociate himself from 'certain alchemists—as they call themselves', and from some of their pursuits: '*Alchymie*, in the common acceptation, and as it is a torture of *Metalls*, I did never believe: much less did I study it. . . . I ever disclaimed *Alchymie* in the vulgar sense.'[6]

His relation to the Fraternity of the Rosy Cross is ambiguous, as is characteristic of most contemporary allusions to that cryptic society. The Rosicrucians began to be heard of first in Germany about 1614; their manifestoes usually bore no names or addresses, and the members preserved their anonymity so deliberately that they provoked both curiosity and suspicion, and they were sometimes dubbed the Invisibles. They claimed to have secret and magical knowledge, especially in the transmutation of metals, the prolongation of life by an Elixir Vitae, and power over elements and elemental spirits. But anyone addicted to alchemical experiments was liable to be called a Rosicrucian. Anthony Wood, not indeed in his first account of Thomas

---

[1] Heinrich Cornelius Agrippa von Nettesheim (1486–1535), alchemist, philosopher, and reputed magician.
[2] *Anthroposophia Theomagica*, pp. 52–4 (Waite, p. 51).
[3] Ibid., p. 50.   [4] M 176, l. 16.   [5] See below, pp. 183–7.
[6] *Euphrates*, To the Reader, A3 (Waite, p. 385).

Vaughan in his Latin history of Oxford, but in the first edition of *Athenae Oxonienses*, says of him:

He was a great Chymist, a noted son of the fire, an experimental Philosopher, a zealous brother of the Rosie-Crucian fraternity, an understander of some of the Oriental Languages, and a tolerable good English and Latin Poet.[1]

Wood calls Sir Robert Moray, who was a serious student of chemistry, 'a great patron of the Rosie-Crucians'.[2] As early as 1648 Eugenius Philalethes dedicated his first book 'To the Most Illustrious and Truly Regenerated Brethren R.C.'; though he does not claim to be of their fellowship, he humbly offers his tribute at a respectful distance: 'Most noble Brethren, I stand in the vestibule of the Temple, nor is my offering placed on the altar but laid in modesty at the threshold.'[3] In his second book, *Anima Magica Abscondita*, he quotes long passages from one who was given the title of Sapiens by 'the Brothers of R.C.'[4] In *Coelum Terrae* he gives the 'sense in punctual, plain English' of an extract from a work by 'one of the Rosy Brothers'.[5] In *Lumen de Lumine* he translates 'A Letter from the Brothers of R.C. concerning the Invisible, Magical Mountain and the Treasure therein contained',[6] and he alludes to the Brethren as 'these famous and most Christian Philosophers: Men questionless that have suffered much by their own discreet silence and solitude'.[7] Still more significantly, Eugenius Philalethes put forth in 1652, with a lengthy 'Praeface' of his own, an anonymous translation from the German of *The Fame and Confession of the Fraternity of R:C:, Commonly, of the Rosie Cross*.[8] In the preface Vaughan begins by affirming his belief in the existence of the society which was widely doubted: 'I am in the *Humor* to affirm the *Essence*, and *Existence* of that admired *Chimaera*, the *Fraternitie* of R.C.', and he protests against the 'clamorous *Defamation* of these innocent and contented *Eremits*'; in their books,

---

[1] *Ath. Oxon.*, 1692, ii. 253.   [2] Ibid. ii. 255.
[3] Waite, p. 3. *Anthroposophia Theomagica* was published in 1650, but the dedication is dated 1648.   [4] Waite, p. 101.
[5] Ibid., pp. 208–10.   [6] Ibid., pp. 259–63.   [7] Ibid., p. 264.
[8] Ibid., p. 490.

he says, he has 'found them *true Philosophers* and therefore not *Chimaera's* (as most think) but *Men*', and he finds that their principles 'are *consonant* to our very *Religion* and *confirm* every *point* thereof'.[1] Yet in this preface he denies that he is himself 'of the Order':

As for that *Fraternity*, whose *History* and *Confession* I have here adventured to *publish*, I have for my own part no *Relation* to them, neither do I much *desire* their Acquaintance.[2]

I shall confess, for my part, I have no acquaintance with this Fraternity as to their Persons; but their Doctrine I am not so much a stranger to.[3]

This disclaimer, however, is not quite conclusive, because members of the fraternity were expected to deny their membership.[4]

Thomas Vaughan, like other alchemists, felt no incompatibility in combining occult philosophy with a profession of the Christian faith, but, anticipating that his religion may be called in question, he gives his answer towards the end of his first book:

It will be question'd perhaps what I am, and especially what my Religion is? Take this short answer. I am neither Papist nor Sectary but a true, resolute Protestant in the best sense of the Church of England.[5]

It is difficult to assess the value attached by his contemporaries to Thomas Vaughan's writings, but he was better known as a writer than his brother. Second editions appeared only of *Magia Adamica* (1656) and *Euphrates* (1671) in this country, but translations of all his works, except of the two ephemeral combats with Henry More, were issued at Hamburg, Stockholm, Frankfurt, Amsterdam, Nuremberg, and Leipzig, at various dates from 1689 to as late as 1789.[6] John Heydon, Eugenius Theodidactus,

[1] *The Fame and Confession*, sig. a–a5 (Waite, pp. 343–7).
[2] Ibid., sig. a4ᵛ (Waite, p. 347).   [3] Ibid., sig. c3 (Waite, p. 365).
[4] Cf. Chambers, ii. li.
[5] *Anthroposophia Theomagica*, p. 62 (Waite, p. 58).
[6] In the Abbé Lenglet du Fresnoy's *Histoire de la Philosophie Hermétique*, 1742, there is confusion between more than one writer who took the *nom de plume* Eugenius Philalethes, besides one who called himself Eirenaeus Philalethes. Of Eirenaeus he says that his real name was believed to be Thomas de Vagan and that Robert Boyle 'étoit en des relations intimes avec cet habile

who claimed intimacy with all the astrologers, dismisses Thomas Vaughan in his *A New Method of Rosie-Crucian Physick* (1658) as 'too young and childish', but did not scruple to purloin a passage from *Lumen de Lumine* in another book of his two years later. Wood says of *Anthroposophia Theomagica* that nothing could be more obscure (*quibus nihil proculdubio obscurius*), and he does not profess to have done more than gather the nature of Vaughan's other books from their titles. Samuel Butler obviously drew on Thomas Vaughan for the first part of his 'Character of an Hermetic Philosopher',[1] and in Canto I of *Hudibras* he describes Ralph, the knight's squire, as one who understood '*Anthroposophus*, and *Floud*, and *Jacob Behmen*'. Swift makes a satirical reference to *Anthroposophia* in *A Tale of a Tub* (1704), and a footnote says of it: 'It is a piece of the most unintelligible fustian, that perhaps was ever published in any language.'[2] On the other hand, Miles Davies, the eccentric author of *Athenae Britannicae: or a Critical History of the Oxford and Cambridge Writers* (1715–16), includes in his list of 119 author-physicians Thomas but not Henry Vaughan, and adds: 'So also there were but three learned Alchymistical Writers: Flud, Vaughan, and Ashmole, with two chief conjurers or sorcerers, Dee and Kelly.'

How far Henry Vaughan shared his brother's interest in the Hermetic literature cannot be gauged. Besides anything he may have read in Thomas's writings, he shows occasional traces of independent knowledge of the writers whom his brother quotes. For instance, he interpolates into his translation of Nieremberg a quotation from 'Another Hermetist' besides the one just cited in his original.[3] His single quotation from Agrippa has already been noted.[4] He interpolates in Nieremberg a quotation from Paracelsus also, which includes the phrase 'the night is the working-time of Spirits', and he turns it to much profit in his wonderful

Artiste', i. 403, 405. This is probably the only authority for the statement about Boyle's regard for our Thomas Vaughan in Hargrave Jennings, *Rosicrucians*, 1870, p. 37.

[1] S. Butler, *The Genuine Remains*, ed. R. Thyer, 1759.
[2] Swift, *Prose Works*, ed. Temple Scott, 1919, i. 92.
[3] M 296.   [4] M 176. See above, p. 148.

poem 'The Night'.[1] The preface to his translation of Nolle[2] suggests that he had some acquaintance with Paracelsian medicine, but this would hardly affect his poetry. Professor Martin has shown beyond a doubt Henry Vaughan's indebtedness to the *Hermetica* for a long passage in 'The importunate Fortune',[3] and this clear case makes Professor Martin's other instances probable.

There are enough parallel sentences in Thomas Vaughan's treatises and Henry's poems to show that the elder brother had some acquaintance with the writings of Eugenius Philalethes, but it is unlikely that he followed his brother far into the maze of his blend of theosophy, alchemy, and occult philosophy. In the absence of more evidence we have to be content with a general impression of the nature and extent of the younger brother's influence upon the poet.[4] Henry, with a more balanced mind, was capable of assimilating what was congenial to him in his brother's ideas and writings without surrendering his independence. There were ideas developed by the Hermetic writers and by Thomas Vaughan that appealed to Henry Vaughan. We need hardly include the conception of the analogy between the macrocosm, 'the greater world', and the microcosm, man 'the lesser', as this was already a commonplace of Elizabethan thought.[5] Again, many Christian writers before

---

[1] M 305. 'The Night', stanzas 5 and 6 (M 522).   [2] M 548.
[3] M 614. L. C. Martin, 'Henry Vaughan and Hermes Trismegistus', *R.E.S.*, July 1942.
[4] The obligations of Henry to Thomas Vaughan and to other occult writers have received much recent attention, e.g. in Miss Elizabeth Holmes's *Henry Vaughan and the Hermetic Philosophy*, 1932; Wilson W. Clough's article with the same title in *P.M.L.A.*, Dec. 1933; three articles by A. C. Judson—'Cornelius Agrippa and Henry Vaughan', *M.L.N.*, 1926, 'Henry Vaughan as a Nature Poet', *P.M.L.A.*, 1927, 'The Source of Henry Vaughan's Ideas concerning God in Nature', *Stud. Phil.*, 1927; R. M. Wardle's 'Thomas Vaughan's Influence on the Poetry of Henry Vaughan', *P.M.L.A.*, Dec. 1936; A. J. M. Smith's 'Some Relations between Henry and Thomas Vaughan', *Papers of Michigan Academy*, 1933; E. L. Marilla's 'Henry and Thomas Vaughan', *M.L.R.*, Apr. 1944.
[5] Cf. Hardin Craig, *The Enchanted Glass: the Elizabethan Mind in Literature*, 1936; Theodore Spencer, *Shakespeare and the Nature of Man*, 1943; E. M. W. Tillyard, *The Elizabethan World Picture*, 1943. Henry Vaughan has 'the greater world' and 'the lesser' in his poem 'Affliction' (M 459), as well as in his translation of *Hermetical Physick* (M 561, l. 15 and 562, l. 4).

Paracelsus had emphasized, as he did, the unity of the world in God and the interpenetration by the Divine spirit of all created beings, whether animate or inanimate. The Paracelsian emphasis upon the 'sympathy' between terrestrial and celestial things was a pious belief with a long history behind it, but, under the influence of the Paracelsians, this idea was much developed, and Henry Vaughan was definitely affected by this development, and, like Thomas, employs the terms usual in this conception. Every terrestrial creature has its antitype or counterpart in the celestial sphere, and it carries the 'signature' or visible indication of that 'correspondence'. Henry Vaughan himself explains the title of the Hermetical books *De signaturis rerum*: 'That is to say, Of those impressions and Characters, which God hath communicated to, and marked (as I may say) all his Creatures with.'[1] To Henry More's remark, 'How fansifull, and Poeticall are you Mr. *Eugenius*', Thomas Vaughan replies: 'Doest thou make the mysterious *Signatures*, and *Symbols* of *Nature*, to be but *fansies*, and *Poetry*?'[2] Without this key we may miss the full significance of Henry Vaughan's looking to all nature to help him towards repentance:

> The blades of grasse, thy Creatures feeding,
> The trees, their leafs; the flowres, their seeding;
> The Dust, of which I am a part,
> The Stones much softer than my heart,
> The drops of rain, the sighs of wind,
> The Stars to which I am stark blind,
> The Dew thy herbs drink up by night,
> The beams they warm them at i'th' light,
> All that have signature or life,
> I summon'd to decide this strife.[3]

And besides having its signature, every sublunary object is in the charge of a star, and may be said to look to its star for direction. As Thomas Vaughan says: 'There is not an *Herb* here *below*, but he hath a *star* in *Heaven above*, and the

---

[1] M 583. Jacob Boehme also wrote a book *De Signatura Rerum*; the first English translation did not appear until the year after the first issue of *Silex Scintillans*.
[2] *The Man-Mouse taken*, p. 75.   [3] 'Repentance', M 448–9.

star strikes him with her *Beame,* and sayes to him, *Grow.*[1]
The poet uses the same language:

> Some kinde herbs here, though low & far,
> Watch for, and know their loving star.[2]

Even Herbert can write: 'Then as dispersed herbs do watch
a potion',[3] but he does not develop the idea as Vaughan
does, and probably it is for him no more than a pretty
fancy, while to Vaughan it is a deeply serious conviction.
Henry Vaughan attributes, literally or at least mystically,
a kind of sentience to herbs, trees, and flowers, and even
stones.[4]

Furthermore, the terrestrial object on its side can attract
the attention of its celestial counterpart, or, as it is sometimes described, exercise 'magnetic' attraction. The plant
attracts its star, the 'magnetisme' of the cock 'works all
night', as it watches 'for the morning hue';[5] and the earthly
object, 'What ever 'tis, whose beauty here below' attracts
the star and makes it 'stream & flow', has 'in it a restless,
pure desire And longing for' the star's 'bright and vitall fire':

> These are the Magnets which so strongly move
> And work all night upon thy light and love,
>   As beauteous shapes, we know not why,
>   Command and guide the eye.[6]

It is significant that these semi-technical Hermetic terms
—*sympathy, influence, magnet, ray, signature*—which are found
in *Silex Scintillans* are never found in *The Temple.* Some
familiarity with the treatises of Thomas Vaughan and other
occult writings throws light upon several poems in *Silex.*
In particular, the fine and interesting poem 'Cock-crowing'
is not fully intelligible without these clues. In the traditional astrology the cock is a 'solary' bird, subject to the
nfluence of the sun, and therefore even in the night is

---

[1] *Lumen de Lumine,* p. 88. Cited by E. Holmes, op. cit., p. 39.
[2] 'The Favour', M 492.   [3] *The Temple:* 'The H. Scriptures' (II), l. 7.
[4] See below, pp. 176–7.
[5] 'Cock-crowing' (M 488). Other words in this poem—*seed, grain, tincture,
house of light* (cf. the title of Thomas Vaughan's book *Aula Lucis, or The House
of Light*)—are constantly found in occult writings, chemical or astrological.
[6] 'The Starre' (M 489).

watching for the first appearance of the sun's rays, and draws those rays by its own magnetism.[1]

The Hermetic writers place particular emphasis upon light as the source of life, and Henry Vaughan is for ever using such words as *light, white, ray, beam,* with fuller connotation than most of his readers recognize. He has passed the Hermetic ideas and terms so integrally into the common language of Christian tradition that they do not disconcert the reader; they are not resented as the technical terms of an unfamiliar philosophy, but are accepted as the poet's individual way of expressing his conviction of the 'commerce' between earth and heaven. The poet is living intimately in two worlds, and sets himself to interpret this world by the other. 'Me thought I heard one singing thus', he says in 'The Search':

> Search well another world; who studies this, ·
> Travels in Clouds, seeks *Manna*, where none is.[2]

The poems of Henry Vaughan, whatever they owe to the Hermetic philosophy, win a far readier acceptance from the reader to-day than his brother's treatises. The poet has assimilated the Hermetic ideas until they harmonize with general Christian thought, while his brother's writings provoke the reader's resistance to a special pleading for a philosophy which has long since become obsolete. In Henry Vaughan the ideas are fused in poetry, in Thomas Vaughan they are still prose, if often beautiful prose; the poet does not argue but assert, the prose-writer is still on the plane of argument.

[1] Cf. E. Holmes, op. cit., p. 39.   [2] M 407, ll. 74, 95–6.

XII

HENRY VAUGHAN, SILURIST

HENRY VAUGHAN'S chosen name of Silurist expresses his devotion to the region of south Wales where he spent almost his entire life. His Welsh birth and breeding, as well as his affection for Welsh scenery, have obviously affected his poetry. It is no less certain that the fact of Welsh being his mother-tongue—his twin brother speaks of English being 'a language the author was not born to'[1]— has left distinct traces on the Silurist's poetry. In a spirited letter to the *Western Mail,* written near the end of her life, Miss Morgan claims Henry Vaughan as 'a thorough Welshman by descent, birth, breeding, and residence in Brecknockshire', and says: 'To those who study Vaughan's poems closely the idea is constantly suggested that he not only spoke but thought in Welsh.' Whether that idea is justified or not, there is evidence of his having some knowledge of Welsh poetry, and it is likely to have influenced his composition of English verse.

In a letter to Anthony Wood, dated 19 March 1680/1, Aubrey remarks that Vaughan had borrowed from Jesus College a copy of Rhesus's Welsh Grammar, and had failed to return it.[2] In his last letter to Aubrey, Vaughan alludes to the 'several sorts of measures & a kind of Lyric poetrie' practised by 'the later Bards', as they are 'all sett down exactly In the learned John David Rhees, or Rhesus his welch, or British grammer'. He explains to Aubrey:

This vein of poetrie they called Awen, which in their language signifies as much as Raptus, or a poetic furor; & (in truth) as many of them as I have conversed with are (as I may say) gifted or inspired with it.[3]

In his prose work *The Mount of Olives* Vaughan quotes three Welsh lines of 'the Brittish Bard' and gives his own

---

[1] See above, pp. 26–7. [2] *Brief Lives,* ii. 201.
[3] Letter of 9 Oct. 1694 (M 675). 'Y naw Awen' are the Nine Muses.

English translation.[1] These lines come from one of the
Englyns of the Months. In Thomas Powell's *Cerbyd Jechyd-
wriaeth* (1657) there are four lines of Welsh verse signed
'Ol. Vaughan',[2] which have been taken to be Henry
Vaughan's. There was a close literary friendship between
Powell and Vaughan, and the latter contributed English
verse-translations from the Latin to Powell's *Humane
Industry* (1661).[3] The Welsh lines in the former book are
not likely to be Vaughan's, as they have been identified
as the last in a series of Englyns on the Lord's Prayer. If
Powell meant Henry Vaughan, the signature may be
intended only to indicate that the lines were brought to
his attention by the author of *Olor Iscanus,* although 'Ol.
Vaughan' would more naturally stand for Oliver Vaughan.[4]

Before dealing with the more important aspects of Welsh
influence upon Vaughan as poet, it may be well to begin
with some instances, in themselves unimportant except as
establishing the general fact of Welsh usage affecting him.
The English reader may have one slight advantage over
the Welsh in recognizing as unfamiliar in English Vaughan's
frequent use of masculine and feminine pronouns referring
to inanimate things, and without any obvious or probable
personification. So far as the use of the possessives *his*
and *her* is concerned, it will be borne in mind that the neuter
possessive *it's* (more rarely *its*) was only slowly establishing
itself in literary use from the very end of the sixteenth
century. It is not found in the Authorized Version of the
Bible (1611) or in any plays of Shakespeare printed in his
lifetime, and it occurs only three times in *The Temple* (1633).
It would, therefore, be still fairly common at the time when
Silex Scintillans was printed, and for yet one more generation, to use *his* and *her* for the possessive pronouns of
things. The Authorized Version freely uses the masculine
and feminine possessives, but never *he* and *she* of things.
Even much earlier there had come to be felt some awkward-
ness in using personal pronouns where there was no

---

[1] M 175 and Martin's note, p. 684. Cf. *Y Cymmrodor*, vol. xi, part 2,
p. 223.　　　　　　　　[2] M 666.　　　　　　　　[3] M 661-4.
[4] Cromwell sometimes signed himself 'Ol. Cromwell'.

conscious personification. Thus, although Tyndale in 1534 translates John iii. 8 'The wynde bloweth where he listeth and thou hearest his sounde', only five years later the Great Bible has 'it listeth' and 'the sound thereof'. Similarly the Authorized Version often resorts to the forms *thereof, therein, therewith,* and the like to avoid the use of a grammatical gender.

Where *his* and *her* were used of things in default of a neuter possessive *its,* there was some uncertainty in English in choosing between the masculine and feminine forms. Convention ascribed masculine or feminine gender to certain things which were more or less clearly personified, like the masculine Time, Death, and the Sun, and the feminine Moon. In translating from the Latin, or even in unconscious imitation of Latin, it was not uncommon to borrow the Latin gender as with Nature, the Soul, the Earth.

What strikes the English reader in Vaughan's usage is that he has *he* and *she* of inanimate things without personifying them, besides the possessives *his* and *her,* often with genders that differ from such English usage as can be said to be common or established. This singular fact must be ascribed to the absence of a neuter gender in Welsh and to Vaughan's generally following the gender of the Welsh equivalents of the words he uses. Thus he treats as masculine not only *sun, time,* and *sea,*[1] which is the common English practice when they are not treated as neuters, but also *rose,* which in English follows the Latin *rosa,* and *cloud, day, fire, truth,* for which there is no clear English precedent. In all these cases the equivalent Welsh words are masculine. He treats as feminine not only *nature* and *earth,* as in English practice, but also *fountain, spring* (of water), and *star,* which are feminine in Welsh but have no tradition of gender in English. In two poems he refers to a star as *she,* and in other poems he refers to the rose and the day as *he;* this goes beyond the English use of possessives that persisted in English poetry when the nouns to which

---

[1] In the A.V. the sea has 'his waves' (Ezek. xxvi. 7), the fountain 'her waters' (Jer. vi. 7), and the earth 'her increase' (Ps. lxvii. 6, Ezek. xxxiv. 27).

they refer were personified.[1] He treats *lake* as feminine; the
Welsh *llyn* is commonly masculine, but is also feminine to this
day, particularly in south Wales, and it is quite likely that
Vaughan knew it only as feminine in the local speech.

Although Vaughan often appears to follow Welsh gender,
especially where there is no established English use, he does
not always do so. He treats *soul* and *vice* as feminine, for
which there is good English precedent.[2] He treats *life* and
death as feminine, although masculine is commoner in
English when Death is personified.[3] A remarkable instance
of his deliberate choice of gender occurs in his translation
of a poem of Boëthius, where he appropriates some lines
from Felltham's translation but alters

> That the World in constant force
> Varies his concordant course

to 'her concordant course'.[4] I.T.'s translation of the same
poem in 1609 also has *her,* although the Latin is the masculine *mundus.* There seems to have been no settled English
usage; the Authorized Version has 'the world hath lost his
youth' (II Esdras xiv. 10) and 'the world would love his
own' (John xv. 19), but Felltham elsewhere has 'The
World's Enchantment, when she smiles on us', and Quarles
in his *Emblems,* which Vaughan is likely to have known,
repeatedly treats the world as feminine,[5] and a Dutch
emblem-engraver represents it as a lady with a high ruff.[6]

A clear case of Welsh influence is Vaughan's constant
rhyming of *s* and *z* sounds. The latter is for the Welshman
not a natural but an acquired sound, and it is likely that
Vaughan pronounced *s* and *z* alike as *ss*. It strikes the

[1] Hooker remarks that God 'caused the morning starre to know his place'.
Thomas Vaughan, like his brother, treats *star* as feminine, and also speaks of
a herb as 'he': see the quotation from *Lumen de Lumine* on pp. 153–4 above.
[2] Cf. Milton: 'Vice with all her baits', *Areopagitica,* and *Comus,* l. 760.
The Welsh *enaid* (soul) and *drygioni* (vice) are both masculine.
[3] *Bywyd* (life) and *angau* (death) are both masculine, but there is also the
feminine *marwolaeth* (death, personified in Rev. vi. 8). Vaughan is more
probably following the Latin *mors*.
[4] Lib. 2, Metr. 8 (misnumbered 7: M 84). Felltham, *Resolves,* ch. cxxxi.
The common Welsh word for world is *byd* (m.), but *daear* (earth) is feminine.
[5] *Emblems,* i. 11, ii. 1, 7, 12, &c. The world is feminine in *Paradise Lost,*
xii. 539.   [6] M. Praz, *Studies in Seventeenth-century Imagery,* 1939, p. 140.

English ear as unfamiliar when he rhymes *doses, roses*; *eyes, ice*; *squeeze, piece*; *price, cries*; *voice, joys*. He has scores of such rhymes, which are only occasionally found in most other English poets. Like most of the Welsh country gentry of his time, he may have spoken with some local accent. For instance, he may have made no clear distinction between *s* and *sh*, when he rhymes *wish'd* and *miss'd, undress* and *fresh*, just as Shakespeare's Fluellen says 'you sall finde' and 'tish ill done'. It may be noted that the literary form of the borrowed English word *fresh* is *ffres*, and *skirmish* becomes *ysgarmes*. There is a perfectly clear distinction in Welsh between the *f* sound (represented by *ff*) and the *v* sound (represented by *f*), but Vaughan may sometimes have been misled by the different English representation of those sounds. He has *lifes* as the plural of *life* and sometimes he has the plural *leafs*, just as Fluellen says *prerogatifes* and *falorous*. James Howell, another Welshman, writes 'They soon will cast their leafs' in *Dodona's Grove* (1640), but Spenser, Shakespeare, the Authorized Version, and Milton always have *leaves*.

Gerard Manley Hopkins was much attracted by what he called 'the consonantal chime' in Welsh poetry, where the consonants echo while the vowel changes.[1] Vaughan's rhyming of *stir* and *far, flesh* and *crush, sport* and *art, priest* and *oppress'd*, conforms to this type, which is technically known as *proest*. There are scores of such rhymes in his poems, and he evidently took pleasure in this interplay of vowels and consonants. And if he rhymes *sense* and *sins*, it may be noted that he probably pronounced the latter word in the Welsh way *sinss*.

In some Welsh metres a stressed rhymes with an unstressed syllable. Vaughan follows no regular pattern in this regard, but he freely uses such rhymes at pleasure; for instance, there are as many as thirteen in a single poem. It would not be safe to infer that he derived this habit from Welsh models, which are stricter than his own practice. Dr. Percy Simpson[2] has shown that it was used by Peele

---

[1] Cf. G. Lilly, 'The Welsh Influence on the Poetry of G. M. Hopkins', *M.L.R.*, July 1943.
[2] 'The Rhyming of Stressed and Unstressed Syllables', *M.L.R.*, Apr. 1943.

and Chapman and, more sparingly, by Ben Jonson. He quotes Samuel Daniel's censure of the English practice in *A Defence of Rhyme* (1603): 'Who knowes not that we can not kindely answere a feminine number with a Masculine Rhyme . . . as *weaknes* with *Confesse, Nature* and *Indure,* onely for that whereby we shall wrong the accent, the chiefe Lord and graue Governour of Numbers.' It should, however, be urged in support of Vaughan that the Welsh care in sounding fully a final unstressed syllable, unlike the common English reduction of it to a half-smothered syllable with an indeterminate vowel sound, makes this kind of rhyme more pleasing to a Welsh than to an English ear. When Vaughan rhymes *and run* with *Domination,* he probably gives a fuller sound to the last syllable of *Domination* than the Englishman does, and therefore the rhyme of stressed with unstressed syllable would be clearly perceptible.

Alliteration plays a conspicuous part in much Welsh poetry, and Vaughan uses it more extensively than most of his contemporaries writing English verse. He will keep it up for many lines together, as in the opening of 'The Water-fall':

> With what deep murmurs through times silent stealth
> Doth thy transparent, cool and watry wealth
> > Here flowing fall,
> > And chide, and call,
> As if his liquid, loose Retinue staid
> Lingring.[1]

Vaughan has a marked fondness for the alliteration of sibilants, which English poets have generally avoided except for some special significance; he will have as many as eleven sibilants in a couple of lines.[2] This, however, does not appear to be characteristically Welsh.

Assonance is also a feature of Welsh poetry. Vaughan is, indeed, content with almost any degree of assonance. He constantly rhymes *n* and *m* sounds: *sins, limbs; come, sun; none, home; since, glimpse; dawn, name.* Sometimes he allows himself even greater licence: *weep, seek; locks, drops; dust, husk;*

[1] M 537.
[2] 'The Constellation', ll. 15–16 (M 469). Cf. 'The Proffer', ll. 32–5 (M 487), and 'Repentance', ll. 19–20 (M 448).

forgotten, broken; *people, sickle.* He also freely rhymes singular
and plural, as is not uncommon in some English poets : *sleep,
creeps*; *alone, groans*; *attempts, contempt*; *guests, rest.* It must
be allowed that he is extremely lax in his rhymes.

It has been observed of some Welsh poets that they have
lavished so much pains on polishing the line or couplet or
stanza that they have neglected to organize the poem as a
whole.[1] This deficiency in architectonic faculty is noticeable in Vaughan. There are, indeed, happily a few poems
of his, and those among the best, which show an orderly
development of thought and feeling, but oftener his poems,
while distinguished by fine lines or stanzas, fail to maintain
their high level throughout the poem. Many of them suffer
from diffuseness after the flash of inspiration—the spark
struck from the flint—has spent itself. This lack of coherence
is made more noticeable by his habit of changing the metre,
sometimes more than once, in the course of a single poem.

Passing to matters of higher value, we are safe in relating
Vaughan's fondness for the word *white,* as an epithet for all
that he values most, to the rich connotations of the Welsh
word *gwyn,* which signifies not only white but fair, happy,
holy, blessed. There is no more frequent epithet in Welsh
poetry, it is the word which introduces each of the Beati-
tudes in the Sermon on the Mount, and a Welsh word for
Paradise is *gwynfyd,* the white world. So we can understand
better why Vaughan speaks of 'a white celestial thought',
the 'white days' of primeval innocence, 'those first white
Pilgrims', and 'Those white designs which children drive'.
Next after white, his special fondness is for green, the
colour most universally noticeable in natural scenery. He
sometimes brings white and green together, especially when
he speaks of heaven:

> For thy eternal, living wells
> None stain'd or wither'd shall come near:
> A fresh, immortal *green* there dwells,
> And spotless *white* is all the wear.[2]

---

[1] Cf. H. Idris Bell, *The Development of Welsh Poetry,* 1936, p. 5. What the
writer says of the poet 'Islwyn' on pp. 154–7 fits Vaughan very closely.
[2] 'The Seed growing secretly', ll. 21–4 (M 511).

And he ends 'Palm-Sunday':

> I care not, so I may secure
> But one *green Branch* and a *white robe.*[1]

He looks for joy in

> Day-stars and light,
> Green trees of life, and living streams.[2]

It is characteristic of his thought that he should interpolate
in his versifying of Psalm civ the line: 'Thou giv'st the
trees their greenness.'[3] He appears to dislike what he calls
'settled' colours and prefers what 'is not fixt, but flies, and
flowes'.[4] His only references to red are disparaging, and
he names purple only of the well stained with Abel's blood.
Like Herbert, he avoids the stronger colours, and there
would seem to be some native feeling about this: 'Welsh
words of colour, like Greek, are apt to be somewhat vague,
referring originally, it is probable, to tone rather than tint.'[5]
He follows Herbert in using ' azure ' of the heavens.

A very fine feature of Welsh poetry is *dyfalu,* the piling up
of comparisons, sometimes fanciful and even riddling, but
all intended to present the object with greater effectiveness.
The sixth stanza of 'The Night' is described by Sir H. Idris
Bell as 'a perfect example of *dyfalu*; even thus and no otherwise would Vaughan have written, had he been writing in
Welsh':[6]

> Gods silent, searching flight:
> When my Lords head is fill'd with dew, and all
> His locks are wet with the clear drops of night;
> His still, soft call;
> His knocking time; The souls dumb watch,
> When Spirits their fair kinred catch.[7]

'Son-dayes' offers almost as good an example. As Sir
Harold recognizes, such instances are to be found also in

---

[1] M 502.   [2] 'The Queer', ll. 7–8 (M 539).   [3] M 495.
[4] 'Affliction', ll. 25–8 (M 460).
[5] *Dafydd ap Gwilym: Fifty Poems.* Translated, with introductory essays,
by H. Idris Bell and David Bell, 1942, p. 59.
[6] Ibid., pp. 38–9. I owe much in this paragraph, and throughout this
chapter, to Sir H. Idris Bell, though he must not be held answerable for my
mistakes.   [7] M 522.

Donne and Herbert, but these poets, too, were of Welsh origin. The employment of fanciful images and conceits is, of course, typical of the whole school of 'metaphysical' poets, and it is found in the contemporary 'Gongorism' of Spanish and Italian poetry, though there is no evidence of Vaughan's knowing those languages as Donne and Crashaw did. Any other of the English metaphysical poets might have written such lines as:

> To put on Clouds instead of light,
> And cloath the morning-starre with dust.[1]

But some of Vaughan's antitheses, where two objects or moods are placed in sharp contrast, come very close to the manner of the Welsh poets. Thus he writes:

> And in the depth and dead of winter bring
> To my Cold thoughts a lively sense of spring.[2]

And, rather more subtly, he alludes to his sensation

> When first I saw true beauty, and thy Joys
> Active as light, and calm without all noise—[3]

where *Joys* would normally suggest some degree of *noise*, from which he has an intense aversion.

Above and beyond all these details, which Vaughan may in part owe to his Welsh breeding and his acquaintance with Welsh poetry, there is something more essential and valuable —the Welshman's imaginative vision, both intense and daring, his sensitiveness to the beauty of nature in all her moods, and his wistful yearning for lost youth, for friends departed, and for peace beyond the grave. All these fine qualities illuminate Vaughan's best poems. The most Welsh of all who have written English poetry, he has given us the truest values that his race has to contribute to our common heritage.

[1] 'The Incarnation, and Passion', ll. 5–6 (M 415).
[2] 'Mount of Olives', No. 2, ll. 19–20 (M 476).
[3] Ibid., ll. 1–2.

XIII

SILEX SCINTILLANS

THE preceding chapters should have prepared the way for a just assessment of the poetic value of *Silex Scintillans*. The slow exploration of the events and influences in Henry Vaughan's early life may have taxed the reader's patience, but it will have been justified if it reveals the growth of his mind before he came to write, within the compass of some half-dozen years, the poems by which he is best remembered. We have watched his childhood and boyhood spent in a sequestered countryside of rare natural beauty in which he elected to spend the rest of life after a brief experience of Oxford and London. Immediately after he had reached manhood the outbreak of the Civil War caught him in the impressionable years just as the French Revolution caught William Wordsworth at almost the same age. We have seen how the victory of the Puritan cause afflicted Vaughan with a sense of utter frustration and instability and how hardly it bore on the fortunes of his kinsfolk and friends. His character can only be inferred from his writings, since there is no portrait nor any contemporary characterization of him except for Wood's brief description of him as 'esteemed by Scholars an ingenious Person, but proud and humorous'—epithets which he uses of other poets of his time.[1] From early years Vaughan had practised the poetic art, at first in frank imitation of Randolph and Cleveland, Cartwright and Habington. His discipleship of Donne, that never went very far, was over by the time he composed *Silex Scintillans*, which reveals little of that influence remaining. There was, indeed, a new and closer discipleship of George Herbert, but Vaughan's best and most distinctive achievements will be on themes of his own choice and treated in his own way. At this stage of our inquiry, and for the purpose of assessing his best work, we can disregard the merely imitative work of his

[1] *Ath. Oxon.*, 1721, ii. 926.

immaturity and those poems in *Silex Scintillans* in which his inspiration flags or deserts him while he continues to moralize gently and on a pedestrian plane. We concentrate now on those poems which are unspoiled by topical allusions and which are, by comparison, independent of time and place and circumstance. It is these greater poems that establish his claim to recognition as a true poet, and it will be seen that their main source and inspiration is an illuminated vision of the universe, newly apprehended.

Before attempting to describe the nature of that visionary power, we should notice that the poet was best able to reach those moments of vision in solitude and in quiet communing with nature. There are many indications that this 'proud and humorous' person, though affectionate by disposition, felt the need at times to seclude himself from human intercourse. He shrank from placing too much reliance upon the company of others, even of those he loved. He grudged the time spent on 'Excesse of friends':[1]

> Shall I thy mercies still abuse
> With fancies, friends, or newes?[2]

'Away with friends,'[3] he exclaims, and even prays to be protected from them:

> Lord, God! I beg nor friends, nor wealth
> But pray against them both.[4]

He tells Sir Charles Egerton in dedicating to him *Flores Solitudinis*: 'when you please to looke upon these *Collections*, you will find them to lead you from the Sun into the *shade*, from the open *Terrace* into a private *grove*, & from the *noyse* and *pompe* of this world into a silent and solitary *Hermitage*.'[5] He was peculiarly sensitive to the distraction of noise. It was one of the reasons why the stars attracted him that the motion of these 'fair, order'd lights' was 'without noise'.[6] He valued 'humble joys' that were 'without all noise',[7] and

---

[1] 'Misery', l. 25 (M 472).   [2] 'And do they so?', ll. 33–4 (M 433).
[3] 'Rules and Lessons', l. 104 (M 438).
[4] 'Day of Judgement', ll. 37–8 (M 403).   [5] M 214.
[6] 'The Constellation', ll. 1–4 (M 469).
[7] 'The Shepheards', ll. 35–6 (M 471).

he begins the second poem that bears the significant title
'Mount of Olives':

> When first I saw true beauty, and thy Joys
> Active as light, and calm without all noise
> Shin'd on my soul, I felt through all my powr's
> Such a rich air of sweets, as Evening showrs
> Fand by a gentle gale Convey and breath
> On some parch'd bank, crown'd with a flowrie wreath;
> Odors, and Myrrh, and balm in one rich floud
> O'r-ran my heart, and spirited my bloud,
> My thoughts did swim in Comforts, and mine eie
> Confest, *The world did only paint and lie.*[1]

It was also in solitary communing with nature that
Vaughan's thoughts developed most fruitfully. It is worthy
of note that he appears to have composed 'They are all gone
into the world of light' out of doors as he watched the
after-glow of 'those faint beams in which this hill is drest,
After the Sun's remove'.[2] Nature had for him a 'healing
power' as it had for Wordsworth when recovering from
the aridity that seized him after the acute disappointment of
his political hopes. The natural beauty of Vaughan's Welsh
home moved him to write of 'the now Primros'd fields',
the shifting lights on the hills, the flowery banks of his
beloved Usk, a rose that buds 'in the bright East' which
discloses 'the Pilgrim-Sunne',[3] and at sunset 'that blushing
Cloud'

> Whose lively *fires* in swift projections glance
> From hill to hill, and by refracted chance
> Burnish some neighbour-*rock*, or tree, and then
> Fly off in coy and winged *flams* agen.[4]

Only an observant lover of nature could have written in
the opening poem of *Silex Scintillans*:

> The unthrift Sunne shot vitall gold
> A thousand peeces,
> And heaven its azure did unfold
> Checqur'd with snowie fleeces,

---

[1] M 476.   [2] M 484.
[3] 'The Search' (M 405).   [4] 'The Recovery' (M 644).

> The aire was all in spice
> And every bush
> A garland wore; Thus fed my Eyes
> But all the Eare lay hush.[1]

Yet, dearly as Vaughan loves this natural beauty for its own sake, he seldom describes it at any length, but passes on to tell of its moral and spiritual significance for him. For example, in one of the longest and most observant of his natural descriptions, 'The Waterfall', the 'mystical, deep streams' that race away from the pool in which the waters falling from a great height have momentarily gathered, speak to him of 'sublime truths, and wholesome themes'. The waters have not found their goal after the plunge into 'this deep and rocky grave' but 'Rise to a longer course more bright and brave'; just as at the head of the waterfall they had 'staid Lingring, and were of this steep place afraid', so the soul that draws back in fear at the approach of death will find her destined end, not in the grave but in the fuller life beyond. And the poem ends:

> O my invisible estate,
> My glorious liberty, still late!
> Thou art the Channel my soul seeks,
> Not this with Cataracts and Creeks.[2]

Vaughan is aware that he might seek content with what presents itself to the bodily eye, 'Did not a greater beauty rule mine eyes'.[3] Therefore he prays:

> Grant I may so
> Thy steps track here below,
>
> That in these Masques and shadows I may see
> Thy sacred way,
> And by those hid ascents climb to that day
> Which breaks from thee
> Who art in all things, though invisibly.[4]

He is conscious of the veil that commonly 'shadows' the

---

[1] 'Regeneration', stanza 6 (M 398).   [2] M 538.
[3] 'The hidden Treasure', l. 23 (M 520).
[4] 'I walkt the other day', ll. 48–54 (M 479).

ENGRAVED TITLE-PAGE OF *SILEX*
SCINTILLANS (1650)

unseen world, and can only hope for its occasional and partial withdrawing at rare moments of vision:

> This veyle thy full-ey'd love denies,
> And onely gleams and fractions spies.[1]

Yet in reflective contemplation of the open face of nature he can hope for a rich reward

> When on some *gilded Cloud,* or *flowre*
> My gazing soul would dwell an houre,
> And in those weaker glories spy
> Some shadows of eternity.[2]

Vaughan realized that he could best cultivate this 'wise passiveness' in the uninterrupted calm and solitude of night-time or of the early dawn before 'the world's up, and ev'ry swarm abroad'.[3] It was night-time that was the occasion of the most arresting of all his great affirmations, 'I saw Eternity the other night.'[4] And he asks the shepherds of Bethlehem

> How happend it that in the dead of night
> You only saw true light,
> While *Palestine* was fast a sleep?[5]

One of the few poems of his that maintain their high level from beginning to end is 'The Night', which takes its *motif* from the story of Nicodemus who 'came to Jesus by night'. In this poem Vaughan reveals what the night-time means to him:

> Dear night! this worlds defeat;
> The stop to busie fools; cares check and curb;
> The day of Spirits; my souls calm retreat
> Which none disturb!
> *Christs* progress, and his prayer time;
> The hours to which high Heaven doth chime.[6]

He ends the poem with a phrase he has learnt from some

---

[1] 'Cock-crowing', stanza 7 (M 489).   [2] 'The Retreate' (M 419).
[3] 'Rules and Lessons', l. 31 (M 436).   [4] 'The World' (M 466).
[5] 'The Shepheards', ll. 5–7 (M 471).
[6] 'The Night' (M 522). R. Sencourt (*Carmelite and Poet,* pp. 126, 186) gives an interesting parallel to Vaughan's 'deep, but dazling darkness' from the writings of St. John of the Cross.

mystical writer and with an answering aspiration of his own:

> There is in God (some say)
> A deep, but dazling darkness; As men here
> Say it is late and dusky, because they
> See not all clear;
> O for that night! where I in him
> Might live invisible and dim.[1]

Besides his poems 'The Starre' and 'The Constellation', Vaughan repeatedly brings the stars into his poems and they generally inspire him. He is likely to have known the Apocryphal verse: 'And the stars shined in their watches, and were glad; when God called them, they said, Here we be; they shined with gladness unto him that made them.'[2] There appears to be an echo of that verse in the poem 'Midnight', which begins:

> When to my Eyes
> (Whilst deep sleep others catches,)
> Thine hoast of spyes
> The starres shine in their watches,
> I doe survey
> Each busie Ray,
> And how they work, and wind,
> And wish each beame
> My soul doth streame,
> With the like ardour shin'd;
> What Emanations,
> Quick vibrations
> And bright stirs are there?
> What thin Ejections,
> Cold Affections,
> And slow motions here?[3]

There is also Vaughan's love of the dawn for its spicy freshness and its stillness; '*Mornings* are *Mysteries*.'[4] In one of the most brilliant of his poems, 'The Dawning', he discusses what hour of day or night best befits Christ's second coming. Such a speculation may seem to us

unprofitable, but we must allow that he makes fine poetry
of it:

> Ah! what time wilt thou come? when shall that crie
>   *The Bridegroome's Comming*! fil the sky?
> Shall it in the Evening run
> When our words and works are done?
> Or wil thy all-surprizing light
>   Break at midnight?
> When either sleep or some dark pleasure
> Possesseth mad man without measure;
> Or shal these early, fragrant hours
>   Unlock thy bowres?
> And with their blush of light descry
> Thy locks crown'd with eternitie;
> Indeed, it is the only time
> That with thy glory doth best chime,
> All now are stirring, ev'ry field
>   Ful hymns doth yield,
> The whole Creation shakes off night,
> And for thy shadow looks the light,
> Stars now vanish without number,
> Sleepie Planets set, and slumber,
> The pursie Clouds disband, and scatter,
> All expect some sudden matter,
> Not one beam triumphs, but from far
>   That morning-star.

Having decided for the hour of sunrise as 'the only time'
for so stupendous an event, he concludes:

> So when that day, and hour shal come
> In which thy self wil be the Sun,
> Thou'lt find me drest and on my way,
> Watching the Break of thy great day.[1]

Another inspired poem, 'The Morning-watch', full of
Vaughan's characteristic thoughts and expressed with more
memorable phrases than he commonly achieves, begins in
these impassioned tones:

> O Joyes! Infinite sweetnes! with what flowres,
> And shoots of glory, my soul breakes, and buds!

[1] M 451–2.

All the long houres
Of night, and Rest,
Through the still shrouds
Of sleep, and Clouds,
This Dew fell on my Breast;
O how it *Blouds*,
And *Spirits* all my Earth! heark! In what Rings,
And *Hymning Circulations* the quick world
Awakes, and sings;
The rising winds,
And falling springs,
Birds, beasts, all things
Adore him in their kinds.
Thus all is hurl'd
In sacred *Hymnes*, and *Order*, The great *Chime*
And *Symphony* of nature.[1]

It does not, therefore, surprise us that the first of Vaughan's counsels in 'Rules and Lessons' is an enlargement upon what is commended in the Book of Wisdom, 'that we must prevent the Sun, to give thee thanks, and at the dayspring pray to thee':

Rise to prevent the Sun; sleep doth sins glut,
And heav'ns gate opens, when this world's is shut.

Walk with thy fellow-creatures: note the *hush*
And *whispers* amongst them. There's not a *Spring*
Or *Leafe* but hath his *Morning-hymn*; Each *Bush*
And *Oak* doth know *I AM*; canst thou not sing?[2]

It was well within the Christian tradition that Vaughan should meditate upon what Bacon calls 'the book of God's work' as well as upon 'the book of God's words':

For as the Psalmes and other Scriptures doe often inuite vs to consider, and magnifie the great and wonderfull workes of God: so if we should rest onely in the contemplation of the exterior of them, as they first offer themselues to our sences; we should do a like iniurie vnto the Maiestie of God, as if wee should iudge or construe of the store of some excellent Ieweller, by that onely which is set out toward the streete in his shoppe. . . . For our Sauiour saith, *You erre not knowing the Scriptures, nor the power of*

[1] M 424.   [2] M 436.

God: laying before vs two Bookes or volumes to studie, if we will be secured from errour: first the scriptures, reuealing the will of God; and then the creatures expressing his power; whereof the later is a key vnto the former.[1]

Many of the Christian mystical writings which Vaughan knew had gone far more deeply into this region of thought than Bacon, and Vaughan learnt much from Plato and the Neo-Platonists, and something from the Hermetic writers. Perhaps also there are traces of a pre-Christian animist belief that attributes a living soul to natural objects. Vaughan's thinking is eclectic, and properly he does not indicate its sources in his poetry. He does not argue but, keeping to his province as poet, he asserts and testifies to what he has seen and felt. Nor is it the province of the present writer to estimate whether Vaughan's view of the universe is tenable to-day, but only to present it so far as it can be gathered from his writings.[2]

There is, at any rate, an impressive completeness about Vaughan's conception of the world which brings into direct and constant relationship not only God and man, earth and heaven, the living and the departed, but also the whole of creation, both animate and inanimate, in 'the great Chime And Symphony of nature'. They are all held together in

> That busie Commerce kept between
> God and his Creatures, though unseen.[3]

There are 'correspondences' and 'sympathy' between celestial and terrestrial objects, which include not man only, and bird and beast, but also tree and herb and stone. Vaughan sees in the creatures' answering to the Divine intent for them a kind of worship in which man should consciously lead the way. So far he follows Herbert:

> Man is the worlds high Priest: he doth present
> The sacrifice for all; while they below
> Unto the service mutter an assent,
> Such as springs use that fall, and windes that blow.[4]

---

[1] *Of the proficience and aduancement of Learning, diuine and humane*, 1605, f. 31ᵛ.
[2] Grierson offers some criticism of Vaughan's view (*Metaphysical Lyrics*, pp. 233–4). [3] 'The Stone', ll. 20–1 (M 515).
[4] 'Providence', ll. 13–16 (O.E.T., p. 117).

But Vaughan carries this thought farther than Herbert, for whom it was perhaps little more than a pious fancy. This 'obedience' of the creatures is for Vaughan almost a conscious adoration of the Creator, which puts man to shame. Quoting at the head of one poem Beza's translation of St. Paul's words, *Etenim res Creatae exerto Capite observantes expectant revelationem Filiorum Dei*, he begins:

> And do they so? have they a Sense
>   Of ought but Influence?
> Can they their heads lift, and expect,
>   And grone too? why th' Elect
> Can do no more: my volumes sed
>   They were all dull, and dead,
> They judg'd them senslesse, and their state
>   Wholly Inanimate.
> Go, go; Seal up thy looks,
>   And burn thy books.[1]

He could even wish himself a bird or tree, 'some poor high-way herb' or stone, that he might render such obedience as they do:

> Thy other Creatures in this Scene
>   Thee only aym, and mean.[1]

He contrasts their fulfilment of the Divine purpose with man's waywardness and instability, and humbly reads a lesson from birds and bees, from the flowers and the loadstone:

> I would (said I) my God would give
> The staidness of these things to man! for these
> To his divine appointments ever cleave. . . .

> Man hath stil either toyes, or Care,
> He hath no root, nor to one place is ty'd,
> But ever restless and Irregular
>   About this Earth doth run and ride,
> He knows he hath a home, but scarce knows where,
>   He sayes it is so far
> That he hath quite forgot how to get there.

<hr />

[1] M 432.

He knocks at all doors, strays and roams,
Nay hath not so much wit as some stones have
Which in the darkest nights point to their homes,
    By some hid sense their Maker gave;
Man is the shuttle, to whose winding quest
    And passage through these looms
God order'd motion, but ordain'd no rest.[1]

The thought of man's kinship with the other creatures
moves Vaughan to a sympathy with the humblest of
them. He will learn from the ass and admires 'his simplicity'.[2] In 'The Timber' he bemoans the fall of a noble
tree and feelingly contrasts its former life with its present
prostration:

Sure thou didst flourish once! and many Springs,
Many bright mornings, much dew, many showers
Past ore thy head: many light *Hearts* and *Wings*
Which now are dead, lodg'd in thy living bowers.

And still a new succession sings and flies;
Fresh Groves grow up, and their green branches shoot
Towards the old and still enduring skies,
While the low *Violet* thrives at their root.

But thou beneath the sad and heavy *Line*
Of death, dost waste all senseless, cold and dark;
Where not so much as dreams of light may shine,
Nor any thought of greenness, leaf or bark.[3]

In 'The Book' he imagines the long story of the constituents
that have made up the volume—the 'papyr' that once was
seed, then grass, then 'made linen'; the tree which once
'flourish'd, grew and spread, As if it never should be dead',
and since its felling has provided the boards for the book;
and the 'harmless beast' which has provided the sheepskin
covering of the boards. Though papyrus and tree and
sheep have all ended their natural life, 'They live unseen,
when here they fade':

Thou knew'st and saw'st them all and though
Now scatter'd thus, dost know them so.

---

[1] 'Man', ll. 8–10, 15–28 (M 477).
[2] 'The Ass' (M 518) and *Mount of Olives* (M 162, ll. 10–14).   [3] M 497.

> O knowing, glorious spirit! when
> Thou shalt restore trees, beasts and men,
> When thou shalt make all new again,
> Destroying onely death and pain,
> Give him amongst thy works a place,
> Who in them lov'd and sought thy face![1]

This appears to be Vaughan's generous interpretation of the scriptural phrase, 'the times of the restoration of all things' (Acts iii. 21), though few Christian thinkers have developed the idea so far as he has done.

Especially remarkable is his repeated insistence on a kind of sentience residing in stones, 'which some think dead'.[2] They share with the rest of *res Creatae* in expecting their 'date' of deliverance and restitution.[3] Accordingly, in 'Palm-Sunday', he includes stones in his acclamation:

> Trees, flowers & herbs; birds, beasts & stones,
> That since man fell, expect with groans
> To see the lamb, which all at once,
> Lift up your heads and leave your moans!
> For here comes he
> Whose death will be
> Mans life, and your full liberty.[4]

This is something beyond the poetic or symbolic words of Christ's reply to the Pharisees' objection to the acclamations of the multitude: 'I tell you, that if these should hold their peace, the stones would immediately cry out!' Herbert had used this saying of Christ and Vaughan follows him, but goes much farther.[5] 'Stones,' he says, 'though speechless, are not dumb,'[6] and have their part in nature's chorus of adoration:

> So hills and valleys into singing break,
> And though poor stones have neither speech nor tongue,
> While active winds and streams both run and speak,
> Yet stones are deep in admiration.[7]

---

[1] M 540.   [2] 'The Stone', l. 39 (M 515).
[3] 'And do they so?', l. 16 (M 432).
[4] M 501. Something seems to have gone wrong with the text in the third line. Miss Guiney suggested 'quick' for 'which', and Martin conjectures 'whist'.
[5] Herbert, 'The Altar'; Vaughan, 'Jesus Weeping' (M 502).
[6] 'The day of Judgement', l. 16 (M 531).
[7] 'The Bird', ll. 13–16 (M 497).

Wordsworth describes in *The Prelude* how he had entertained very similar thoughts in early manhood:

> I was only then
> Contented when with bliss ineffable
> I felt the sentiment of Being spread
> O'er all that moves, and all that seemeth still.[1]

> To every natural form, rock, fruit or flower,
> Even the loose stones that cover the high-way,
> I gave a moral life, I saw them feel,
> Or link'd them to some feeling: the great mass
> Lay bedded in a quickening soul, and all
> That I beheld respired with inward meaning.
> Thus much for the one Presence, and the Life
> Of the great whole. . . .
> I had a world about me; 'twas my own,
> I made it; for it only liv'd to me,
> And to the God who look'd into my mind.[2]

Vaughan repeatedly emphasizes the constancy of the
creatures in fulfilling the Divine intent—the orderly proces-
sion of the heavenly bodies and the life according to nature
of all created beings and things. Richard Hooker also had
eloquently maintained man's dependence upon the stability
of the natural order:

Now if nature should intermit her course, and leaue altogether,
though it were but for a while, the obseruation of her own lawes:
. . . if celestial spheres should forget their wonted motions; . . . what
would become of man himselfe, whom these things now do all
serue? See we not plainly that the obedience of creatures vnto the
lawe of nature is the stay of the whole world?[3]

But there is no suggestion in Hooker of a conscious
obedience on the part of the creatures, and no contrast is
drawn with man's lawlessness, which for Vaughan was so
distressingly exemplified in the disorders of the Civil War
and its sequel.

Again, Vaughan's conception of the whole universe
being indissolubly interconnected, and of the perpetual

---

[1] *The Prelude*, 1805–6 version, ii. 418–21. [2] Ibid. iii. 124–31 and 142–4.
[3] *Of the Lawes of Ecclesiasticall Politie*, i. iii. 3.

'commerce' maintained between earth and heaven, links
man with his departed kinsfolk and friends. It will be
remembered that some of the most striking poems in the
1650 volume were occasioned by the death of a younger
brother. The poet expresses his faith that his brother lives
in the unseen world and continues to influence him:

> Joy of my life! while left me here,
>   And still my Love!
> How in thy absence thou dost steere
>   Me from above![1]

The dead were like the stars that send their rays to illumine
our path:

> Gods Saints are shining lights: who stays
>   Here long must passe
> O're dark hills, swift streames, and steep ways
>   As smooth as glasse;
>   But these all night
>   Like Candles, shed
>   Their beams, and light
>   Us into Bed.

> They are (indeed,) our Pillar-fires
>   Seen as we go,
> They are that Cities shining spires
>   We travell to.[1]

By the time that Vaughan was composing the second
part of *Silex Scintillans* others, including probably his first
wife, had passed beyond the veil, and once more he likens
the departed to stars:

> They are all gone into the world of light!
>   And I alone sit lingring here;
> Their very memory is fair and bright,
>   And my sad thoughts doth clear.

> It glows and glitters in my cloudy brest
>   Like stars upon some gloomy grove,
> Or those faint beams in which this hill is drest,
>   After the Sun's remove.

[1] M 422. See below, p. 195.

I see them walking in an Air of glory,
   Whose light doth trample on my days:
My days, which are at best but dull and hoary,
   Meer glimmering and decays.

O holy hope! and high humility,
   High as the Heavens above!
These are your walks, and you have shew'd them me
   To kindle my cold love,

Dear, beauteous death! the Jewel of the Just,
   Shining no where, but in the dark;
What mysteries do lie beyond thy dust;
   Could man outlook that mark![1]

The poet goes on to liken the recollection of the dead to the bird-song which abides in the mind after the bird has flown out of sight and hearing. He allows that these are 'strange thoughts' that 'transcend our wonted theams, And into glory peep', but he treasures them. He is ill at ease in the thraldom of this world and looks for complete freedom only in the next:

O Father of eternal life, and all
   Created glories under thee!
Resume thy spirit from this world of thrall
   Into true liberty.

As Vaughan says, in another fine poem 'Man', the restlessness of man on this earth, in which 'God order'd motion, but ordain'd no rest', has no cure except the constant recollection that 'he hath a home' in the eternal order.[2] This thought finds perfect expression, and with a simplicity that Vaughan seldom attains, in his poem 'Peace', which is so short that it can be quoted in full:

My Soul, there is a Countrie
   Far beyond the stars,
Where stands a winged Centrie
   All skilfull in the wars,
There above noise, and danger
   Sweet peace sits crown'd with smiles,
And one born in a Manger
   Commands the Beauteous files,

[1] M 483.   [2] M 477.

He is thy gracious friend,
  And (O my Soul awake!)
Did in pure love descend
  To die here for thy sake.
If thou canst get but thither,
  There growes the flowre of peace,
The Rose that cannot wither,
  Thy fortresse, and thy ease;
Leave then thy foolish ranges;
  For none can thee secure,
But one, who never changes,
  Thy God, thy life, thy Cure.[1]

There is a quiet serenity about these timeless poems of
Henry Vaughan that is their chief attraction. The vexations
of the time that had so often fretted him and brought discord and harsh notes into his less successful poems have
here faded into the background as he stays himself on the
thought of the ultimate deliverance of the soul in the peace
of the infinite and the eternal. He has given a felicitous
English rendering of St. Augustine's central conception:
'Fecisti nos ad Te, et inquietum est cor nostrum, donec
requiescat in Te.'

[1] M 430.

XIV

HENRY VAUGHAN, DOCTOR IN PHYSIC

IN his letter to Aubrey of 15 June 1673, Henry Vaughan, after saying that his brother's employment was 'in physic & Chymistrie', continues: 'My profession allso is physic, wch I have practised now for many years with good successe (I thank god!) & a repute big enough for a person of greater parts than my selfe.'[1] It used to be thought that Vaughan had begun to practise in the forties of the century, and this view is still tenable, but some facts of those years which were not known to earlier biographers seem to point to a later date. The forties must have been largely taken up with his secretaryship to Judge Lloyd and with military service. He could hardly have obtained the necessary training for medical practice at home, and he was certainly at Newton for parts at least of 1647 and 1648. In the early fifties he was partly incapacitated by a prolonged and dangerous sickness, and what vitality he possessed was devoted to writing; no less than seven of his nine books were published between 1650 and 1655. This looks as if the first available time for continuous medical training was after his recovery about the year 1655. It should, however, be noted that by the time he published his translation of *Hermetical Physick* in 1655 he had made some acquaintance with Galen and Paracelsus.[2]

Anthony Wood, in his account of Vaughan in his Latin history of 1674, follows the mention of Vaughan's addiction to literature and the publishing of *Olor Iscanus* in 1651 (he does not mention *Silex Scintillans*) with these words which virtually reproduce the sentence quoted above from the letter to Aubrey: 'Ad Medicinae studium deinceps conversus est, & ob felicem ejus praxin in pretio nunc temporis apud suos habetur.'[3] Wood repeats this sentence in the second edition of *Athenae Oxonienses*: 'Afterwards applying his Mind to the study of Physic, [he] became at length

[1] M 668.   [2] M 548.   [3] *Hist. et Antiq.* ii. 321.

eminent in his own Country for the practice thereof.'[1]
Probably Wood had no other authority for this statement
than the letter to Aubrey, in which case 'deinceps' or
'Afterwards' is only an inference, not an explicit statement
of Vaughan's, though probability is on its side.

It is likely enough that Henry Vaughan was already
attracted to medicine before he gave himself seriously to
qualifying himself professionally. His brother Thomas,
after ceasing to be rector of Llansantffraed, had taken to
'physic & Chymistrie'; there is no evidence of his having
at any time practised as a doctor, though medical theories
and recipes are found in his notebook. Mr. Blunden
believes himself to find evidence of Henry Vaughan's being
already a doctor when he was composing Silex Scintillans:
' "Henry Vaughan, M.D." and a little brass plate on a
surgery door, must sometimes occur to the fancy as one
reads Silex Scintillans.'[2] He carefully collects many instances
of physical or medical metaphors in Silex, such as 'eye-
salve', 'salves and syrups', 'New Cordials, new Cathartics',
'a sugerd Dosis of Wormwood', 'pills', 'spit out their
phlegm', and allusions to the medicinal use of dead flowers.
But this is less conclusive than at first appears; George
Herbert, whom Vaughan so closely follows in Silex, had
many of these—'salve', 'cordial and corrosive', 'julips and
cordials' (he uses the word cordial in seven poems), 'pills of
sublimate' (a more technical description than any that
Vaughan uses in Silex), 'fractures well cur'd', 'consuming
agues', 'spit out thy flegme', and in three poems he alludes
to the 'purging' value of the rose 'after death for cures'.
And Donne earlier had freely used medicinal metaphors.
It is, indeed, characteristic of the metaphysical poets to draw
illustrations from such knowledge as an intelligent and well-
informed layman might have of professions other than his
own. Both Herbert and Vaughan had enough personal
experience of sickness to compel their attention to its
conditions. Such metaphors as Vaughan used in Silex do

[1] Ath. Oxon., 2nd edn., 1721, ii. 926. Wood omitted the account of
Henry Vaughan in the first edition.
[2] E. Blunden, On the Poems of Henry Vaughan, p. 11.

not necessitate his having, at the time of writing these poems, any more medical interest or knowledge than Herbert had; the terms they use are not out of the reach of the non-professional man. A far more esoteric term, the 'great port-vein',[1] the *porta vena* conveying blood to the liver, is found in 'Daphnis', but this poem was written after Thomas Vaughan's death in 1666, when Henry had been practising for some years.

Henry Vaughan's early interest in the healing art is shown in his translating for inclusion in *Olor Iscanus* the two treatises of Plutarch and Maximus Tirius with the identical title, 'Of the Diseases of the Mind and the Body', but they are only short general essays with little practical application. A far more important indication of his growing interest is his translation of Heinrich Nolle's *General System of Hermetic Medicine*.[2] 'Hermeticall Physick, by . . . Henry Nollyns. Englished by Hen: Vaughan, gent.' was registered at Stationers' Hall on 16 January 1654/5, exactly nine weeks before the augmented *Silex Scintillans* was registered. This was followed by a translation of Nolle's *De Generatione Rerum naturalium* under the title *The Chymists Key to Open, and to Shut; or the True Doctrine of Corruption and Generation*, 'Written by Hen. Nollius, Published by Eugenius Philalethes'.[3] Wood must have read Henry Vaughan's letter carelessly, as he attributes the translation to Thomas

[1] M 657, l. 45.
[2] *Systema Medicinae Hermeticae generale*. Ab Henrico Nollio, Philochymiatro. Frankfurt, 1613.
[3] Nolle published his *De Generatione* at Frankfurt in 1615 (M 703). There is some doubt about the year of the publication of *The Chymists Key*. Wood, *Hist. et Antiq.* ii. 321, dates it 1656, but in *Ath. Oxon.*, 1692, ii. 254 and in later editions it is given as 'Lond. 1655'. Grosart, ii. 308, gives 1657 and prefaces his list by saying (p. 305): 'I have now for the first time to furnish from the actual books themselves a complete and accurate list of the Writings of Thomas Vaughan, as follows.' He reverses the order of the title, giving the words as 'to shut, and to open'. As he gives also a collation, it may be presumed that he had a copy of the book before him. Like other writers, he overlooked Henry Vaughan's claim to be the translator of Nolle's 'discourse dè generatione' (M 668), and he does not include the book in his *Complete Works of Henry Vaughan*, nor is it in Martin's edition. The *D.N.B.* attributes the translation to Thomas Vaughan and gives its date as 1657. I have been unable to trace any copy of *The Chymists Key* in any public library or to discover an entry of its registration at Stationers' Hall.

Vaughan;[1] Henry does not include it among his brother's works but he lists among 'What past into the presse from me', between *Flores Solitudinis* and *Thalia Rediviva*, 'Nollius his Systema medicinae Hermeticum, & his discourse dè generatione done into English'.[2]

As Eugenius Philalethes was the editor of *The Chymists Key*, it is probable that he was the moving spirit and that he persuaded his brother Henry to undertake the translation of both works of Nolle. Heinrich Nolle (Nollius) describes himself on one of his title-pages as doctor of philosophy and medicine and professor in the University of Steinfurt. His books were already forty years old when Henry Vaughan translated them. Vaughan, especially at the time of his writing religious verse and prose, may have been attracted to this author by the strong infusion of piety in *Hermetical Physick*. Nolle puts first among the qualifications of a physician that he 'must be a sound Christian, and truly religious and holy',[3] and the patient also must have penitence and faith in God.[4] The fact that Vaughan often expands such passages with comments of his own shows that he is in sympathy with his author. The attitude is characteristic of the 'spagyric'[5] or Hermetic physicians. Paracelsus, 'the great Father and leader of the *German* Philosophers' as Nolle calls him,[6] used religious language, and his successors, whether sincerely or not, followed suit. A religious philosophy underlay their scientific theories and was, so they claimed, the motive that impelled them to search the secrets of nature which could be revealed only to the God-fearing.[7]

Paracelsus is reputed to have burnt the books of Galen at his first lecture in Basel. He and his successors deprecated reliance on the usual text-books and on those whom they

[1] *Hist. et Antiq.* ii. 321 and *Ath. Oxon.*, ed. Bliss, iii. 725.
[2] M 668.   [3] M 579.   [4] M 590.
[5] *Spagyric*, 'used, and probably invented by Paracelsus' (*O.E.D.*), noun and adjective, was commonly employed in the seventeenth century to denote alchemy, alchemist, and alchemical.   [6] M 571.
[7] Cf. W. Pagel, 'Religious Motives in the Medical Biology of the XVIIth Century', *Bulletin of the Institute of the History of Medicine*, Apr. 1935, and 'The Religious and Philosophical Aspects of van Helmont's Science and Medicine', ibid., Supplement no. 2, 1944.

called 'the Dogmatical Physicians' as contrasted with 'the true Philosophers',[1] and gave themselves to independent empirical research. They were sceptical of any attempt to explain life, which they regarded as, like God himself, inaccessible to human reason. They distrusted deduction by logical processes from *a priori* doctrines, and instead aimed at making sure of the premisses by experiment. They carried over from the past some belief in magic, which included all natural events or phenomena of which they could make no convincing analysis. Many of their ideas would to-day be dismissed as superstitious, but this did not debar them from making some useful contributions to the knowledge of medicine. Sometimes, even in their superstitions, they were on the track of important discoveries, though they failed to make them. Also, as a consequence of their addiction to chemistry and metallurgy, the Hermetists introduced the use of metallic medicine, whereas attention had previously been almost entirely confined to vegetable remedies.[2] And if they attached importance to astrology, and even believed in 'astral diseases'[3] (a term used by Paracelsus), many of the most enlightened orthodox physicians of the day like Sir Theodore Mayerne could not rid themselves wholly from a belief so strongly entrenched in common opinion. Sir Thomas Browne gently rationalizes some of these beliefs; he argues that 'should we blindly obey the restraints both of Physitians and Astrologers, we should . . . confine the utility of Physick unto a very few daies', but that there was good sense in observing that in the heat of summer the body 'cannot so well endure the acrimony of purging Medicines'.[4] The continued belief in such superstitions as the basilisk's evil eye was not seriously harmful, and Nolle quotes the opinion of Crolle that sometimes 'the Imaginants superstition' of his body being infected by a *Basiliscus Coeli* may have the effect he fears.[5] There may also be detected in Nolle's treatise some-

[1] M 564, l. 35; 549, l. 12; 580, l. 26.
[2] M 582. Cf. Hecker, *Epidemics of the Middle Ages*, 1844, p. 273: 'The severe metallic remedies of the Spagyric school.'
[3] M 566, 586.   [4] *Pseudodoxia*, IV. xiii.   [5] M 591.

thing like homœopathy—'that famous principle of the Hermetists : *Every like is cured by its like*'[1]—and faith-healing.[2] But, more important than any particular theories, was the emphasis put upon the need of patient and continuous experiment in place of accepting uncritically the received notions.[3]

Nolle shows himself a very moderate and reasonable type of Hermetist, like those whom he specially commends, Joseph Quercetan, 'a most expert Physician, and a learned Philosopher, whom as my master in this science I worthily honour',[4] and 'Oswaldus Crollius, a truly learned and expert Physician'.[5] He agrees with Crolle that 'whosoever desires to be eminent in the Art of Physick . . . must (above all things) be unbiassed and addicted to no Sect, nor any one Author whatsoever, but passe through them all in pursuit of the sincere truth . . . *Nullius addictus jurare in verba Magistri*'.[6] He must learn from all schools: 'Now as I preferre the *Hermetical* science to the medicines of these men [the Galenists]: so (their Errours being first laid aside), I unite it with the Physick of the more sober *Galenists*, that theirs by consociation with ours, may become perfect and irreprehensible.'[7] Nolle has no concern with those alchemists 'who seeke to extract from other things by their sophistical operations a great treasure of Gold, which onely nature can supply us with', for this attempt 'is most commonly the task of Sophisters and Impostors'.[8] He cannot, indeed, wholly dismiss the hope that a 'universall medicine' may be found, but he does not pretend that it has yet been discovered.[9]

---

[1] M 581.   [2] M 591–2.

[3] It is, of course, true that many of the best orthodox physicians set greater store by experiment and observation than by the traditional text-books; for instance, Thomas Sydenham's 'most striking characteristic, intellectually, was his independence and repudiation of all dogmatic authority in matters of science. . . . His aim was not to frame hypotheses about the operations of nature, but to observe them directly, as Bacon advised' (*D.N.B.* s.v. Thomas Sydenham).

[4] M 551. Joseph du Chesne (Quercetanus), 1544–1619.

[5] M 584. Oswald Crolle (*ob.* 1609); his best-known book, *Basilica Chymica*, is quoted at length by Nolle (M 584–7, 591–2).   [6] M 551.

[7] M 550–1.   [8] M 550.   [9] M 558, l. 2; 578, l. 5; 579, l. 24.

Vaughan adopts the same tolerant attitude as Nolle in the preface to his translation:

For my owne part, I honour the truth where ever I find it, whether in an old, or a new Booke, in *Galen*, or in *Paracelsus*; and Antiquity, (where I find it gray with errors) shall have as little reverence from me, as *Novelisme* . . . I wish we were all unbiassed and impartiall learners, not the implicite, groundlesse Proselyts of Authors and opinions, but the loyall friends and followers of truth.[1]

And in an interpolated sentence in his translation Vaughan states a further reason which attracts him to the Hermetists, namely, their devotion to experimental research:

Now all the knowledge of the *Hermetists*, proceeds from a laborious manual disquisition and search into nature, but the *Galenists* insist wholly upon a bare received *Theorie* and prescribed Receits, giving all at adventure, and will not be perswaded to inquire further then the mouth of their leader.[2]

It is, however, a little doubtful if Vaughan possessed the spirit of scientific research. In matters of religion, at any rate, he seems to have questioned the value of inquiry:

> Let me thy Ass be onely wise
> To carry, not search mysteries;
> Who carries thee, is by thee lead,
> Who argues, follows his own head.[3]

> Those secret searches, which afflict the wise,
> Paths that are hidden from the *Vulturs* eyes
> I saw at distance, and where grows that fruit
> Which others onely grope for and dispute.
>   The worlds lov'd wisdom (for the worlds friends think
> There is none else), did not the dreadful brink
> And precipice it leads to bid me flie,
> None could with more advantage use, then I.[4]

He describes himself as one 'whose search lov'd not to peep

[1] M 548.   [2] M 550, ll. 10–15.
[3] 'The Ass' (M 518). Cf. 'Asinus mysteria portans' (*Erasmi Adagia*, no. 2204).
[4] 'The hidden Treasure' (M 520). I have for clearness modified the punctuation of ll. 6–7. The allusion in the second line quoted is to Job xxviii. 7.

and peer I' th' face of things'.[1] In 'Vanity of Spirit' he tells
how such search had brought little or no reward:

> I summon'd nature: peirc'd through all her store,
> Broke up some seales, which none had touch'd before,
>   Her wombe, her bosome, and her head
>   Where all her secrets lay a bed
>   I rifled quite, and having past
>   Through all the Creatures, came at last
>   To search my selfe, where I did find
>   Traces, and sounds of a strange kind.[2]

The last passage is very close to language used by Thomas
Vaughan: 'But me thinks Nature complains of a Prostitu-
tion, that I goe about to diminish her majesty, having almost
broken her Seale, & exposed her naked to the World.'[3] It
sounds as if Henry had at one time engaged in such alchemical researches as his brother, but had abandoned them. More
significant than these early allusions, which may refer to
religious speculation, is the passage in a letter to Aubrey in
his sixtieth year, when he had long been a doctor:

> That the most serious of our profession have not only an
> vnkindnes for, butt are persecutors of Astrologie: I haue more
> than once admired: butt I find not this ill humour amongst the
> Antients, so much as the modern physicians: nor amongst them all
> neither. I suppose they had not travelled so far, & having once
> enterd upon the practise, they were loath to leave off, and learn to
> be acquainted with another world. for my owne part (though I
> could never ascend higher,) I had butt litle affection to the skirts
> & lower parts of learning; where every hand is graspinge & so
> litle to be had. butt neither nature, nor fortune favoured my
> ambition.[4]

Vaughan's modesty and his disclaimer of considerable learning or interest in research are evident here.

In Vaughan's day the controversy between the rival
medical schools of the Hermetists and the academical doctors was at its height. William Du Gard in his translation
of Comenius's *The gate of the Latine tongue unlocked* (1656)

---

[1] 'I walkt the other day', ll. 8–9 (M 478).
[2] M 418. The thought is not unlike Herbert's 'Vanitie', 1, *Works*, p. 85.
[3] *Anima Magica Abscondita*, p. 13.
[4] M 672–3. Cf. 'The Search', l. 95 (M 407): 'Search well another world.'

writes, 'At this day *Spagirick* (or *Hermetick*) Physic is in request', but Lord Herbert of Cherbury, who collected many medical works, says: 'As for the Chymic or Spagyric Medicines, I cannot commend them to the use of posterity.'[1] Vaughan, like Nolle, appears to show a preference for the Hermetists, but also, like Nolle, some independence and willingness to learn from other schools. We have no means of knowing whether in his practice he followed the general lines of Nolle's *Hermetical Physick* or whether he saw reason to qualify his approval in the light of experience and of contemporary advances in medical knowledge. One may hope that, with his open mind, he recognized the importance of the contributions to knowledge that were being made by such men as Harvey, Boyle, and Sydenham. It is tempting, if also hazardous, to suppose that there is an allusion to Harvey's discovery of the circulation of the blood in Vaughan's rendering of an ode of Boëthius:

> As *blood* let out forsakes the *Heart*
> And perisheth; but what returns
> With fresh and Brighter spirits burns.[2]

There is no mention of the blood and the heart in this poem of Boëthius.

There is, unfortunately, no evidence as to where and when Vaughan obtained his qualifications for medical practice, and the source of his medical degree has so far baffled all inquirers. The 'M.D.' on his tombstone has been known to all who have written about him, but there is much new evidence of his being described as doctor from 1677 consistently, though there is at present no evidence of his being so described before that date. On the title-page of *Hermetical Physick*, where a medical description would have been appropriate, the translator is given as 'Henry Vaughan, gent.', and *Thalia Rediviva* has no author's name on its title-page. In a series of legal documents from 1650 to 1671 he is described as 'Gent.' He is similarly described in the wills of his father-in-law Richard Wise (1668) and of his daughter Frances (1670), but when the latter will

---

[1] *Autobiography*, ed. S. Lee, 1906, p. 30.
[2] Boëthius, iv. vi. ll. 68–70 (M 633).

was proved in 1677 administration was granted 'Henrico Vaughan in Medicina Dri'.[1] In a warrant issued at Brecon at his request on 15 January 1689/90 and in an indenture of the following 28 January he is 'Dr. Henry Vaughan'.[2] A Caveat of 30 April 1691 registers the claim 'Henrici Vaughan Medici Doctoris' to present to the benefice of Llandefalle. Among the depositions made in 1693 about the disputed will of Thomas Powell of Maesmawr, two of the deponents refer to 'Dr. Henry Vaughan', but Vaughan himself does not use this title in either of the two depositions he makes, the first as witness to the will, and the second testifying to the testator being of sound mind; he describes himself only 'as Physitian who did attend him in his sicknesse'.[3] In the grant of administration to his widow on 31 May 1695 he is named as 'Medicinae Doctor',[4] and in a Bill of Complaint, dated 15 August 1695, he is called 'doctor in physick now deceased'.[5]

Henry Vaughan could have obtained a medical degree only from a university, British or continental, or from the Archbishop of Canterbury. His name is not found in the official registers of Oxford,[6] nor did he tell Aubrey in any of his letters of his having an Oxford degree. The Oxford registers show that both under the Commonwealth and at the Restoration medical degrees were often given without the prescribed residence and exercises to those who had rendered valuable medical service in the Civil War, but Vaughan's name is not in these lists. Miss Guiney obtained negative answers from the British universities and Trinity College, Dublin, and also from the Dutch universities.[7]

---

[1] Hereford Probate Registry.

[2] Minute Book of Brecon Quarter Sessions, and Chanc. Pro., Mitford 355. 174. Similarly in Brecon Qu. Sessions, 3 Oct. 1693 and 9 Jan. 1693/4.

[3] Hereford Probate Registry.

[4] Llandaff Registry Office: Breconshire wills.

[5] Record Office, Wales 11.21: Brecon Circuit, Bundle 122, 1696.25.

[6] I have gone through the manuscript Registers of Oxford University (Registrum Congregationis, Q 16, Qa 17, Qa 18, Bd 19) from 1640 to 1677, and have also examined Wood's manuscript list of medical graduates for this period (Bodl. MS. Wood E. 8).

[7] It does not appear that Miss Guiney inquired of Italian universities or of Montpellier. The librarian of the Medical School in the University of Montpellier has kindly informed me that there is no record of Henry

The list of incorporations recorded in Wood's *Fasti Oxonienses* indicates a close connexion between Oxford and the medical schools on the continent, especially at Leyden and Padua. Peacock's *Leyden Students* shows a surprisingly large number of persons with British surnames graduating there, but Vaughan's name is not among them. It would be tempting to identify him in the following entry in the State Papers: 'May 7, 1656. Licence for — Vaughan to go to Holland',[1] but the absence of Christian name and the commonness of the surname make the identification very hazardous.

Henry VIII granted to the Archbishop of Canterbury in 1531 the power to grant degrees in divinity, medicine, and arts; one of the most famous men of science of Vaughan's time, John Hooke, was created a doctor of physic by a warrant from Archbishop Tillotson. But Henry Vaughan's name is not to be found at Lambeth. It should be remembered that from 1645 to 1660 there was no archbishop and no one else was authorized to exercise his rights of granting degrees.

The College of Physicians was entitled to see that 'no man, though a graduate in Physick of Oxford or Cambridge, may, without Licence under the said College seal, practise Physick in London', nor in any other part of England 'in case he hath not taken any Degree in Oxford or Cambridge'.[2] But the regulations against unlicensed practitioners were not strictly enforced even in London until 1663, when a particularly vigorous President of the College came into office, and it is probable that in a remote county like

Vaughan there. By the kindness of University officers, and with the assistance of the British Council, I have received negative answers from Padua and Pisa. The registrar of Padua reports the registration on 10–14 March 1659 of 'Gulielmus Valgranus fil. dom. Enrici Anglus', but this can hardly be a mistake for Henry Vaughan. His name does not occur in the visitors' album of Padua University, although one 'Thomas Vaughan Cambro-Britannus' signs on 7 Aug. 1659 (Horatio F. Brown, 'Inglesi e Scozzesi all' Università di Padova', *Monografie storiche sullo Studio di Padova*, 1922); I owe this reference to Mr. E. S. de Beer. The registrar of Bologna has promised an answer soon.

[1] Cal. S.P.D., 1655–6, p. 582.
[2] *Angliae Notitia*, 1700, p. 394.

Breconshire the college was unable to secure its privileges. Henry Vaughan's name is not among the licentiates in Munk's *Roll of the College of Physicians*, nor is it in the Records of the Society of Apothecaries of London.

By an Act of 1511 it became the duty of diocesan bishops to license non-graduates of Oxford or Cambridge to practise medicine after having them examined by four doctors of physic, but the diocesan system was out of action during the Commonwealth and Protectorate, just when Vaughan probably began to practise. The Bishop of St. Davids in his return of 1665 to Archbishop Sheldon's interrogatories, requiring him *inter alia* to certify the 'names, degrees and qualities of all practisers of Physick' in his diocese, and to state whether they were licensed or not, did not include Henry Vaughan.[1]

It was already becoming customary in the seventeenth century for practitioners to be popularly styled doctor without being graduates. The astrologer John Pordage (1607–81) describes himself in his will as 'doctor in physick', and his posthumous book *Theologia Mystica* (1683) has 'M.D.' on the title-page, although in a former work of his he describes himself on the title-page only as 'Student in Physic'. Another astrologer, John Heydon, was 'usually styled Doctor'.[2] Wood mentions 'Dr. Curie or Carew, a non-conformist divine and a curer of deafness';[3] this is Nicholas Cary of Monmouth, ejected in 1662, who graduated in arts from Cambridge, but nothing is known of his obtaining a medical degree. A more reputable example is the Cambridge physician William Butler, *facile princeps* in his profession, who attended Henry, Prince of Wales, in his last illness: 'He was usually styled Doctor, though he never took the degree of M.D.'[4] Dr. Cecil Wall states that some

[1] Mr. A. W. Haggis, of Worcester College, Oxford, who has been making an extensive research into the conditions of medical degrees and licences in the seventeenth century, was good enough to tell me that he had examined the registers and other documents of all the English and Welsh dioceses and had not come across any evidence that Henry Vaughan had received a licence to practise medicine from any episcopal authority.

[2] *D.N.B.* ix. 769.   [3] Wood, *Life and Times*, iii. 448.

[4] *D.N.B.* s.v. William Butler (1535–1618).

who held diocesan licences 'began to style themselves M.D.'[1] It seems, however, most unlikely that a man of honour like Henry Vaughan would have adopted the custom of none too scrupulous astrologers, or have suffered popular use to give him a degree to which he was not entitled. We may assume, therefore, that at any rate for the last twenty years of his life he was a medical graduate of a British or continental university. But he may have begun to practise without a degree. Some colour is given to this view by his making in 1655 a contemptuous reference to academical doctors, as was not unusual among the Hermetist physicians. In his translation of Nolle, where his author is emphasizing that 'he onely is the true Physician, created so by the light of Nature', who devotes himself to 'a Physicall practise or triall' by his own experiments and observations, Vaughan contrasts 'the coyl of Academical licentiated Doctors'.[2] He would hardly have used this expression if he was himself already a graduate in medicine or was expecting shortly to become one.

It is evident from Vaughan's letter to Aubrey in 1673, already quoted, that he was happy and successful in his practice, and seven years later there is similar testimony. Aubrey tells Wood that his Breconshire cousin 'has the Practice of Physic over all those Parts',[3] and nearly a year later he tells him that Vaughan 'has great & steady practise there'.[4]

Vaughan, no doubt, professionally attended the village people, but his repute as a doctor stretched far beyond Llansantffraed, and the only patients of whom we happen

[1] *British Medical Journal*, 2 Nov. 1935. I owe this reference to Mr. Haggis, who questions whether it was only episcopal licentiates who adopted this style.
[2] M 581 (this clause is interpolated by Vaughan). On the other hand, Grosart (iv. 336) is mistaken in saying, in reference to the passage (M 588-9) about an unfriendly doctor: 'As I find nothing corresponding with the personal allusions in Nollius, it seems clear that the Silurist in this place stated his own grudge or grievance against some eminent medical dignitary.' Grosart looked at Nolle's *Naturae Sanctuarium*, not at his *Systema*, the book which Vaughan was translating. The passage was faithfully reproduced from Nolle's *Systema*, and is not an interpolation by the translator.
[3] Bodl. MS. Wood F. 39, f. 354.
[4] Bodl. MS. Ballard xiv, f. 80. It is uncertain whether Aubrey had any more recent information than Vaughan's letter of 15 June 1673.

to know were among the well-to-do. In his letter of 15 June 1673 to Aubrey he writes: 'Yours of the 10th of June I received att Breckon, where I am still attendinge our Bishops Lady in a tertian feaver, & cannot as yet have the leasure to step home.'[1] The Bishop of St. Davids, William Lucy, grandson of the Sir Thomas Lucy of Charlecote in Shakespeare's youth, had restored Christ College, Brecon, as his official residence. His wife, Martha, daughter of William Angell of Crohurst, Surrey, died in the following January and was buried in the Collegiate Church. In a letter dated from Crickhowell on 14 September 1693 Vaughan excuses himself from attending a summons of the Judge of the Brecon circuit on the score of 'my present engagement with Mr. Serjeant Le Hunt's Lady, who is most dangerously sick in a putrid fever'.[2] The Serjeant's wife was a daughter of Sir John Herbert of Crickhowell, and perhaps related to Vaughan's former schoolmaster. Mrs. Le Hunt died four months after. On 3 February 1693/4 Vaughan made a deposition as to the mental fitness for making a will of his neighbour and kinsman, Thomas Powell, of Maesmawr, whom he had attended in his last illness and whose will he had witnessed. It may be that an even more extensive range of his practice is indicated by the allusion in his letter of 9 December 1675: 'Your letter of the 27th of November I received butt the last week, my occasions in Glamorganshire having detained me there the best part of the month.'[3] In view of his successful following of his profession there seems warrant for Miss Guiney's imaginative description: 'One can picture him on his hardy Welsh pony, drenched in the mountain mists, close-hatted, big-cloaked, riding alone, and looking abroad with those mild eyes which were a naturalist's for earth and sky, and a mystic's for the spiritual world.'[4]

---

[1] M 667.   [2] See below, p. 234.   [3] M 671.
[4] There is a similar description of the doctor on his rounds, happily communing with nature in the solitude which he loved, in Dr. John Brown's *Horae Subsecivae*, 2nd series, 1861.

XV

THE MIDDLE YEARS

THERE is little evidence for determining the dates either of the death of Henry Vaughan's first wife or of his second marriage. The Llansantffraed registers for that period are no longer extant.[1] Miss Guiney was at one time inclined to think that the poem beginning 'Joy of my life! while left me here, And still my Love!' in the *Silex* of 1650 commemorated the death of Vaughan's first wife Catherine, and she noted that Spenser begins the 82nd sonnet of his *Amoretti* with the same words, 'Joy of my life.' The words are more appropriately used of a wife than of a brother, however beloved. But this poem of Vaughan is not only preceded by two poems which clearly refer to a brother, but is followed, after two intervening poems, by another elegy written 'Twelve hundred houres' since the brother's death, and ending with the consoling reflection, 'Yet I have one *Pearle* by whose light All things I see.' The pearl may be his wife, or, as others think, the Bible.[2]

There are, however, some good reasons for thinking that Catherine Vaughan died between the publication of the first and second parts of *Silex Scintillans*. In the Epistle Dedicatory of *The Mount of Olives*, dated 1 October 1651, to Sir Charles Egerton, Catherine's uncle, the author urges that 'Though I should have no other *defence*, that near *relation* by which my *dearest friend* laies claime to your *person* might in some measure excuse' his publishing the book under the shelter of Sir Charles's name.[3] The present tense of 'laies claim' shows that the 'dearest friend' is alive, and there are contemporary precedents for a man using this description of his wife. Francis Bassett of Tehidy, who was

---

[1] The Faculty Office lists of marriage licences have an hiatus from 23 May 1633 to 16 Jan. 1646/7 (which may cover the date of Vaughan's first marriage), and another between 10 Mar. 1650/1 and 21 Aug. 1660 (which may cover the date of his second marriage). There is, however, no reason to suppose his marriages were by licence, not by banns.

[2] 'Silence, and stealth of dayes!', ll. 3, 29–30 (M 425).   [3] M 138.

with Sir Bevil Grenville at Stratton Hill fight in 1643, addressed a letter to his wife: 'To my dearest, dearest Friend, Mrs. Bassett at the Mount, speede this, haste, haste.' It must be allowed that if Vaughan had married his second wife, Elizabeth Wise, who too, like Catherine, was Sir Charles Egerton's niece, by October 1651, the words might refer to her. Or the 'dearest friend' might be Egerton's neighbour, Richard Wise, the father of Catherine and Elizabeth. The reference is, therefore, far from certain. There is also reason to suppose that Catherine Vaughan was living after her husband's dating his dedication to Egerton. It appears to be she who was staying in London with the Thomas Vaughans, who were married in September 1651. Thomas alludes in his notebook to 'a great glass full of eye-water, made at the Pinner of Wakefield, by my dear wife and my sister Vaughan, who are both now with God'.[1] There are no sisters of Thomas Vaughan that we know of except the one who had already married William Parry and bore his surname; he must, therefore, almost certainly be referring to his sister-in-law, Henry Vaughan's first wife. Thomas's wife Rebecca died in April 1658, and he made the note about the eye-water soon after her death, so that the latest possible date of the death of 'my sister Vaughan' is 1658. It may well be no more than a coincidence that the register of St. Giles in the Fields records the burial on 20 January 1653/4 of one 'Katherine Vaughan'.[2] Thomas Vaughan is described in a lawsuit of 1661 as 'of St. Giles in the Fields', but the only previous places of residence in London that we know of from his notebook are Paddington, Holborn, and the 'Pinder' or 'Pinner of Wakefield', which was in the parish of St. Pancras.[3] A more certain reference

[1] B.M. MS. Sloane 1741, f. 106 (Waite, p. 449).
[2] There is also in the St. Giles's register the baptism on 22 Mar. 1653/4 of 'Rebecca Vaughan'. Miss Guiney thought it possible that Henry Vaughan's wife, Catherine, died in childbirth at Thomas Vaughan's lodgings and that the child was given her aunt's Christian name. But, in spite of the names Catherine and Rebecca being found in the Vaughan family, the surname Vaughan is too common and the connexion of Thomas Vaughan at this date with the parish of St. Giles too uncertain to make any such conjecture probable.
[3] There was an inn, 'The Pinder of Wakefield', in Grays Inn Lane, about

to Catherine Vaughan's death is the lament of 'the surviving
turtle' in the poem 'Fair and yong light!' which appeared
in the augmented *Silex* of 1655.[1]

When, in his elegy on Charles Walbeoffe, who died in
September 1653, Henry Vaughan alludes to 'my sad retire-
ments',[2] he may be referring to a period of mourning after
his first wife's death, but it more probably refers to his
sickness, which, as we know, belongs to this time, and we
may compare the words used on the title-page of *Flores Solitudinis* (1654), 'Collected in his Sicknesse and Retirement.'[3]
The allusion to 'thy solitary years' in the poem 'Joy'[4]
(*Silex Scintillans*, 1655) may be to the interval between his
first wife's death and his second marriage. If we can trust
the evidence of his son Thomas, given in an action about
forty years later, Henry Vaughan married again 'soon after'
the death of Catherine; but Thomas was only a child at the
time of his mother's death and in the lawsuit he was seeking
to damage his father's reputation.[5]

Henry Vaughan did not need to look far for someone to
mother his four surviving children. He took to wife Elizabeth
Wise, Catherine's younger sister, whose baptism on 12 April
1630 is recorded in the Coleshill register. She, too, bore her
husband four children, who are named in this order in the
genealogy drawn up by the Welsh herald, Hugh Thomas—
Grisell, Lucy (there was also a Lucy by the first marriage),
Rachel, Henry.[6] Henry's age is given as 26 at his ordination in 1687,[7] which would date his birth in 1661, and, as
three sisters preceded his birth, the marriage of the poet and
Elizabeth Wise is likely to have been about 1655.

It is somewhat surprising that so strict a churchman as
Henry Vaughan should have married his deceased wife's
sister, but no allusion is anywhere made to this canonical

half a mile north of Grays Inn; it was in the parish of St. Pancras and was
'destroyed by a hurricane' in 1724 (Samuel Palmer, *St. Pancras*, 1870, pp. 16,
310). There was also a Pinder of Wakefield Alley opposite Grays Inn, in the
parish of St. Andrew's, Holborn, but the former is probably meant. St. Giles
in the Fields was one of the parishes which bounded St. Pancras on the south.

[1] M 513. See above, pp. 107–8.   [2] M 609, l. 21.
[3] M 211.   [4] M 491, l. 28.   [5] See below, pp. 228–31.
[6] MS. Harl. 2239, f. 81, given in Chambers, II. xix.
[7] *Llandaff Records*, ed. J. A. Bradney, 1909, iii. 38.

disability. The 99th Canon of 1604 prescribed that Archbishop Parker's Table of prohibited degrees should be set up in every parish church. It was based on the principle that affinity, or relationship by marriage, was as much a bar to matrimony as consanguinity, or relationship by blood. The Church of England followed the rules of the Western Church, but the archbishop's authority to grant dispensations was restricted to such cases as were not 'repugnant to the Holy Scriptures'.[1] In normal times the State recognized the Church marriage laws and left matrimonial cases to the ecclesiastical courts, but appeal was possible to the temporal courts which did not admit the legal authority of Parker's Table. The Commonwealth passed its Act for Marriages in August 1653, prescribing civil marriage, but did not touch the matter of the prohibited degrees; it may, however, have given little attention to such matters, and the ecclesiastical courts were out of action, and the Table of Kindred and Affinity shared the fate of the prohibited Prayer Book. Even when the Table was operative marriage with a deceased wife's sister was not void, but voidable, that is, it could be made void by regular process after trial, if persons properly concerned brought the case into court. There were not likely to be any difficulties raised if, as is most probable, Vaughan's second marriage took place before 1660. After the Restoration and the revival of the ordinary ecclesiastical courts such a marriage, if challenged, might have been annulled or, if contemplated but not yet entered into, a clergyman might have refused to celebrate it. There is, for example, the distressing case of Charles Blount, the deist: 'On his application to the most learned civilians, and the archbishop of Canterbury, he was informed, that such a match could not take place. On this, the lady positively refused her consent, and Mr. Blount in a fit of despair shot himself through the head. August 1693.'[2]

---

[1] There was no archbishop from 1645 to 1660.

[2] *Ath. Oxon.*, ed. Bliss, iv. 56; editorial note, on the authority of Warton. Such marriages were made 'absolutely null and void' by the Marriage Act of 1835, but marriage with a deceased wife's sister was legalized in 1907, and with a deceased brother's widow in 1921.

Henry Vaughan's father is described as being 'very decrepit, and about 70 years old' at the time of his making his Complaint on 7 November 1656 in a suit about a sale of lands by which he wished 'to raise money to pay his debts'.[1] In spite of his age and infirmity he suffered arrest twice in these years, and on the second occasion was lodged in Brecon jail. The former occasion arose out of his failure to settle accounts 'for several sums of money' owing to Brecon tradesmen.[2] The other occasion arose out of his connexion with the tithe and glebe of the rectory. At the Restoration Commissioners of Account were appointed for the county of Brecon to inquire into the alleged misuse of tithes during the years of the Commonwealth and Protectorate. They required 'A perfect Accompte of ye farmers of ye Teith of Llansanfred And to whome they payde since ye yeere 1649'. In the accounts furnished to the Commissioners on 20 August 1662 the entry for 1656 is simply 'Thomas Vaughan ye elder farmer for ye sayd teith in the yeare 1656', followed by a blank, instead of any figure of receipt or payment.[3] This deficiency of information led the Commissioners to ask Thomas Vaughan's son and heir for an explanation, which is given in the following letter, now printed for the first time:

To the honored gentlemen: the Commissioners sittinge att New Radnor: present this.
Gentlemen
Some few dayes since there was a processe left att my house (in my absence) without any account, either from whome it came, or for what cause, butt havinge learnt since, that it was sent hither by yor Commande, I resolved to make my Addresse accordinglie. And (in truth) I had not fayled to wayt upon you my selfe, if weaknes, & other violent effects of a late feaver, had not resisted my real intentions.
The Cause of this service I coniecture to be about one years profits of Lansanfred Church, wch were granted to my father & to Mr William Jones of Buckland Jointenants for them, & both deceased. My father, whoe had some reason to looke after the

---

[1] Chanc. Pro., Hamilton 448.   [2] See above, p. 96.
[3] Lambeth, Sequestered Livings 1650–62, MS. 1027 County of Brecon, f. 36.

profits of this Church, they being (by right) my brothers (whoe for his loyalty to his late Majesty was sequesterd & persecuted for his life,) had often petitiond the Committees then in being, to allow him the profits of the Church towards the paym^t of a considerable summe of money, wch was well knowne, to be due to him from my brother, butt this he could never effect, the persons then in power being all his adversaries. Att last in the yeare –56, (as I suppose,) it was graunted to him; butt Mr Jones was made Joint-tenant with him. And att the years end my father insisting still for allowance & delayinge the paym^t the Committees sent their Agent Thomas Williams, whoe with some foote-souldiers tooke my father prisoner & carryed him to Brechon goale, where he remayned till the rent was payed, wch by the graunt were thirtie pounds. The bearer heerof payd twenty pounds of it att the Hay unto Thomas Williams the agent & the other ten were paid unto the said Williams att Brechon, & the bearer (as he saith) upon the payment received an Acquittance, & gave it my father, butt I cannot find it amongst all his papyrs, wch are still in my Custodie. butt the bearer is ready to make oath of the paym^t if you please to receive it. Gentlemen, this is all that I know off, or am concernd in this matter; & how litle this will amount unto, I referre unto yor Judgements. The processe I have sent by the bearer, with a civil confidence, that you will take it up. butt if you see any cause to doe otherwise, I shall observe ye Commands of that honorable Court I am serv'd into, & remayne

Gentlemen!

Yo^r very humble servant

HENRY VAUGHAN

To the honored gentlemen: the Commissioners sittinge att New Radnor: present this.[1]

We may hope that Vaughan's explanation was accepted by the Commissioners and that nothing further was asked of him; it is characteristic of members of the Vaughan family that receipts and deeds were wont to be missing when they were asked for. But if he suffered no financial loss, he would not readily forget the indignity that had befallen his old father, when, within a year of his death, he was marched off by Parliamentarian soldiers to Brecon jail.

[1] Lambeth, Sequestered Livings 1650–62, MS. 1027, f. 36b. Undated, but endorsed 1662. The letter still has a small red wax seal, of which the design is a heart transfixed by an arrow, with drops falling from it; it seems like a variant of the emblem in *Silex Scintillans* (engraved title-page, 1650).

Thomas Vaughan the elder did not long survive these troubles, which seemed to increase with the years. He died in the early summer of 1658. The inventory 'of all the goods, cattels and chattels' was prised on 25 June at only 'Five Pounds of current English money'.[1] As he died intestate, administration was granted to his eldest son Henry and George Vaughan of the town of Brecon, whose relationship, if any, to the Vaughans of Newton is not known. They were required to give a bond for £60 to the Reverend Thomas Aubrey, official of the Archdeaconry Court of Brecon, from which they would be released so soon as they furnished a satisfactory account of their administration and had paid all debts 'as farre as the said goods of the said deceased shall thereunto extend'.[2] It was customary to fix the amount of the bond at double the amount of the estate of the deceased. In any case £60 is a surprisingly small sum, but it will be remembered that the Newton estate belonged to Thomas Vaughan's wife. In a suit of 1659 Henry Vaughan is described as 'heir at law' of his father and 'being but heir apparent in the right of his mother and as her tenant for the present'.[3] Eventually Newton would be his, but we do not know how long his mother, who had inherited that estate at the age of five, survived.

The Restoration must have been very welcome to Henry Vaughan and have dispersed many of the clouds which had darkened his life ever since he came to manhood. He was now approaching his fortieth year and he had adopted a profession which brought him happiness and success. The Puritan régime, under which he had suffered and which he so hotly resented, was at last over, and Church and King had come into their own again. The Restoration was too long delayed to mend the broken fortunes of some of his friends.

Matthew Herbert, his old schoolmaster, who had been ejected from his two rich livings as far back as 1646, died three months before Charles II came in, and his widow Johan, petitioning the House of Lords on 11 June 1660,

[1] See above, p. 17. [2] Bond in the Hereford Probate Registry.
[3] Chanc. Pro., Collins 579, 112.

alludes to her husband's having suffered 'several imprison-
ments . . . leaving wife and children destitute and with many
debts to pay'.[1]

Thomas Powell, after remaining in the neighbourhood
for some years after his eviction from the rectory of Cantref,
'went beyond the Seas', according to Walker, but 'to what
Place, or what time he staid there, I know not'.[2] In the
dedication of his *Quadriga Salutis* (1657) to 'the Lady Eleanor
Williams of Gwerneval', a staunch royalist, Powell writes:
'I do not know whether I shall live to finish a better Piece
than this, being long since taken away from the book by
secular cares and encumbrances, to make up the breaches
of a ruinous fortune', and in the margin he puts 'Forced to
be secular priests'. He did, however, live just long enough
to be reinstated at Cantref, to take the degree of Doctor of
Divinity at Oxford by a mandamus from the king,[3] and to
be made a canon of St. Davids. It was expected that he
would have been made a bishop, but he died in London on
the last day of 1660 'in the two and fiftieth yeare of his
age', and, as Vaughan tells Aubrey, he 'lyes buried in S.
Dunstans church in fleetstreet'.[4] A posthumous work of
his, *Humane Industry* (1661), contains Dr. Powell's acknow-
ledgements to 'Mr. *Hen. Vaughan Silurist*' for his verse-
translations and also a tribute to 'that pious and Seraphic
Poet, Mr. *George Herbert*'. Twelve years later Vaughan tells
Aubrey that there are three manuscript works of Powell's
'left in my Custodie, & not yet printed', namely, translations of Puteanus and Malvezzi, and, what would more
interest Vaughan himself and posterity, 'A short account of
the lives, manners & religion of the Brittish Druids and the
Bards &c.'[5] If Powell had lived longer, his wise encouragement might have preserved Vaughan a poet for a few more
years.

If his brother Thomas was not to return to the rectory
of his native place, no appointment was likely to have
given more pleasure to Henry Vaughan than the institution

---

[1] House of Lords MSS. Comm. 7th Rpt., Appx. i, p. 96 (*cit. ap.* Richards,
ii. 343).   [2] *Sufferings of the Clergy*, ii. 337.
[3] M 670.   [4] Ibid.   [5] Ibid.

to Llansantffraed of Thomas Lewes, the evicted rector of
Llanfigan, by Bishop Lucy on 15 September 1660 on the
presentation of Sir Henry Williams, Bt., of Gwernyfed.
But Sir Henry's right to present was contested by Alice
the widow of Sir George Vaughan who had presented
Thomas Vaughan in the forties; the matter was brought
before the bishop, and, with the consent of both parties and
also of Lewes, Dr. Edward Games was appointed on the
presentation of Anne Vaughan and Frederick Vaughan,
Sir George's brother. It was the easier for Lewes to give
way, as he was at once presented by the widow of his old
patron, Edward Kemeys, to his former rectory of Llanfigan.[1]
Dr. Games lived only one year after his appointment to
Llansantffraed. After the incumbency of Philip Roberts for
four years only, the living was again vacant in 1668, and
the next rector was to live at Llansantffraed for the rest of
Henry Vaughan's life and for twenty-two years beyond that.
The new rector, Hugh Powell, a son of Vaughan's old friend,
Dr. Thomas Powell, became also Precentor of St. Davids;
he held the living from 1668 to 1717, being over 90 at the
time of his death. We may suppose that Vaughan welcomed
having his friend's son for his rector, but the rector became
involved in the domestic troubles which befell Vaughan in
his last years.[2] Hugh Powell was connected by marriage
with the house of Tretower and had also links with families
related to Henry Vaughan—Walbeoffe, Aubrey, and Morgan
of Wenallt. The intricacies of relationship are the greater
because of the frequency of second marriages, but it may
be well to set them out as they affected the connexion of
the Tretower family with Scethrog in Vaughan's immediate
neighbourhood.

Hugh Powell married a daughter of Morgan John of
Wenallt by his wife Frances, a daughter of Charles Vaughan
of Tretower, the poet's uncle. Mrs. Hugh Powell had previously married Charles Williams, whose father David Williams had bought the 'mansion-house' of Scethrog; Charles
Williams's mother was a sister of Vaughan's friend, Charles

---

[1] Richards, ii. 509, and Theo. Jones, iii. 216.
[2] See Chapter XVII.

Walbeoffe of Llanhamlach. As her first husband, Charles Williams, had no children by her, Mrs. Hugh Powell inherited Scethrog, and when her daughter by her second marriage, Margaret Powell, married Charles Vaughan, of the Tretower line, Scethrog passed to the Vaughans and became their principal residence, remaining in the family till the line came to an end in 1783. This Charles Vaughan was a direct descendant of Charles Vaughan of Tretower, but in the female line. His grandmother, Margaret Vaughan,[1] married Thomas Morgan of Maes Gwarthey, Llanelly, and when her brother Edward died without issue in 1656 she inherited Tretower. Her son, Vaughan Morgan, described as 'of Tretower', was succeeded at his death in 1684 by his son Charles who took the surname of Vaughan. So there came to be living in the parish of Llansantffraed the senior representative of the house of Tretower as well as Henry Vaughan of a junior line. By this time, it may be presumed, Tretower was passing into decay and the Scethrog house was preferred as a home.[2]

Henry Vaughan's father-in-law, Richard Wise of Coleshill, Warwickshire, died in October 1668, and by his will, made on 20 July and proved on 24 October, he remembered the Vaughan family. He made legacies to 'Lucy eldest daughter of my son-in-law Henry Vaughan, Gent.', to Frances and Catherine, the poet's second and third daughters, and to 'Thomas eldest son of the said Henry Vaughan'. These were all the children of Henry Vaughan by his first wife. There is also a legacy to 'my daughter Elizabeth Vaughan', the poet's second wife, but nothing to their children. The will continues: 'And whereas I have hereby devised less legacys unto my daughter Elizabeth Vaughan

---

[1] Margaret Vaughan was a daughter of William Vaughan (*ob.* 1654), son of Charles Vaughan of Tretower (*ob.* 1636). The genealogies differ as to whether her son Vaughan Morgan was father or grandfather of the Charles Vaughan who married Margaret Powell; both were named Charles Vaughan. Theo. Jones (iii. 176) makes Margaret Powell's husband a grandson of Vaughan Morgan and therefore fifth in descent from Charles Vaughan (*ob.* 1636). This seems a generation too remote, as Margaret Powell was only third in descent from Charles Vaughan (*ob.* 1636), and Vaughan Morgan is described as an infant in a lawsuit of 1673 (Chanc. Pro., Bridges 88.53).

[2] See below, pp. 251–2.

and to my granddaughter Lucy than I have bequeathed unto the residue of my grandchildren, I doe hereby declare the reason to be because they have already received such several summes of money from me as will make up theirs to the said several legacies hereby given to twenty pounds apiece.'[1]

Only two years after Richard Wise's will was proved, one of the legatees, Frances, Henry Vaughan's second daughter by his first wife, 'being sicke in body and of perfect memory', made a nuncupative or oral will 'in the month of Septbr or Octobr 1670' in the presence of her stepmother and two other women, Elizabeth John and Jane Rosser.[2] Before the stricter provisions of the Statute of Frauds of 1677, a minor, being a female of not less than twelve years, could devise personal property not exceeding £30, and at common law a will devising personal estate needed not to be made in writing. Nuncupative wills were ordinarily made only when the testator was believed to be *in articulo mortis*. Frances Vaughan 'gave & bequeathed to her sister Lucy Vaughan the younger Ten Pounds' and five pounds apiece to her brother Thomas and her sister Catherine, and she then declared that the twenty pounds which she now bequeathed was a legacy she was entitled to under the will of her grandfather Richard Wise.

Frances Vaughan's will was not proved until 1677, when administration was granted to Dr. Henry Vaughan, her father. The seven years' interval between making and proving the will may be due to the fact that Wise's legacy to Frances did not accrue till the later date; he bequeathed to her the rents and profits of certain lands 'for and during the space of one year next after the terme of six yeares after my decease'. If it were not that Frances makes her first bequest to 'her sister Lucy Vaughan the younger', we should take the legatee to be her own eldest sister Lucy, but 'the younger' may mean her half-sister, also Lucy, and it will be noted that her stepmother was a witness of the nuncupative will. If the beneficiary is the half-sister, it is

---

[1] Lichfield Probate Registry.
[2] Hereford Probate Registry. The will was originally in the Consistory Court of the Archdeaconry of Brecon.

a welcome sign that the friction between the children of the two marriages was not yet acute. Frances's own sister Lucy, though she is named as 'Lucy Vaughan' in Wise's will in 1667, may by 1670 have been married to Charles Greenleafe and so provided for.

In 1673 begins the correspondence of Henry Vaughan and John Aubrey which is the principal first-hand evidence about the poet's life. Aubrey's own knowledge of Vaughan was not considerable. They had communicated or met in 1656, when they discussed Llangorse Lake,[1] and Aubrey had some unfortunate dealings with Henry Vaughan's father.[2] After his father's death John Aubrey succeeded to several lawsuits and he notes: 'Sept. 1655, or rather I think 1656, I began my chargeable and tedious lawe suite on the entaile in Brecknockshire and Monmouthshire.'[3] This involved many visits to Wales, which may have given him opportunities of seeing the Vaughans, but he does not record visits much later. He became out of touch with the Vaughans, as is evident from the letter which he wrote to Edward Llwyd on 17 June 1673, not having had an answer from Henry Vaughan to his letter of 3 June, though actually Vaughan's letter was already on its way. Aubrey asks Llwyd about 'the 2 Vaughans, Twynnes', 'what bookes they writt, & what p'ferments, if liveing & where buryed, as also w^t were theyr employmts'.[4] Aubrey did not know what were their professions or even if they were alive. Thomas had been dead seven years.

The exact degree of cousinship of Aubrey to Henry Vaughan is uncertain. Aubrey is certainly wrong in saying of the twins, Henry and Thomas Vaughan, that 'their grandmother was an Aubrey',[5] but at any rate they were related through the Walbeoffe marriages. Charles Walbeoffe, Henry Vaughan's first cousin, married Mary, daughter of Sir Thomas Aubrey of Llantrithyd, and Charles's son, also Charles, married Elizabeth, daughter of Thomas Aubrey,

---

[1] See above, p. 24. [2] See above, p. 91.
[3] J. Bretton, *Memoir of John Aubrey*, 1845, p. 18.
[4] Bodl. MS. Wood F 39, f. 211.
[5] *Brief Lives*, ii. 268. See below, p. 244, for Aubrey's mistake.

Esquire. In both his letters of 1673 to Aubrey, Vaughan sends him greetings from 'My Cousin Walbeoffe', and adds that she 'would be very glad to see you in these parts'.[1] This is Mrs. Charles Walbeoffe, senior, who survived her husband and her two sons. In his second letter Vaughan mentions also 'Sir John with his Son & Lady', who is Mrs. Walbeoffe's brother, Sir John Aubrey, father of 'Rosania' (Orinda's fancy name for Mary Aubrey), with his wife and their son John, afterwards second baronet. Enough has been said to show that the value of the Vaughan–Aubrey correspondence is almost wholly what Aubrey extracts from Vaughan, since on his side he knew nothing of the recent doings of the Vaughans.

Vaughan is pleased at Aubrey's desiring to have details about his brother and himself for Wood's intended history of Oxford and Oxford men. With touching modesty he writes in his first answer: 'I am highly obliged to you that you would be pleased to remember, & reflect vpon such low & forgotten thinges, as my brother and my selfe.'[2] And in the letter of two years later, after the Oxford history has appeared, he says: 'That my dear brothers name (& mine) are revived, & shine in the Historie of the Vniversitie; is an honour we owe vnto your Care & kindnes.'[3] We may note that he always puts his brother's name before his own. Fourteen years later, when Wood had been writing direct to Vaughan for information to use in his forthcoming *Athenae Oxonienses*, Vaughan complains of inaccuracies and omissions in the Latin history: 'If you intend a second Edition of the Oxford-historie, I must give you a better account of my brothers books & mine; wch are in the first much mistaken, and many omitted.'[4] So far as Thomas Vaughan was concerned, Henry had no just ground of complaint, as Wood included in his 1674 book all the books that Henry named to Aubrey, and added *Euphrates* which was not in that list. Wood also supplied the dates of publication which Henry Vaughan had not given, and he reproduced faithfully Henry's information about Thomas's

---

[1] M 669, 671.   [2] M 669.   [3] M 672.
[4] Letter to Wood, 25 March 1689 (M 674).

career. Henry had twice confessed that he did not know
where his brother died, and Aubrey was at pains to get the
facts from Sir Robert Moray.[1] But, for some unexplained
reason, Wood's account of Henry Vaughan, both in 1674
and 1692, is far less satisfactory. In 1674 he appends a
short account of Henry to his long account of Thomas, and
embodies in it all that Henry had told Aubrey about his
life, but mentions two books only—*Olor Iscanus* and *Thalia
Rediviva* 'now ready for the presse'. There is no mention of
Silex Scintillans, and, indeed, Aubrey too, before hearing
from Vaughan, could tell Wood only of 'a poeme called
Olor Iscanus' and 'another book of Divine Meditations';
whether Aubrey by 'Meditations' means *The Mount of Olives*
or *Silex Scintillans* is not clear, and he knows so little of
Olor Iscanus that he thinks it is a single poem. Wood did
even less justice to Henry Vaughan in 1692 than in 1674,
in spite of his having recently corresponded with him.
While he gives a full account of Thomas Vaughan, he omits
any account of Henry and only alludes to him casually in
connexion with other writers. It was not till the second
edition of *Athenae Oxonienses* in 1721 that a full account of
Henry Vaughan appeared, mentioning '*Silex Scintillans*: or,
the bleeding Heart'.[2]

Aubrey's letters to Vaughan, written at long intervals,
open up other subjects of inquiry. Will Vaughan furnish
him 'with any thing that may deserve the notice of' the
Royal Society, of which Aubrey is a member? Vaughan
disclaims any scientific eminence or even any aptitude or
desire for 'speculations into Nature'.[3] Again, can Vaughan
help him with materials for making horoscopes of two
distinguished Welshmen who had died eighty years ago?
Vaughan undertakes that he will 'not omitt the most curious
search' but is not hopeful of being able to satisfy him.[4]

[1] See above, p. 145.
[2] *Ath. Oxon.*, 1721, ii. 926. Wood's excuse for his description 'the bleeding
Heart' must be the engraved title-page of 1650 with the emblem of a heart
struck by a steel implement.   [3] Letter of 28 June 1680 (M 672).
[4] Ibid. Aubrey had scribbled on Vaughan's letter of 9 Dec. 1675 about
himself and his brother, 'Cast their Nativities', but he did not include the
Vaughans in his *Libri geniturarum*.

Both Aubrey and Wood write to Vaughan several times in 1688 and 1689 for information about Dr. John David Rhys (Rhesus), a Brecknockshire physician who produced a notable Welsh grammar in 1592, and about his patron Sir Edward Stradling of St. Donat's, who bore the expense of publication, and his adopted son Sir John Stradling, who was also an antiquary and a friend of Camden's. Both Rhesus and Sir Edward Stradling died in 1609, so that it would have been difficult for Vaughan to collect any intimate information about them such as Wood delighted in recording.

Wood jotted down in his diary the dates of his letters referring to *Athenae Oxonienses*, and Vaughan's name occurs repeatedly, though it is long before any response is forthcoming. Thus Wood enters in 1688: 'Oct. 14 Su. to Mr. Aubrey . . . to send a letter to Olor Iscanus for the obit of Dr. John David Rhese', and again on 4 November 'to Silvester Vaghan for John David Rhese', and yet again on the following 28 February 'for epitaph of Dr. John David Rhese [and] about Sir Edward and Sir John Stradling', and, still more impatiently, on 28 March 'to send to Olor Iscanus to answer my letters!'[1] In fact, an answer, dated 25 March 1689, was on its way, but with no epitaph of Rhesus.[2] Aubrey also remembers that he wrote to Vaughan on 'that very day yᵗ yᵉ Pr. of Orange came to London' (18 December 1688), 'but never recd answer; he was wont to be free enough of his Pen. I will write to him again.'[3] When Vaughan at last wrote to Wood on Lady Day 1689, he asked indulgence for his delay in answering a letter of Wood's which he received 'in the declination of a tedious and severe sickness with a very slow recovery'; he undertakes to do all he can to satisfy Wood 'as soon as I can gett abroad'.[4] He alludes, too, to having heard from Aubrey 'in the beginning of my sickness', but till now he had continued 'so very weak and such a forlorn Clinic' that he

---

[1] *Wood's Life and Times*, ed. Clark, iii. 252, 294–5. Aubrey was apt to be impatient with those who did not answer his letters promptly. Even to Wood he writes: 'My good friend Mr. Wood, what a God's name are you asleep or dead, or what is become of you?'
[2] M 674.   [3] Bodl. MS. Wood F. 39.   [4] M 674.

could not answer him. So then we learn that Vaughan had been bed-ridden from about Christmas to Lady Day, six years before his death. A month after his first letter to Wood he made another attempt to answer his questions. This letter is here printed for the first time.

April 25th
—89.

Worthy S^r

I received yours by our Carrier & in order to give som satisfaction to yor Quæres about the Stradlings: I have sent a leter to my learned friend M^r. John Williams (sometimes of Jesus College:) now Archdeacon of Cardigan, from whom I expect a good account As for John David Rhesus, I find by yor last leter that you are like to run into a great mistake, when you take him for the Authour[1] of the welch Dictionarie: wch he was not. Our Doctour John David Rhesus was not a Divine, butt a physician, & of the Roman communion. He took his degree att the vniversity of Siena in Italy, where he had his Education, & was a person of great parts and curious learning. This much for the p^rsent; you will have more hereafter. He wrott (indeed) the welch grammer, & an Italian one dedicated to a Venetian Senatour, with som other rare Tractates, wch are all lost. butt the Authour of the welch Dictionary lived a great while after him & was of the same Communion with vs & a Dignitarie of this Church of England, as you have righly [*sic*] recorded.

I doubt not butt my Cousen Awbreys leter from me, gave (then) a true account of what I, or my brother had written & published. butt in the Latin Edition of the history of Oxford, I doe assure you, it is quite otherwise; butt I shall redress that.

With my hearty respects
I shall remain
S^r
Your very ready Servant
HEN. VAUGHAN.

To the Reverend M^r. Antonie Wood att his lodginge near to Merton College in Oxford: Present this.[2]

[1] Wood has written in the margin, 'I said no such thing!' He has underlined in red ink the salient facts, which he afterwards embodied in his account of Rhesus in *Ath. Oxon.* Underneath Vaughan's signature Wood has written 'Olor Iscanus'.

[2] Bodl. MS. Autog. c. 9, f. 81. Mr. Aleck Abrahams purchased this letter from a bookseller in Red Lion Passage and generously gave it to the Bodleian on 14 May 1910. For John Williams, see below, p. 215.

What little Vaughan was able to tell Wood about Rhesus was used in *Athenae Oxonienses*, though Wood made further attempts to get more information from him. Aubrey reports to Wood on 29 June 1689: 'I will write to him again', and on 5 September: 'I much wonder I have not received an answer from my cosen Henry Vaughan about your queres. I sent a second letter about Whitsuntide last.'[1] Aubrey drew a last letter from Vaughan on 9 October 1694 in answer to an inquiry about 'the antient Bards'. Although Vaughan was now 73 years old and within six months of his death, the handwriting is firm and clear. Aubrey put enough value upon the letter to transcribe it in his *Templum Druidum*,[2] as well as to preserve the original in his collection. The letter shows the old man's fondness for the traditions and legends of the Welsh countryside, a credulous side of his mind which is strangely blended with his following of a learned profession, but there are many parallels in his century. It must have been a relief to turn his mind from the domestic troubles of his later years and to discourse with his cousin about older and happier memories. He had long ceased to exercise his poetical gift, but the writer of this last letter still has the mind of a poet and tells his dreams as only a poet can.

[1] Bodl. MS. Wood F. 39, f. 358.
[2] Bodl. MS. Top. Gen. c. 24, f. 112. The original letter is in Bodl. MS. Aubrey 13, f. 340; it is printed by Martin, pp. 675–6.

XVI

THALIA REDIVIVA

AFTER publishing the augmented *Silex Scintillans* in
1655, and the second treatise of Nolle, Vaughan
appears to have abandoned authorship. The reception of
his books may have offered him little encouragement, and,
besides, there were the pressing claims of his professional
life. He never fulfilled the promise announced in *Hermetical
Physick* that, 'if God will blesse me with health, and his
performing assistance', he would 'shortly communicate to'
the English reader 'a most accurate Treatise of *Meteors*,
their Generation, Causes, qualities, peculiar Regions and
Forms: what spirits governe them, and what they signifie
or fore-shew', written 'according to the *Hermetic* principles'.[1]
This full description indicates the kind of Paracelsian treatment of the subject which Vaughan intended in 1655, but
his mind may have moved away in later years towards a less
fanciful approach to nature.

Another literary project was put before him by Aubrey
in 1675. Dr. Robert Plott, the Keeper of the Ashmolean
Museum at Oxford, was contemplating a natural history of
England and Wales and sought to get the collaboration of
Aubrey and others. On 27 November 1675 Aubrey, who
was living in London, wrote to Wood at Oxford, asking
him to tell Dr. Plott 'that I have writt out the Natural
History of Wiltshire and of Surrey, and a sheet or two of
other counties, and am now sending to my cosen Hen.
Vaughan (Silurist, Olor Is.) in Brecknockshire, to send me
the Naturall History of it, as also of other circumjacent
counties: no man fitter'.[2] Vaughan's response to this suggestion is in his letter of the following 9 December:

'Tis a noble & excellent Designe that yor learned friend D^r

[1] M 561. It is possible that Vaughan means a translation of a work on
meteors. Nolle is not known to have written one. Thomas Vaughan alluded
in *Euphrates* (1655) to his intention of publishing 'our Meteorology' (Waite,
p. 386); he may have intended a work in collaboration with his brother.
[2] Bodl. MS. Tanner 456, f. 19.

Plott hath now in hand, & I returne you my humble & hearty
thanks for Communicatinge it with me. I shall take Care to assist
him with a short account of natures Dispensatorie heer, & in
order to it, I beg you would acquaint me with the method of his
writinge.[1]

More than five years passed without Vaughan's receiving
the instructions for which he very properly asked. On
13 April 1680 Aubrey wrote from London to Wood asking
him to request Plott 'to send some of his queres to me to
send to my cosen Hen: Vaughan, who . . . may and will
write a Naturall History of those Parts. Dr. Plot promised
to send them to me, but has forgot it'.[2] Nearly a year later,
on 19 March 1680/1 Aubrey again wrote to Wood: 'When
you see Dr. Plott, minde him to send me halfe a dozen
printed Queres, wch I would send to my Cosen Hen:
Vaughan in Brecknockshire, whom I have engaged to
follow his method.'[3] At last on 2 April 1681 Aubrey asks
Wood to thank Plott for the queries, 'which I send to my
cos. H. Vaughan (Olor Iscanus) whom I have engaged to
doe Brecknockshire according to his method'.[4] Nothing
seems to have come of Vaughan's collaboration, although
his devotion to his native county, its flora and fauna and
antiquities, besides his gift of writing in an attractive and
individual style, would have enabled him to make an
interesting contribution.

In his letter of 15 June 1673 to Aubrey, giving him for
Wood's use a list of 'what past into the presse from me',
Vaughan continues:

To these you may adde (if you thinke it fitt,) Thalia Rediviva,
a peece now ready for the presse, with the Remaines of my
brothers Latine Poems (for many of them are lost,) never published before: butt (I believe) wilbe very wellcome, & prove
inferiour to none of that kind, that is yet extant.[5]

Loyalty to his brother Thomas and admiration for his
work appear to count for more with Henry Vaughan than
any ambition to come again himself before the public as a

---

[1] M 672.   [2] Bodl. MS. Wood F. 39, f. 354.
[3] Bodl. MS. Ballard xiv, f. 80.   [4] Bodl. MS. Wood F. 39, f. 358.
[5] M 668.

poet. The choice of the title, too, would suggest Thomas
rather than Henry Vaughan, because Eugenius Philalethes
had declared Thalia to be 'my Mistris',[1] and he had represented her in *Lumen de Lumine* as appearing to him in
radiant beauty and conversing with him on the secrets of
nature. The word Θάλεια comes from a verb which means
to sprout and bloom, and Thomas reports her as saying to
him, 'I am alwaies *green*, and I shall never *wither*.'[2] For a
motto Henry Vaughan goes, as so often, to Virgil. The
Latin poet was fain to sing of kings and battles and other
heroic themes, but Thalia, the Muse of lyrical or pastoral
poetry, 'blushed not to inhabit the woods'.[3] The title
Thalia Rediviva—the lyrical Muse come to life again—
signifies Henry Vaughan's return to his old allegiance to
poetry, of which he had given nothing to the world since
he completed *Silex Scintillans* at the age of 34. He would be
57 when *Thalia Rediviva* appeared in 1678.

There is some obscurity about the publication of *Thalia
Rediviva*, as there is about that of *Olor Iscanus*; in both cases
publication was long postponed and someone other than
the author was in the end responsible. *Thalia* did not appear
until five years after Vaughan had told Aubrey it was 'ready
for the presse'. And when it appears the author's name is
not on the title-page, which has for its sub-title 'The *Pass-
Times* and *Diversions* of a Countrey-Muse, In Choice Poems
On several Occasions', the last five words being also used for
the page-heading throughout the book for both Henry's and
Thomas's poems. The commendatory poems of 'Orinda'
and 'Tho. Powel, D.D.', both long dead, are dedicated to
'Mr. *Henry Vaughan* the Silurist'.[4] Powell's poem could
hardly have been intended for this volume, as he addresses
'a young *Tyrtaeus*' who sang martial songs, of which there
are none in *Thalia*, but he alludes also to Etesia and Timan-

---

[1] *Lumen de Lumine*, p. 6 (Waite, p. 246).
[2] Ibid., p. 7 (Waite, p. 247).
[3] 'Neque erubuit silvas habitare Thalia' (Virg. *Ecl.* vi. 2). Horace (*C.* vi.
25) addresses Apollo as 'doctor argutae fidicen Thaliae'. More often Thalia
is represented as the Muse of Comedy.
[4] Vaughan himself used 'Silurist' without the definite article on his title-
pages.

der who are not mentioned in any book of Vaughan's
before *Thalia*, though they may have been in *Olor Iscanus*
as projected in 1647. The third and fourth commendatory
poems are signed respectively 'N. W. Jes. Coll. *Oxon*.' and
'I. W. A.M. Oxon.' They are likely to be Nathaniel and
John Williams, brothers, both of Jesus College, and much
younger than Vaughan. Nathaniel was only just of age in
1678, having matriculated six years before at the age of
15. According to Wood, he 'went away without com-
pleating his degree', and commenced author at the age of
18 with *A Pindarique Elegy on the famous physician Dr.
Willis* (Oxford, 1675), and followed it up next year with
Imago Saeculi. He died in or near his native town of Swansea
in 1679. It could only be a very young man who would
write of Vaughan, aged 57, as 'in his declining years'.[1] His
elder brother John was in his thirtieth year in 1678 and in
that year was made a prebendary of St. Davids. Two years
later he resigned the prebend on being collated to the archdeaconry of Cardigan in the same diocese. The tone of
his poem, like his brother's, suggests that he is the poet's
junior. He is the 'learned friend' to whom Vaughan was
afterwards to refer Aubrey for information about the Stradlings.[2] It is probable that John Williams is the 'J. W.' who
signs the dedication of *Thalia* to Lord Worcester and the
'I. W.' who signs 'To the Reader'.[3] It would seem that, just
as *Olor Iscanus* was 'Published by a Friend' after some prolonged diffidence on the author's part, so *Thalia Rediviva*
was edited by a friend, 'J. W.', five years after the author
had stated that it was ready for printing.

The choice of the person to whom the book is dedicated

[1] M 599, l. 21.　　　　　　　　　　　　[2] See above, p. 210.
[3] The capitals *I* and *J* were interchangeable; e.g. in the prefatory pages of
Overbury's *The Wife*, 1616, a poem signed I. F. is followed by another signed
J. F. and headed 'Eiusdem in Eandem'; similarly J. S. and I. S. are in the title-
page and dedication respectively of *Masquerade du Ciel*, 1640. Sir Charles
Firth suggested Nathaniel Williams of Swansea for N. W. and John Williams,
second son of Sir Henry of Gwernyfed, for J. W. The latter matriculated
from Brasenose College in 1642 at the age of 17, but does not appear to have
graduated as the J. W. of *Thalia* did (M 602). Chambers, ii 344, mentions
other conjectures; he rightly dismisses John Walbeoffe as there is no evidence
of his being an Oxford graduate.

would normally be the author's, but perhaps in this case it is the editor's. Henry Somerset, third Marquess and seventh Earl of Worcester, and soon to be created first Duke of Beaufort, was the representative of the richest and most powerful family in the Principality. Both his grandfather and his father took a leading part in the Civil War, spending vast sums in the raising of regiments for the king, and Raglan Castle was the last royalist stronghold in Wales to surrender in the first Civil War. It will be remembered that Henry Vaughan had a strain of Somerset blood.[1] We may be thankful that the wording of the dedication is not Vaughan's, as it is more fulsome even than was usual in that age in its comparison of Lord Worcester to Augustus Caesar, who found more satisfaction in distributing 'Lawrels among his Poetick Heroes' than in all his victorious wars.

In the preface 'To the Reader' the editor appears to be conscious that some apology is needed for the publication of a second gleaning, seeing that Vaughan had put his best work in his earlier volumes, about which it is rather extravagantly said that the author's reputation 'is better built in the sentiment of several judicious Persons, who know him very well able to give himself a lasting Monument, by undertaking any Argument of note in the whole Circle of Learning'.[2] But if any shall presume to think that 'even these his Diversions' (the word is picked up from the title-page) are 'not worth the publishing', it is enough to say that they were accounted 'valuable' by 'the matchless *Orinda*' and 'deserv'd her esteem and commendations'. Orinda's poem 'upon these and his former *Poems*' immediately follows. The first half of her poem treats of the verses to Amoret and 'the best of Unions' which followed when the poet wedded his Amoret; this implies that Orinda was writing before Vaughan lost his first wife. The second half speaks of 'thy sacred Muse', which 'we admire almost t'Idolatrie', which suggests that Catherine Vaughan was alive when the first part of *Silex Scintillans* appeared. Orinda makes no allusion to any of the contents of *Olor Iscanus*, and the presumption is that she wrote this commendatory

[1] See above, p. 6. [2] M 596.

THALIA REDIVIVA

poem before the publication of *Olor* in 1651. How then
can she be held to commend the contents of *Thalia Rediviva*? Only if a substantial part of it was already known to
her in manuscript. An examination of *Thalia* gives good
reason for accepting this as true. It is made up almost
entirely of early work and is an after-gleaning of poems
which might have found a place, some of them in *Silex
Scintillans*, and the more secular of them in *Olor Iscanus* as
originally planned in 1647. The poems which are demonstrably early work have been already discussed along with
the contemporary poems of *Olor Iscanus*.[1] Of the secular
poems in *Thalia Rediviva* not more than half a dozen at
most were written after 1650. There are no means of
dating 'To *Mr. M. L.* upon his reduction of the *Psalms* into
Method'[2] or 'To *I. Morgan* of *White-Hall Esq;* upon his
sudden Journey and succeeding Marriage'.[3] John Morgan
of Wenallt in the parish of Llandetty was Vaughan's neighbour and kinsman, but the date of his marriage is not
known. Four of the poems can be certainly dated. The
elegy on Charles Walbeoffe follows his death in September
1653.[4] 'Daphnis' commemorates Thomas Vaughan who
died on 27 February 1665/6, and at the close of that year is
the poem 'Upon sudden news of the much lamented death
of Judge *Trevers*'.[5] Arthur Trevor was Puisne Judge of the
Brecknock circuit from 1661 till his death; his will was
proved on 11 January 1666/7. David Lloyd in his *Memoires*

---

[1] See above, pp. 86–8.
[2] M 608. Grosart's reference, ii. 204, to Matthew Locke's setting of the
Psalms to music (never apparently published) has been commonly accepted,
but it is far from certain that 'Method', which has no musical associations,
relates to musical treatment, and the words 'you were not understood' (l. 18)
would be more naturally used of a literary composition. Many writers in
that age set themselves to paraphrase or write metrical versions of the
Psalms, sometimes with commentary, and it is probable that Vaughan, who
nowhere shows any interest in music, refers to one of these. The musical
terms of ll. 12–15 are as naturally applied to language as to music, as in the
verses prefixed to John Trapp's *Commentarie on the Minor Prophets*, 1654:
> So sweet is Scripture's harmony that we
> By it do argue its Divinity:
> But yet we understand the Musick better
> When you Harp on it, both by note and letter.

[3] M 617. [4] M 609. [5] M 622.

includes, among those who had suffered for their loyalty to Church and King, Arthur Trevor 'a lawyer of the Temple, that died lately and suddenly'.[1] The latest poem in *Thalia* is 'To the Editor of the matchless *Orinda*',[2] which must refer to Sir Charles Cotterel's authorized edition of *Poems* 'By Mrs. Katherine Philips' in 1667, three years after the authoress's death.

Of the seventeen poems included in the section called 'Pious Thoughts and Ejaculations' (recalling the sub-title of *The Temple* 'Sacred Poems and private Ejaculations') one only is dated, 'The Nativity. Written in the year 1656'.[3] 'The true Christmas',[4] which follows, lamenting the purely secular observance of the day, probably belongs to the same period when the religious observance of Christmas was prohibited. The allusions to 'Music, Masque' and 'Showe' would have point in the latter years of Cromwell's rule when, in spite of the Parliamentary suppression of stage-plays and masques, Shirley's masque of *Cupid and Death* was privately performed before the Portuguese ambassador in 1653, and on 22 November 1656 Davenant began his famous entertainments of 'Declamations and Musick', a kind of modified opera, at Rutland House with the Lord Protector's tacit approval.

The Latin poem '*Servilii Fatum*, sive *Vindicta divina*'[5] has a cryptic allusion to one of the leading regicides. It may have been composed soon after Charles's execution or at the death of a regicide. The poet, echoing a song of Boëthius in which he says that 'a second death' awaits men who have once been illustrious,[6] foretells a divine judgement on those who sentenced King Charles. Sir Edmund Chambers takes Servilius to be Q. Servilius Casca, 'the

---

[1] *Memoires,* 1668, p. 144. The suddenness of his death and the long connexion with Brecon make it certain that Arthur Trevor is the man commemorated by Vaughan, not (as all editors from Grosart have said) Sir William Trevor, of Denbighshire origin, who died at Leamington Hastings in 1656, and who had no connexion with Brecon. As to the inconsistent spelling of *Trevers* in title and *Trever* in ll. 3 and 5, cf. Clarendon's spelling of John Earle, the future bishop, as Earles (*Life,* 1759, pp. 26–7).

[2] M 621.   [3] M 645.   [4] M 646.   [5] M 648.

[6] *De Consolatione,* Lib. II. vii. Cf. Vaughan's concluding lines: 'qualisque in Corpore vixit, Talis it in tenebras bis moriturus homo.'

"envious Casca", who was the first to "rear his hand" against Caesar', and the contemporary reference to be to Bradshaw or Ireton rather than to Cromwell.[1] General Ireton died on 26 November 1651 and was given a state funeral in Westminster Abbey. Bradshaw was the lord president of the parliamentary commission which tried the king, and his signature stands first in the death warrant. He died, still convinced of the justice of the sentence, on 31 October 1659 in the deanery of Westminster, his official residence ever since he was appointed president, and was buried in the Abbey, from which his body, with those of Cromwell and Ireton, was ignominiously exhumed at the Restoration. Vaughan's vindictive outburst is partly redeemed by his lines on the flowers that deck the graves of the just, which, as Sir Edmund suggests, recall Shirley's poem, printed in 1659, with its fine close:

> Onely the actions of the just
> Smell sweet, and blossom in their dust.

Some of the poems in the section 'Pious Thoughts', such as 'The Bee' and 'To Christian Religion',[2] were evidently written before the restoration of the Church. Others, such as 'Discipline' and 'The Request',[3] seem less descriptive of Puritan England than of the licence which followed the king's return and which must have distressed Vaughan's sober mind. But most of the poems in this section are near in tone, and probably also in date, to those in *Silex Scintillans*; few reach as high a level, and that may be the reason why Vaughan did not include them in the augmented *Silex*. 'The Shower', 'Retirement', 'The Revival', and 'The Day-spring',[4] if they were written by 1655, would have deserved inclusion in that volume.

[1] Grosart (i. 331) took Vaughan to mean Q. Servilius Caepio, proconsul, who was killed by the inhabitants of Asculum at the outbreak of the Social War in 90 B.C., though he also rightly suggested that the name was 'a mask, not now to be raised, for some contemporary of the poet's'. Chambers's far apter reference to Casca and to Bradshaw was contributed by him to *The Athenaeum*, 29 Mar. 1902, in answer to an article by Miss Guiney, 'Cromwell and Henry Vaughan', in the same issue, maintaining that Vaughan was aiming at the Protector.

[2] M 652-5.   [3] M 641, 647.   [4] M 641-3.

The place of 'Daphnis' in *Thalia Rediviva*,[1] immediately
after the group headed 'Pious Thoughts', may be due to
its preceding the poems of Thomas Vaughan. It is the only
poem which is given a special prominence by having its
title in capitals. It is described as 'An Elegiac Eclogue',
and the pastoral names and the general style are borrowed
from Virgil, especially from his fifth Eclogue, 'Daphnis'.
Vaughan had always shown his special love for Virgil, and
in this poem he comes nearest him and has produced a poem
of remarkable beauty and merit, perhaps the most distinguished of his poems except for the best in *Silex Scintillans*. But the poem, as it stands, presents some difficulties,
and hardly seems to be a unity. The reference to Thomas
Vaughan is unmistakable in the passage about his burial
near the Thames by 'Noble Murrey', and in the early
memories of the days when the twins belonged to old
Amphion's 'beautiful Flock'; and 'true black Moores' refers
to the controversy of Eugenius Philalethes with Henry
More. Yet much in the earlier parts of the Eclogue appears
to refer to one who died young:

> So Violets, so doth the Primrose fall,
> At once the Springs pride and its funeral.
> Such easy sweets get off still in their prime,
> And stay not here, to wear the soil of Time.
> While courser Flow'rs (which none would miss, if past;)
> To scorching Summers, and cold Autumns last.[2]

Just so Henry Vaughan had called his young brother William, dying at twenty, 'this Prim-rose'.[3] Thomas, dying 'in
the seaven & fortieth year of his age',[4] cannot well be
likened to spring flowers and 'the early forward things'.
Moreover, the Daphnis whom Virgil commemorated was
still young at the time of his death.[5] The Daphnis of
Vaughan's poem is 'happy' in his journey's end coming
'before the Night', which may mean before the king's
execution and the complete ruin of Church and State, and

---

[1] M 656.   [2] 'Daphnis', ll. 25–30 (M 656).
[3] 'Thou that know'st for whom I mourne', l. 10 (M 417).
[4] Letter to Aubrey (M 670).
[5] Virg. *Ecl.* v. 54: 'Et puer ipse fuit cantari dignus.'

before 'The dregs and puddle of all ages' overwhelmed the land.[1] Such expressions would answer to Henry Vaughan's view of public events in the late forties, but would ill fit the years when his brother Thomas was happily employed in the service of the restored king. The echoes, conscious or unconscious, of 'Lycidas' are also more likely to have originated at an earlier date than 1666.

A possible solution of these inconsistencies in the poem, as it stands now, is that it was originally written on the death of William Vaughan or of some other young friend who died before 1649, and that it was not included in *Olor Iscanus* because it was unfinished and its author was not satisfied with it, nor in the first part of *Silex Scintillans* because its classical tone would have harmonized ill with the deeply and explicitly Christian elegies there. The author would keep it by him, as authors are always loath to destroy their offspring and as Henry Vaughan kept poems which had been excluded from *Olor Iscanus*, and at his brother Thomas's death he sought to adapt it, not altogether successfully, to commemorate his twin brother.[2] A further difficulty is the absence from 'Daphnis' of any Christian expression. This might have been expected before the summer of 1648, or Vaughan may by 1666 have passed from the rather austere and rigid Christian mood which ruled him in the years when he was writing *Silex Scintillans*. The latter seems unlikely, as his letters to the end of his life and the epitaph which he wrote for himself show his Christian feeling, even if, as is likely, it has mellowed and is less severe than in the early fifties. Or it may be only that his lifelong devotion to Virgil made him content with following his model and adopting its pastoral convention, with the happy example of 'Lycidas' before him.

If, then, 'Daphnis' suffers a little, for whatever cause, from some inner inconsistency, it has passages of real beauty such as the Virgilian close which describes the

[1] Cf. preface to *Poems*, 1646: 'the Dregs of an Age' (M 2).

[2] Miss Guiney diffidently suggested that ll. 33–102, and, more certainly, ll. 113–18 were additions made in 1666 to an earlier poem, but in her later letters to Miss Morgan she shows herself still hesitating about this difficult solution.

oncoming of the night,[1] or the customary injunction to
the mourners in the true elegiac style:

> Cast in your Garlands, strew on all the flow'rs
> Which *May* with smiles, or *April* feeds with show'rs.
> Let this days Rites as stedfast as the Sun
> Keep pace with Time, and through all Ages run,
> The publick character and famous Test
> Of our long sorrows and his lasting rest;
> And when we make procession on the plains,
> Or yearly keep the Holyday of Swains,
> Let *Daphnis* still be the recorded name
> And solemn honour of our feasts and fame.[2]

In an obscure little book, published two years after
Vaughan's death, there is a last flicker of his poetic flame.
The Excise-Man 'by Ezekiel Polsted, A.B.' deals satirically
with the qualities and honours of that unpopular officer.
There is a commendatory poem signed 'John Morgan
senior de Wenallt in Com. Brecon', who is probably the
'I. Morgan of White-Hall' (Wenallt, White Hill), to whom
Vaughan addressed a poem on his marriage. Morgan's lines
are succeeded by the following trifle, which carries on Pol-
sted's satirical vein, and it has the more point because Henry
Vaughan's name appears in the list of the Commissioners
of Taxes for the county of Brecon for 1689/90:

To the
Officers of the Excise.

> We owned your Power, and the Pleasures too
> That, as their Center, ever meet in you;
> But your monopolizing Sense, affords
> A Ravishment, beyond the Pow'r of Words:
> To Silence thus confin'd, I must obey,
> And only freely say, that I can nothing say.
> *Henry Vaughan*, Silurist.[3]

---

[1] M 660, ll. 177–84.

[2] M 658, ll. 103–12. The allusion in l. 109 is to the Rogationtide proces-
sion through the fields; cf. Herrick, 'To Anthea':

> Dearest, bury me
> Under that Holy-oke, or Gospel-tree:
> Where (though thou see'st not) thou may'st think upon
> Me, when thou yeerly go'st procession.

[3] Bertram Dobell drew Miss Morgan's attention to this rare book.
Vaughan's lines have not appeared in any edition of his works.

Note. Two other attributions may be noticed here. Miss Morgan inclined to assign to Vaughan the verse epitaph in Llansantffraed church to Games Jones of Buckland, Recorder of Brecon, who died on 18 May 1681 at the age of 31. There is no external evidence of its being by Vaughan. The curious may see a transcription of the epitaph, and judge of it for themselves, in Theo. Jones, *Hist. Breck.*, 1809, ii. 532, where no authorship is suggested. In her article, 'Cromwell and Henry Vaughan' (*Athenaeum*, 29 Mar. 1902), Miss Guiney quoted as Vaughan's an English version of a Latin poem 'Upon the burning of London Bridge'. The English version, which follows the Latin poem, is signed 'H. V.', in Bodl. MS. Ashm. 36–7, f. 207. In the same MS. are two other Latin poems, on Augustus and Strafford, with English versions, all unsigned, in the same hand as the London Bridge poem. Miss Guiney took the hand to be Vaughan's and attributed them to him. Mr. Falconer Madan, to whom she referred the question of the handwriting, judged it to be unlike the writing of Vaughan's letters in the Bodleian. Later, Miss Guiney found part of the English version of the Augustus poem quoted in *King Charles his Starre* (1654) by Arise Evans, who gives it as William Lilly's translation of a poem by Mantuan. Miss Guiney then abandoned her attribution of these poems and versions to Vaughan.

XVII

LAWSUITS AND FAMILY DISSENSIONS

HENRY VAUGHAN's later years were troubled with a succession of lawsuits, the most painful of them arising out of acute family dissensions. The first suit was vexatious rather than important and had no connexion with domestic strife. At the Quarter Sessions of January 1688/9 the Justices of the Peace ordered a warrant to be issued against James and Thomas Gunter and two others 'for entering riotously into the house of Dr. Henry Vaughan and takeing away his horse'.[1] They were required to give security for good behaviour and to appear at the next Quarter Sessions. There is no further reference to the matter in the minutes and it may be presumed that the nuisance was not repeated. It may be no more than a coincidence that the next litigation also concerned a horse, which Vaughan had bought from his friend William Wynter.

The Wynters of Llanfihangel Talyllyn, a village to the north of Llangorse Lake, were traditionally Roman Catholic. William Wynter's father, Edward, had had his estate sequestrated in 1653, but William, who succeeded him in 1669, had conformed to the Church of England. There was every worldly inducement to conform because, under the penal law, a Roman Catholic was liable to have his estate sequestrated and assigned to the nearest relative who conformed. William Wynter's wife Eleanor came of a recusant family at Treivor in Monmouthshire and she adhered to the old faith. It was, no doubt, the difference in religion that led to the bitterness of the litigation which followed Wynter's death in the autumn of 1690. He had shown friendliness to Vaughan and in 1689 had presented the poet's younger son Henry to the rectory of Penderyn in the county of Brecon, and had also granted to Henry Vaughan senior the next presentation to the vicarage of Llandefalle. To safeguard his rights

[1] Minute Book of Brecknockshire Sessions, 15 Jan. 1688/9.

Vaughan entered a Caveat on 30 April 1691, warning the
Bishop of St. Davids not to institute any one to that benefice
'except on the presentation of Henry Vaughan Medici
Doctoris the true and undoubted patron by the grant of
William Wynter armiger'.[1]

Vaughan had bought from William Wynter 'a dandy
horse' for £21. 10s. 0d. According to Mrs. Wynter 'not one
peny' of this debt had been discharged at the time of her
husband's death, although when Wynter asked him for it
three days before his death he promised to pay it, and when
Wynter appealed to Mrs. Vaughan, Mrs. Wynter 'heard her
promise' that her husband would pay. The widow sued
Henry Vaughan in the Brecon town court. He maintained
that his debt was 'fully paid and satisfied to the said Wynter
before his death', but that the widow 'takes advantage' of
him because he has no receipt to show. He maintained also,
for reasons which will appear below, that, even if the debt
were still unpaid, it was due not to the prosecutrix but to
her younger children for whom he was a trustee. Eleanor
Wynter secured a verdict and execution at law against him.
And when in November 1693 Vaughan instituted proceedings in Chancery against Mrs. Wynter in the matter of the
trust, she expressed her belief on oath that he would not
have sued her or 'troubled himself with a pretended trust' if
she had agreed to discharge him of the debt for the dandy
horse.[2]

In the Chancery proceedings Vaughan stated in his Complaint, dated 15 November 1693,[3] that the late William
Wynter was unwilling that his wife 'who was of the Romish
Church' should 'for the advancement of her eldest son who
was of the same persuasion' intermeddle with the provision
he was making for his four younger children. Wynter had,
therefore, 'about December 1688' asked Henry Vaughan,
Hugh Powell rector of Llansantffraed, and John Prosser to
be guardians of the younger children and to 'manage their

---

[1] From Hereford Probate Registry, cited by W. B. Rye in *The Genealogist*,
iii. 36.
[2] Chanc. Pro., Bridges, 300. 30. The Answer of Mrs. Wynter is subscribed,
'Elinor Winter her marke. Sworn at Monmouth.'   [3] Ibid.

portions during their minority'; the father was evidently anxious that the children should not be brought up in their mother's faith or suffer financially by their mother's favouritism towards the eldest son. A deed, made by Wynter with his wife's knowledge, conveyed to the trustees a debt of £500 due to him under bond from Thomas Williams of Talgarth (whose daughter was married to Wynter's eldest son) and also his personal estate, which Vaughan took to be about £1,000, in trust for Wynter himself for life and then to go to the trustees, who were to pay to the children when they came of age—£200 to Walter and £100 to each of his sisters, Mary, Elinor, and Margaret. According to Vaughan's sworn statement, Wynter and himself had signed the deed, which was duly attested, but Hugh Powell and Prosser had refused to sign. And when, after Wynter's death, Vaughan appealed to Powell and Prosser to assist him in carrying out the trust, they refused on the ground that they had not signed the deed and therefore were not answerable. They even went so far, he says, as to combine with Mrs. Wynter to deprive the children of their fortunes; they, or one of them, gave the deed to Mrs. Wynter who then 'cancelled, burned, or destroyed, or at least concealed it from your Orator'. She now says, he continues, that Wynter made a will giving his widow full control of the provision for the children, and he suspects that the will 'was made or contrived by one Hanford, a popish priest' when the testator was not of sound mind and memory. Mrs. Wynter's behaviour he describes as 'contrary to all equity and good conscience', and it will be 'the ruine and destruction of the said Infants' and also of himself, as he will be unable to fulfil the obligations of the deed. He asks, therefore, that Powell and Prosser will either join him in carrying out the provisions of the deed or assign their interests in it to himself, and that Mrs. Wynter be required to give him the deed 'if it is still extant' and to render 'a true inventory of the whole estate'.

In her sworn Answer Elinor Wynter begins by asserting 'the manifold imperfections, errors, and insufficiencies' of Vaughan's Bill of Complaint. Her jointure was £60 a year, not £200, as he had stated,[1] and her husband's personal estate was 'worth about £30 only', with no debts due to him except the £500 bond, Vaughan's debt for the dandy horse, and one other debt. The eldest son Edward (Vaughan had misnamed him Edmund) was not 'of the Romish Church' but, as she had heard and believed, had 'taken the oathes to their maiesties' (that is, to William and Mary). She held that the deed of which Vaughan talked was superseded by her husband's having made better provision for his children in the will he made on 25 September 1690. It is 'false and feigned' that her husband was not of sound mind when he made the will, which was not 'contrived by a popish priest' but was 'penned and drawne by one Mr. John Morgan, a councellour att law'. One of the four witnesses to the will was Mrs. Henry Vaughan, and the Overseers were Mrs. Wynter's brother Hugh James, Dr. Vaughan, Hugh Powell, and John Prosser. She says, too, that Vaughan, 'so far from thinking anything was wrong with the will before she brought the suit' about the horse, went with her to Brecon to assist her in getting it proved. As for the deed, her husband, shortly before his death, had handed to her 'a deed or writeing', relating to the younger children's provision, and directed her to burn or destroy it, 'which she lawfully did'. She thinks that if Vaughan were to be given the upper hand over her 'it may bee a heard [hard] matter for her said younger children to get their legacies paid from him'. If he should succeed in making out that he had any rights, she hopes the Court may require him to give good securities for the due performance of the trust, 'so that the younger children may not be defrauded by the complainant's management and officiousness'.

The attributions of bad motives, which both sides made against their opponents, may be disregarded, but it is evident that Vaughan's statement of facts was seriously inaccurate about the amount of Wynter's estate and about the will not

[1] Her statement is corroborated by the fact that her 'jointure estate' at Talgarth was let to one Roger Havard in 1715 for £58. 14s. 6d. In a list of recusants for that year is 'Eleanor Winter, late of Llanfihangel Tal-y-llyn, and now of Monmouth, Widow' (J. O. Payne, *English Catholic Nonjurors*, p. 11).

being drawn by a lawyer. The unwillingness of Prosser and the rector to have any further concern with the deed is likely to be due to their thinking that the provision for the children in the will, of which they were Overseers, superseded the deed.

The habit of litigation was such a constant feature of Welsh life that Vaughan may not have been very seriously troubled by the Wynter lawsuits, but the suits arising out of family dissensions must have occasioned him the keenest distress. His children by his first marriage believed that their interests were being sacrificed to those of the children by the second marriage. If this was true, Elizabeth Vaughan may have been more to blame than her husband. Thomas, Henry Vaughan's elder son and heir, was foremost in the contentions, and already by 1688 the dispute between him and his father had reached such acute strain that the father made a great sacrifice for the sake of peace. By an indenture dated 28 January 1688/9 between him and his wife on the one part and his son Thomas on the other it was covenanted that, 'partly in consideration of the natural love and affection he bore' to his son, Henry and Elizabeth Vaughan 'would at any time upon the reasonable request of his son' convey to Thomas Vaughan and his heirs the whole estate of Newton 'free from all manner of incumbrances'. On his part, Thomas Vaughan agreed that he would, 'within the space of six months' after the execution of the conveyances, make payments of £100 each to the children by the second marriage, namely, to Grisell and her husband Roger Prosser, to Luce and Rachel, both of them at this time unmarried, and to Henry. He was also to allow his father £30 a year for life (and to his stepmother £20 a year after her husband's death) and 'liberty to keep and graze two cows and one horse yearly upon the said premises during their lifetime, and to cut down and carry away from the premises sufficient timber to amend and rebuild the house and outhouse of the said Dr. Vaughan in the village of Skethrogg'.[1]

Accordingly, the premises were 'soon after' conveyed to Thomas Vaughan, and his father rebuilt the cottage. The

[1] Chanc. Pro., Mitford 355. 174.

Scethrog cottage was pulled down some forty years ago, after being for long untenanted and in a ruinous state, but the lintel stone has survived with the inscription $\frac{H^{VE}}{1689}$ which corroborates the date of the rebuilding for the occupation of Henry and Elizabeth Vaughan.[1] The lintel is now placed at the foot of Vaughan's gravestone in Llansantffraed churchyard. A photograph of the cottage, taken shortly before it was demolished, shows two doors and a single window on the ground-floor of the front, with two dormer windows in the only story above; there is a single upper window on the side of the house which shows, and there are chimneys at either end of the roof. To leave the home in which he had been born and had spent most of his life for an insignificant cottage can have been no small sacrifice for Henry Vaughan to make in the interest of peace. Yet Thomas Vaughan, in a suit which he brought against his father four years later, alludes grudgingly to the covenant as having been made 'by the insinuation and persuasions' of his stepmother 'under pretence of keeping peace & quietness in the family', and in order 'to raise a portion' for her own children.[2]

Bad blood continued because Thomas Vaughan did not fulfil his undertakings to his half-sisters and half-brother. Before 1693 Luce had married Jenkin Jones of Llangasty Talyllyn,[3] whose mother was a daughter of Henry Vaughan's old friend Charles Walbeoffe, and Rachel had married John Turbeville of Llangattock. The husbands would see to it that their wives got their portions which were still unpaid. At the time the indenture was made Thomas Vaughan had entered into a bond to pay Roger Prosser the £100 due to him and his wife Grisell, and similar bonds to his sisters Luce and Rachel, then unmarried; all three bonds were witnessed by their father. When the years passed without these payments being made, at last, in the Great Sessions of

---

[1] Miss Guiney identified the stone in 1895. It did not belong to the Newton house as is suggested in Chambers, II. xx.

[2] Chanc. Pro., as before.

[3] A kinsman of the Puritan preacher, Jenkin Jones of Llandetty. See below, p. 251.

Brecon in the spring of 1693, Jenkin Jones and his wife Luce put their bond in suit and obtained judgement against Thomas Vaughan. And in the Trinity term of the same year John Turbeville and his wife Rachel began a Chancery suit in respect of Rachel's bond and caused Thomas Vaughan to be apprehended. According to Thomas Vaughan, his half-brother Henry and his brother-in-law Prosser were also threatening that they would 'suddenly put their bonds in suit either in the Exchequer or the Court of Great Sessions of the county of Brecon'; 'these confederates', as he calls them, 'threaten to have your Orator cast in prison'. He thereupon began a Chancery suit against his father, praying 'for writs of injunction for stay of proceedings at law' against him, and for writs of *sub poena* against his father, step-mother, half-brother, half-sisters and their husbands.

In his Complaint, dated 5 July 1693,[1] Thomas Vaughan alleged that his expectation of entering into peaceful occupation of Newton had not been realized because his father and stepmother 'have combined and confederated' to deprive him of the enjoyment of Newton, 'in a most clandestine manner having gott into the chamber where the Plaintiff lay and broken open his trunk and have taken away the said articles and indenture of enfeoffment and cut the signatures therefrom'. This alleged deprivation of valuable evidence he regrets the more because he claims that his father before or after his first marriage executed deeds by which the issue of that marriage would benefit, and he therefore asks that his father and stepmother 'shall be called upon to set forth and discover their covenants with your Orator' and any other relevant deeds. He also asks that his half-sisters and their husbands shall declare 'whether any or either of them broake open your Orator's trunke where the deeds were and conveyed the same away'. He states, too, that he is 'remedilesse' because some of the witnesses he would have called 'are now gone to remote places beyond the seas'.

In spite of Thomas Vaughan's injurious language against his father and other members of the family, the matter appears to have been settled out of court and the lawsuits

[1] Chanc. Pro., Mitford 355. 174.

abandoned, as on the following 11 November an agreement
was reached. On that day a deed was signed 'between Henry
Vaughan the elder and Elizabeth his wife and Henry
Vaughan the younger of one part and Thomas Vaughan of
the other', by which Henry Vaughan the elder conveyed to
Thomas and his heirs for ever the Newton estate, charged
with £30 a year to the father and with £20 a year to his wife
if she survived him.[1] At the Brecon Sessions in the following April, just a year before the poet's death, a Fine was
levied between the same parties acknowledging Thomas
Vaughan's right to the estate, which is described as consist-
ing of '1 messuage, 1 garden, 60 acres of land, 20 acres of
wood, 20 acres of furze and heather, with appurtenances, in
the parishes of Llansanffreed and Llanvigan'.[2] Blackstone
describes a Fine as 'a final agreement', 'an amicable composition or agreement of a suit, either actual or fictitious, by
leave of the king or his justices'.[3] Its opening words were
generally, 'Haec est finalis concordia', and with these words
of good omen this account of the painful proceedings may
well end.

The case of Catherine Vaughan, the third daughter of
Henry Vaughan by his first wife Catherine, is even more
painful than that of her brother Thomas. She suffered from
a hand having been burnt in infancy, and later in life from
lameness, so that, by her own account, she was unable to
support herself. When, again according to her own account,[4]
her father had refused to assist her, she applied to the Overseers of the parish, who were empowered by the Elizabethan
Poor Law of 1601 to relieve the impotent poor, but they
refused to assist her from the rates because they judged her
father to be able to give her what she needed. She then
took her grievance to the magistrates, and she relates having 'made her complaint att severall meetings of the Justices
of the peace', but, though they made an order, her father

[1] Record Office: Documents of the Principality of Wales: Wales 11. 21.
[2] Feet of Fines: Brecon, April Session, 1694.
[3] Cited in the *O.E.D. s.v.* Fine.
[4] National Library of Wales: Brecknockshire file of the Great Sessions for
1693 and 1694. The Librarian kindly supplied Miss Morgan with transcripts
of the documents here cited.

continued to refuse 'vpon the request and order of ye Justices'. She then petitioned the Justices of the Great Sessions at Brecon in April 1693 in the following terms:

To the right honourable his Majesties Justices of the great Sessions for the seuerall Counties of Brecon Glamorgan and Radnor.

The humble petition of Catherine Vaughan

Sheweth vnto your Lordshippes

That your petitioner is a poore impotent person having one hand burnt in the fire when shee was vppon the breasts, and of late lame in one foot soe that shee cannot gett any thinge to relieue herselfe; may it please your Lordshipps to be advertized that her ffather is a gentleman of estate, and a Doctor of phisicke and refuseth both vppon the request and order of ye Justices of the peace to relieue his daughter, the Parishe also refuseth because her ffather is able, and fitter to relieue her, soe that she is on all hands remediles, and sure to perish for want: May it therefore please your Lordshipps to commiserate her sad and deplorable condition and order her ffather to giue her necessary maintenance and your petitioner will pray for your prosperity and happiness with increase of honour whilst &c.

CATHERINE VAUGHAN.

The result of her petition is the following Order of Mr. Justice Powlett:

Having ordered Henry Vaughan of Newton Doctor of Phisick to attend me about this peticōn he came and in the presence of Daniel Williams Esqr. promised to allow the peticōner his Daughter Six pounds a year for her maintenance and that in order to it he will pay to Hugh Powell Minister of Lansainfreed Thirty shillings imēdiatly for the first Quarter and Thirty shillings at the beginning of every other Quarter during his life to be payd by Mr. Powell to the peticōner by half a crown a weeke And if this be not performed I recommend it to the Justices of Peace of the County of Brecknock to make all necessary orders for performance of it.

Apr. 21. 1693.   WM. POWLETT.

It would appear that the local magistrates, who were likely to know more of Catherine Vaughan's character and way of living, were less favourably inclined to her than the visiting Judge of Assize, since they had exercised no pressure on

Henry Vaughan before this petition of April 1693, even if indeed they had ever issued an Order, as Catherine averred in her petitions to the Great Assize. When she approached them again after her first petition, she got less than no support from them, as she declares in the second petition which she brought before the next meeting of the Great Sessions in September:

The humble petition of Catherine Vaughan
Sheweth vnto your Lordships that your petitioner had nothing to this day from Doctor Henry Vaughan her ffather acordinge to your Order made the last great Sessions but two shillings and sixe pence, and although she served her ffather with the order, and made her complaint att seuerall meetings of the Justices of the peace they used no meanes to force her father to performe your order, but some of them rather frightinge her and threatning to imprison her and binde her for seekinge relieffe: May it therefore please your good Lordshipps to consider howe your order is slighted on all hands, and to commiserate the sad and lamentable condition of your petitioner being an object of Charity by taking such speciall course for the reliefe of petitioner as your Lordshipps shall conceiue fitt, otherwise your petitioner must inevitably perishe for want, and your petitioner will euer pray, &c.
                                        CATHERINE VAUGHAN.

Henry Vaughan excused himself from attending on the score of urgent professional duties in the following letter addressed 'To the trulie honoured: Mr. Justice Paulett. Humbly these':

Honoured Syr!
That I am accused by adversaries of all sorts & renderd to your Lordship as a person guiltie of all they can devise & declare against me: I doe not at all doubt; but I hope that you will give ear to what I allso have to say & shall make good.
According to the promise & agreement made to & with your Lordship, I payed & tenderd half a crown weekly to the petitioner, butt she refused it. butt of thirty shillings to be payd her att one tyme, I know nothing & never made any such promise.
Bysides all this, your Lordship will give me leave to tell you that among heathens noe parents were ever compelld to maintain or relieve disobedient & rebellious children, that both despise & vilifie their parents, & publickly give out most scandalous &

reproachfull lyes concerning them: which this pious petitioner hath done, & still doth. How far this may enter into your Lordships brest, or whither it willbe of any weight, or value with your Lordship, I am vncertain: butt I am sure that among Christians & in all civil governments it is, or should be looked vpon as a practise directly against his precepts & commands, who is the great Judge of all our actions.

My Lord,

What ever your Lordship intends, or will resolve to doe: I shall with such respects & civilities as are due to your person & the place you sitt in: receive & digest them. butt must not prostrate my self to the designs or devices of vnreasonable adversaries, or informers. I had wayted vpon your Lordship, butt my present engagement with Mr. Serjeant Le Hunts Lady, who is most dangerously sick in a putrid fever with most malignant symptoms detein me heer: & will (I hope) obtein your pardon: which shallbe thankfully acknowledged by

Your Lordships most
humble servant
HENRY VAUGHAN.

Crickowel:
Septemb: 14th 93.[1]

Meanwhile, on 12 September, Mr. Justice Powlett had given order: 'Let Mr. Daniel Williams and the rest of the Justices of Peace now in Town be desired to attend me at my Chamber about this business at the rising of the Court in the afternoon.' It appears from his letter that Henry Vaughan had inadvisedly attempted to deal with the matter personally instead of strictly following the judge's Order of 21 April which required him to pay thirty shillings at the beginning of each quarter to the rector for him to give Catherine Vaughan half a crown a week. The relations between father and daughter were so strained that she had resented receiving half a crown from him, perhaps because she wrongly believed that she was entitled to receive an initial payment of thirty shillings in a lump sum at once; she does not claim this in her second petition, and we learn of it only through her father's letter. The judge was not likely to approve

---

[1] Nat. Libr. of Wales: Brecknockshire Sessions, 2nd Session of 1693: Welsh Papers, Bundle 178. This letter has not been previously printed.

Vaughan's variation from the terms of his first Order, and on 15 September, the day after receiving Vaughan's letter, he made his second Order in more stringent terms than the first:

At the Grand Sessions holden at Brecon this fifteenth day of September 1693

Vpon reading of the peticon of Katherine Vaughan daughter of Henry Vaughan Dr. in Physick exhibited the last Sessions and of the order therevpon made both which are hereunto annexed and upon view of the sayd Katharine Vaughans person and prooffe of her inability to keep herself by her labour and upon Complaint that her sayd father hath not payd thirty shillings to Hugh Powell minister of the parish of Lansainfreed according to his promise and Agreement menĉoned in the sayd Order nor anything done by the Justices of this County at their Quarter Sessions last held for this County to compell her sayd father to performe his sayd agreement or to provide for her according to Law forasmuch as the Children of parents able to maintaine them are to be maintained by their parents and are not to be chargable vpon the parish where they dwell in case they are and become impotent or otherwise vnable to maintaine themselves It is Ordered by this Court That it be again referred to the Justices of Peace of this County in their next Quarter Sessions to convene the sayd Dr. Vaughan before them and therevpon to order her reliefe according to Law and his owne promise and agreement menĉoned in the sayd Order and to see their own order effectually performed and to signify what they shall do therein to this Court at the next Grand Sessions And Daniel Williams Esqr Richard Jeffreys and [a blank] Justices of the Peace of this County or any or either of them are desired to bind over the sayd Dr. Vaughan in the meantime to appeare before them at their next Quarter Sessions for the purposes aforesayd and to stand to such Order as they thinke fitt to make therein.

The Justices of the Peace found themselves obliged to review the case afresh under pressure of the Order of the Great Sessions, and at the next meeting of Quarter Sessions, held at Hay on 3 October, they made the following Order:

Llansainfread. Upon readinge of the peticon of Catherine Vaughan, Spinster, Daughter of Henry Vaughan of Llansainfread in the County aforesaid gent setting forth that she was poore & impotent, not able to maintaine herself & that her said father did refuse to maintaine her or allow anythinge towards her relieffe, And alsoe upon readinge of an Order of reference or Recommendačon of the matter made to their Maiesties Justices of the peace of the said County by the Right hon. their Maiesties Justices of the Great Sessions of this County & alsoe this Court havinge enquired into the condičon of the said petitioner, and alsoe to the ability of her said father Itt is ordered by this Court that the said Henry Vaughan doe pay quarterly from henceforth into the hands of Hugh Powell Clericus Rector of the said parish the sume of twenty shillings to be by the said Mr. Powell laid out towards the relieffe of the said Catherine Vaughan untill further order, And that the said Henry Vaughan doe duly obey & performe this order upon the payne & penalty contained in the Statute against persons offendinge in like Cases. And the Churchwardens and Overseers of the poore of the said parish are hereby ordered to give forthwith due notice of this order to the said Henry Vaughan & upon his neglect or refusall to obey & perform the same to give notice thereof to the Justices of the peace of the limitts in order to have the penalties by him incurred duly leavied for the relieffe of yᵉ said petičoner.¹

It will be noted that the magistrates order a quarterly payment of twenty, not thirty shillings, a further indication that they took a less favourable view of Catherine's case than Mr. Justice Powlett had done at the Great Sessions. They repeated their Order at the January meeting of the Quarter Sessions,² and at the next meeting, on 17 April 1694, they reduced the quarterly payment to fifteen shillings, '& upon payment thereof the former order to be discharged'.³

It is not likely that Henry Vaughan was even now wholly quit of this unhappy business. It is fair to him to record that in the deed of 28 January 1688/9, by which he was to transfer Newton to his eldest son, one of the stipulations was that, as a charge upon the estate, Thomas Vaughan was to pay after his father's death a sum to provide his sister Catherine with 'sufficient meat, drink, washing, lodging, and clothing during her life'. And if, as seems evident, Catherine was

¹ Nat. Libr. of Wales: Brecon Qu. Sessions, 5 Wm. & Mary, 3 Oct., p. 75.
² Ibid., p. 79.
³ Ibid., p. 80. For the later story of Catherine Vaughan see below, pp. 247-8.

difficult and implacable it may be merciful to recall what Bacon says of those who are afflicted with bodily infirmities:

Deformed persons are commonly even with nature, for as nature hath done ill by them, so do they by nature, being for the most part (as the Scripture saith) void of natural affection; and so they have their revenge of nature. Certainly there is a consent between the body and the mind, and where nature erreth in the one, she ventureth in the other: *Ubi peccat in uno, periclitatur in altero.*

XVIII

THE END

IT is much to be hoped that the family Concordia of April
1694 procured to Henry Vaughan greater peace for the
last year of his life, and that he had no further cause to
charge his 'disobedient and rebellious children' with
despising and vilifying their parents and uttering 'most
scandalous & reproachfull lyes concerning them', though
his daughter Catherine could hardly fail to be other than a
care and embarrassment to him to the end, as she was to
other members of the family after his death. Vaughan was
now in his seventy-third year, and his father, on reaching
the age of seventy, had been described as 'very decrepit'.
Ill-health had pursued the poet long after his recovery from
the prolonged sickness that nearly ended his days in the
period between writing the first and second parts of *Silex
Scintillans*. In 1662 he describes himself as kept at home
by 'weaknes, & other violent effects of a late feaver',[1]
and on Lady Day 1689 he writes of 'a very slow recovery'
from 'a tedious and severe sickness', which had begun
before Christmas.[2] He was, however, sufficiently restored to resume his professional duties, and there is
evidence of his visiting his patients within eighteen
months of his death.[3]

The end came in 1695 on St. George's Day, 23 April,
which had been the death-day of Shakespeare and was to be
that of Wordsworth 155 years after Vaughan's. In his last
sickness, we may hope that he could still see through the
windows the Breconshire Beacons and hear the waters of the
Usk that he had loved and celebrated, just as, when Walter
Scott lay dying, 'the sound of all others most delicious to his
ear, the gentle ripple of the Tweed over its pebbles, was dis-
tinctly audible as we knelt around the bed, and his eldest son
kissed and closed his eyes'.[4] At any rate it was within sight

---

[1] See above, p. 199.   [2] M 674.   [3] See above, p. 194.
[4] Lockhart, *Memoirs of the Life of Sir Walter Scott*, ch. xxix.

of mountains and river that Henry Vaughan's body was laid
in Llansantffraed churchyard. In this fulfilment of his wish
he was more fortunate than his brother Thomas, buried far
from the place where 'his Stars first saw him'.[1] Nearly half
a century before his death Henry Vaughan had expressed his
wish in the opening poem of *Olor Iscanus*:

> But *Isca*, whensoe'r those *shades* I see,
> And thy *lov'd Arbours* must no more *know* me,
> When I am layd to *rest* hard by thy *streams*,
> And my *Sun sets*, where first it *sprang* in beams,
> I'le leave behind me such a *large, kind light*,
> As shall *redeem* thee from *oblivious night*,
> And in these *vowes* which (living yet) I pay
> *Shed* such a *Previous* and *Enduring Ray*,
> As shall from age to age thy *fair name* lead
> 'Till *Rivers* leave to *run*, and *men* to *read*.[2]

So long as men read, the Swan of Usk will be remembered,
and the river he sang of will have its place in the annals of
English literature, for

> *Poets* (like *Angels*) where they once appear
> *Hallow* the *place*, and each succeeding year
> Adds *rev'rence* to't, such as at length doth give
> This aged faith, *That there their Genii live*.[3]

It may well have been Vaughan's own wish that he should
be buried in the churchyard, not within the church as was
usual in his day for those of any social standing.[4] Departures
from that long-established custom still attracted notice. The
Dean of St. Asaph thought it his 'duty' to inform the Archbishop of Canterbury in 1680 of the recent burial of his
admirable bishop, Isaac Barrow, 'not in the Church but the
Church-yard just without the great doore at the West end of
the Church (the place where long before in the time of his
health he had made choice of to be buried in)'.[5] Four years

---

[1] 'Daphnis', ll. 113–22 (M 659).
[2] 'To the River *Isca*', ll. 25–34 (M 39).
[3] Ibid., ll. 15–18.
[4] Wood (*Ath. Oxon.*, 1721, ii. 927) is mistaken in saying that Vaughan 'was buried in the Parish Church of Llansenfreid'.
[5] Bodl. MS. Tanner 146, f. 43.

before Barrow died, Sir Matthew Hale, Lord Chief Justice,
was buried in Alderley churchyard, 'having left express instructions that he should not be buried in the church, that
being a place for the living, not the dead'.[1] John Evelyn
notes in his *Diary* on 12 February 1682/3 that his father-in-
law, Sir Richard Browne, sometime ambassador in Paris,
who died in Evelyn's house, 'by a special clause in his will,
ordered that his body should be buried in the churchyard'.
Edward Lloyd of the Middle Temple, a Carmarthen mag-
nate, making his will in 1717, directs:

> As for my corruptible body I bequeath it to the earth whence it
> was taken to be privately buried, without any show or ostentation
> whatever in some churchyard; for I think it well said of my
> grandfather Sir William Vaughan:

> > Taint not the Churche, ye that mourn
> > Nor with worms' meat: the yarde shall serve my turne;
> > Only a Shroud for decency I crave,
> > Such as my Saviour, wrapt in Joseph's grave.

The stone which covers Vaughan's grave came probably,
as Grosart suggests, 'from the celebrated quarry of Bwlch-
yr-Arllwys in the adjoining parish of Cwmdu', and is 'of
unusual size and thickness, measuring 7 ft. 2 in. by 2 ft. 10 in.
and 4½ inches thick'.[2] The coat of arms would have ample
precedent in the tombs of the Vaughan family which were
once in Cwmdu church. Above the arms is the bare statement 'Henricus Vaughan Siluris M.D. obiit Ap. 23. Año
Sal. 1695 Ætat. suæ 73'. So far the inscription may or may
not have followed Henry Vaughan's directions, but the rest
is explicitly the epitaph of his own choice, as the next sentence indicates—'Quod in sepulchrum voluit'.[3] Then
follows: 'Servus inutilis: peccator maximus hic iaceo',

---

[1] *D.N.B.* s.v. Matthew Hale (1609–76). In Llangattock churchyard is the
tombstone of a rector, William Skinner, who died in 1757, with this inscription, 'Yr eglwys i'r byw a'r fynwent i'r meirw' (Theo. Jones, iii. 160; 'The
church for the living and the churchyard for the dead').   [2] Grosart, i. xlvi.
[3] Dr. Percy Simpson (*Notes and Queries*, 28 Aug. 1943) points out that
some such word as *poni* needs to be supplied before *voluit*. While agreeing
with him, I replied (ibid., 20 May 1944) that Vaughan may have met the phrase
in an epitaph which Owen Felltham devised for himself, with the heading
Quod in Sepulchrum volui, and appended to the 1661 edition of his *Resolves*.
Vaughan frequently quotes from some earlier edition of this favourite book

TOMBSTONE IN
LLANSANTFFRAED CHURCHYARD

which is an evident reminiscence of the counsel of Christ:
'Sic et vos cum feceritis omnia quae praecepta sunt vobis,
dicite: Servi inutiles sumus: quod debuimus facere, fecimus',
and, perhaps also, of the prayer of the publican: 'Deus pro-
pitius esto mihi peccatori.' Beneath a small incised cross
are the two words 'Gloria Miserere'. Vaughan had ended
his *Mount of Olives* with an ascription of glory in the same
words with which Herbert had ended *The Temple*. And
Vaughan's 'Miserere' strikes again the note of Christian
humility that is recurrent all through *Silex Scintillans*.
There is revealed in his self-chosen epitaph a consistency
maintained throughout life from the first appearance of
Silex till his death. It is an interesting coincidence that
Robert Vaughan, the engraver of the frontispiece of *Olor
Iscanus*, who is not known to be a kinsman of the poet, en-
graved David with a shield bearing 'Gloria—Miserere—
Confiteor' as frontispiece of a notable edition of the Psalms
printed at Oxford in 1644.

Theophilus Jones, writing at the beginning of the nineteenth century, describes the inscription as 'now defaced',
but he prints it correctly except for giving the age as 78.[1]
Miss Guiney, visiting the grave just two hundred years after
Vaughan's death, found it sadly neglected. A letter of hers
to the *Athenaeum*, dated from Boston, U.S., 1 October 1895,
had fruitful consequences. It brought her into contact with
Miss Gwenllian Morgan of Brecon, and they henceforth
collaborated in their researches into the life and writings of
Henry Vaughan. Miss Morgan also became the honorary
secretary of a fund that provided for the repair of the tomb
and for a memorial tablet in the church with an inscription
composed by Dean Vaughan, Master of the Temple. The
tombstone has a crack running across the centre but is otherwise in good order, and the recut lettering is clear. The grave
is almost due east of the church, slightly to the south; over-
hanging it is an old yew-tree.

of his. Dr. Simpson takes Felltham's sentence to mean 'What I have wished
for my grave', and thinks that, if Vaughan borrowed it from Felltham, he
did so uncritically.

[1] Op. cit., 1809, ii. 535; the mistake in the age is repeated in the 1911
edition, iii. 205, and it is given as 75 in iii. 208.

After two centuries and a half the poet's grave is visited by many more lovers of his poetry than at any time since his death. This grateful remembrance seems to fulfil an injunction of his in *The Mount of Olives*: 'If thou hast lost any *dear friends*, have them alwayes before thine eyes, visit their *graves* often, and be not unkind to a *Jonathan* though in the *dust*.'[1] A poet of our time has happily expressed the nature of our debt to the Silurist:

Above the voiceful windings of a river
An old green slab of simply graven stone
Shuns notice, overshadowed by a yew.
Here Vaughan lies dead, whose name flows on for ever
Through pastures of the spirit washed with dew
And starlit with eternities unknown.
Here sleeps the Silurist; the loved physician;
The face that left no portraiture behind;
The skull that housed white angels and had vision
Of daybreak through the gateways of the mind.
   Here faith and mercy, wisdom and humility
   (Whose influence shall prevail for evermore)
   Shine. And this lowly grave tells Heaven's tranquillity
   And here stand I, a suppliant at the door.[2]

[1] M 188.
[2] 'At the Grave of Henry Vaughan', from *The Heart's Journey*, by Siegfried Sassoon, 1928.

HENRY VAUGHAN'S IMMEDIATE ANCESTRY

CHAMBERS (II. xix and 347), following MS. Harl. 2289, f. 81, gives the poet's father as Henry, son of Thomas and Denise Vaughan. This is certainly wrong, as many lawsuits establish the fact that the poet's parents were Thomas Vaughan (*ob.* 1658) and Denise, daughter of David and Gwenllian Morgan. The mistake may have arisen from the Harleian manuscript's having the name Henry at the foot of a page as catchword and again at the head of the next page. The real difficulty is as to whether the poet's father Thomas was a younger son of Charles Vaughan of Tretower (*ob.* 1636) or a younger brother of his. All the seventeenth-century genealogies give Charles as the eldest son of William and Frances Vaughan. Some of them, as was not unusual, give only the eldest sons, the inheritors of Tretower. Some, e.g. MS. Harl. 2289, give Thomas as a younger son of Charles, but MS. Harl. 5058, f. 28, written about 1614 (i.e. some seven years before the poet's birth), gives the children of William and Frances Vaughan as Charles, Thomas, William, and a daughter (unnamed) who married John Walbeoffe.

Another manuscript collection of Welsh genealogies (Bodl. Add. MS. A 281, f. 281), compiled in 1644 and 1645, gives the children of William and Frances Vaughan as Charles Vaughan, 'Thomas Vaughan of Newton', and an unnamed daughter married to John Walbeoffe of Llanhamlach. The children of Charles Vaughan of Tretower are given as 'William Vaughan of Tretower Esq. now living 1644' and an unnamed daughter 'maried to Morgan John of Gwenallt'. On the reverse page the marriage of Thomas Vaughan of Newton is recorded, to an unnamed daughter of David Morgan 'being heiresse of that meanes & now liveing 1644 hath issue'.

There are many indications that Charles Vaughan and the poet's father were of the same generation. Frances's father, Thomas Somerset, was a prisoner in the Tower from 1562 till his death in 1586; it is, therefore, probable that his daughter Frances was born not later than 1563. The poet's father is described in a lawsuit of November 1656 as 'very decrepit and about 70 years of age', which would put his birth about 1586.[1] Frances Vaughan would,

---

[1] Chan. Pro., Hamilton 448. Among the Depositions in the case of *Powell* v. *Vaughan*, taken at Brecon on 14 Oct. 1652, is one by 'Thomas

therefore, be not less than 23, and probably older, at the birth of her third child. Before marrying William Vaughan she had borne a son Roger to her first husband, a Vaughan of Talgarth. If Charles, her undoubted son by William Vaughan of Tretower, was two years older than the poet's father, he would be 20 at the time of his marriage on 1 May 1604 to Eleanor Norton,[1] and Thomas Vaughan (aged about 70 in 1656) could not be his son. Thomas Vaughan married Denise in 1611 or 1612, which is another indication that Charles and Thomas were of the same generation, both of them sons of William and Frances Vaughan.

Besides the variants in the early genealogies, there is only one argument for making Charles Vaughan of Tretower the poet's grandfather, namely, Aubrey's statement about the poet and his twin-brother that 'their grandmother was an Aubrey'.[2] Charles Vaughan's wife, Eleanor Norton, was the daughter of a daughter of Dr. William Aubrey, the famous civilian. If, then, Charles and Eleanor Vaughan were the parents of the poet's father, the twins would have an Aubrey for their great-grandmother. Aubrey was careless about exact relationship; he writes once of 'my grandfather William Aubrey, LL.D.',[3] whom elsewhere he correctly calls his great-grandfather.[4] His letter to Edward Llwyd in 1673[5] shows that he knew little then of the Vaughan family. He was at any rate connected with the Vaughans through the Walbeoffe–Aubrey marriages.[6] It should be added that Henry Vaughan's grandmother on the maternal side, Gwenllian Morgan, was not an Aubrey; she was a daughter of William Howell Richard of Llanhamlach and is sometimes described, for lack of a proper surname, as Gwenllian William or Williams after her father's first name.

Vaughan of Newton in the parish of Llansanfreade co. Brecon, gent. aged 62'; this would put his birth some four years later, *c.* 1590. The common use of 'about' or 'circiter' in such depositions makes precision unobtainable. If he was born in 1590, Frances would be not less than 27 at the time of his birth.

[1] This date for Charles Vaughan's marriage is given in the suit *Morgan* v. *Vaughan* of 12 Feb. 1673/4. It is, of course, possible that the date, being given seventy years after the event, may be wrong, but it suits the bridegroom's probable age, as the heir to Tretower would probably marry young.

[2] *Brief Lives*, ii. 268.   [3] Ibid. i. 5.   [4] Ibid. i. 210.
[5] See above, p. 206.   [6] See above, pp. 206–7.

APPENDIX B

DATE OF HENRY VAUGHAN'S BIRTH

As Henry and Thomas Vaughan were twins, any evidence about one is equally available for the other. It should also be noted that it was still usual, especially in ecclesiastical, legal, and academic records, to date the year from Lady Day. Henry Vaughan, in his letter to Aubrey of 15 June 1673 says: 'My brother and I were borne att Newton . . . in the yeare 1621.'[1] No month or day is named, and if Henry was born at any date between 24 April 1621 and 24 March 1621/2, he would be 73 at his death on 23 April 1695, as is stated on his tombstone. There is a mistaken inference in the account of Henry Vaughan in the *D.N.B.*: 'He and his twin-brother Thomas were born on 17 April 1622 (*Sloane* MS. 1741).'[2] This manuscript is a notebook of Thomas Vaughan containing chemical formulae, interspersed with many entries expressing his devotion to his wife Rebecca who died on 17 April 1658. On the first anniversary of her death occurs this entry against the date 17 April 1659: 'in ipso Anniversario sive Die solenni Nativitatis suae Æternae'. This is a pious expression for her death-day being the commencement of her immortal life.[3] It has been perversely taken to mean that it was both her death-day and her husband's birthday, although *suae* can grammatically refer to Rebecca only and *Æternae* could have no meaning in reference to his birthday. The manuscript nowhere names the year 1621 or 1622. There is, then, no evidence at all of the day and month of the twins' birthday.

The evidence about the year is not quite decisive, but even a man of such vagueness about matters of fact, as Henry Vaughan from many indications certainly was, is not very likely to be wrong about the year of his birth. The University Register gives the age of Thomas Vaughan at his matriculation on 14 December 1638 as 16. If the twins were born at any date between 15 December 1621 and 24 March 1621/2, Thomas would still be under 17 at his matriculation. But Wood may be right when, perhaps resting on Henry's statement that the year of birth was 1621, which he in-

---

[1] M 667.
[2] This date is also given in the *D.N.B.* s.v. Thomas Vaughan.
[3] Cf. the contemporary epitaph of a rector of Pusey, Berks: 'William White, began to live; that is, died; the xxxi. May m.dc.lxxviii.'

corporates in another context,[1] he states that Henry was 'aged 17' at 'his first entry into Jesus coll. in Mich. term 1638'.[2] In the Free School inquisition in 1650 Henry Vaughan is described as 'aged about xxvii yeares';[3] if he was actually 27 he must have been born at least a year later than 1621/2, but 'about' allows of some latitude. In his letter of 7 July 1673 to Aubrey, Henry Vaughan says that his brother 'died in the seaven & fortieth year of his age, upon the 27th of februarie, in the yeare 1666'.[4] As he had told Aubrey in his previous letter of 15 June 1673 that Thomas died 'in the yeare that the last great plague visited London',[5] he probably means February 1665/6, not 1666/7, though there is no confirmation of the earlier date to be had from the will cited in the *D.N.B.*, which is certainly the will of another Thomas Vaughan, late vicar of Cropredy.[6] If Thomas Vaughan had already passed his 46th birthday by 27 February 1665/6, he must have been born before 1621, but Henry may be at fault by one year in reckoning his brother's age at death, seven years after the event. In a deposition taken in January 1693/4 Henry Vaughan is described as 'aetatis suae 71 annor. aut eo circiter'.[7] If he was born any time between the end of January and 24 March 1621/2, he would be just under 72 when he made the deposition, and this would agree with his being 73 at his death fifteen months after.

Having regard to Henry Vaughan's customary vagueness (e.g. about the length of his brother's residence in Oxford, his M.A. degree, and the place of his burial), we find perhaps as much consistency as we might expect from him. We may then, with some diffidence, take him to be right about the year of his birth being 1621 (including the period up to 24 March 1621/2), but we know nothing about the day or month.

[1] *Ath. Oxon.*, ed. Bliss, iii. 722.   [2] Ibid. iv. 425.
[3] Chancery Petty Bag: Charity Inquisitions, co. Brecon, Bundle 20, no. 17. See above, p. 91.
[4] M 670.   [5] M 667.   [6] See above, p. 146.
[7] Hereford Probate Registry: Depositions on the will of Thomas Powell of Maesmawr, who died 3 Dec. 1693.

APPENDIX C

HENRY VAUGHAN'S DESCENDANTS

HENRY Vaughan died intestate and administration was granted to his widow. The 'Inventory of all the goods chattells and credits of the said deceased Henry Vaughan, Doctor of Physick', signed by his widow Elizabeth, his son-in-law Roger Prosser, Water [*sic*] Prosser, and David Thomas, amounted to £49. 4*s*.[1] The small amount is partly accounted for by the fact that Vaughan had made over the Newton estate to his son Thomas with a life interest for himself and his widow. It may also be supposed that his widow had some property in her own right. In any case his inventory was for ten times as much as his father's.[2]

It remains to tell what can be ascertained about Henry Vaughan's descendants. Many of his children were married into families which have already found mention in these pages; it is characteristic of seventeenth-century Welsh life that neighbouring families were closely intermarried. Nothing is known of his eldest daughter Lucy, by his first wife Catherine, after her marriage to Charles Greenleafe of Stretton-upon-Trent. Her name does not occur in her sister Catherine's litigation, and she had probably long since left her native county for Staffordshire. The next daughter, Frances, died unmarried, some five and twenty years before her father.[3] The remaining daughter by the first marriage, Catherine, continued to be troublesome. Within four months of her father's death she filed a Bill of Complaint against his widow and their son Henry, in which she alleged that her father, when settling the Scethrog cottage, which is here named Holly Bush, on his widow and their son Henry, reserved the use of the cottage, or the rent thereof, estimated at 40*s*., to Catherine for her maintenance, but that her stepmother and half-brother kept her out of it and 'refused to discover the conveyance to her'.[4] The defendants were able to refute this by putting in a deed of 16 August 1690, and another of 20 November 1693,[5] dealing with Holly Bush, which made no mention of Catherine Vaughan. It is, however, possible that in the end she went to live there. Catherine was unmarried in 1696,

---

[1] 'Ad bonoⓡ. Henri. Vaughan Medicinae Doctor ob. intest. def. concessa fuit Eliza: ejus relict. Inv. 49:4:' (Llandaff Registry Office: Breconshire wills, 1695.21, Llansantfrayd). [2] See above, p. 17.

[3] See above, p. 206. [4] Record Office: Documents of Wales, 11. 21.

[5] Record Office: Welsh B. & A., Brecon circuit, Bundle 122, 1696. 25.

but a genealogy compiled as late as 1707 by the Welsh Herald, Hugh Thomas, who was born and lived near Llansantffraed, and is therefore likely to have known about the Vaughans, gives Catherine as married, without naming her husband. Miss Morgan was inclined to think that her husband was John Richard of Llansantffraed, who was buried there on 8 March 1717/8; she added, 'I hope that she caught a Tartar of a husband'. The minutes of the Court Leet of Scethrog Manor show that the court was held in 1717 'at the house of John Richard', and in 1720 'at the mansional of Catherine Richard', who is also described in that year as 'Catherina Richard, vid.' (i.e. widow). She is named in the minutes as late as 1737, and in 1740 the word 'died' is written against her name.[1] If Catherine Vaughan, who had repeatedly called herself 'impotent', lived till 1740, she must have been well advanced beyond her eightieth year.[2]

Thomas Vaughan, as a result of the Concordia of 1694, entered into possession of the Newton estate in his father's lifetime. It is not known whether he went to live there, but the Scethrog Manor minutes show for the year 1701–2, among those making payments to the lord of the manor, 'Thomas Vaughan, Gent., for a Tenement of Lands called Newton, 1s. 8d.' In 1717 the same sum was paid for Newton by 'Hugh Powell, clerk', who is presumably the aged rector of Llansantffraed in the last year of his life. Thomas Vaughan's wife Frances (her maiden name is not known) died in 1723. He survived her by nearly ten years and was buried on 13 January 1732/3.[3] G. T. Clark credits him with one son who died without issue. This

---

[1] MS. Manor of Scethrog. Details communicated to Miss Morgan by the owner of the MS., Sir John Lloyd. The *O.E.D.* gives no example of *mansional* as a noun, but *mansion*, besides meaning 'the chief messuage of the Lord of a Manor', was used also of much humbler dwellings, e.g. 'a low cottage . . . hauing in it two mansions' (1553).

[2] In a lawsuit, *Elizabeth Vaughan infant* (daughter of Walter Vaughan of Brecon) v. *Charles and Catherine Powell*, among the tenants of the infant's estate 1734–7 is one Catherine Vaughan in the parish of St. John Evangelist; her rent appears to be £1. 4s. with an extra charge of 12s., and she is continually in arrears. If Henry Vaughan's daughter Catherine was born c. 1650, and is to be identified with this woman, she would be about 87 in 1737. There were other families of Vaughan in Brecon, and for this and other reasons the identification seems improbable. G. T. Clark, *Genealogies of Glamorgan*, p. 240, names Catherine Vaughan's husband William Harris, but he makes her the sixth child of Henry Vaughan by his second wife, and there are other manifest errors in his genealogy; he does not name his authority for it. Cf. Chambers, II. xviii.

[3] A Thomas Vaughan witnessed the will of Thomas Rogers *alias* Prosser in 1700; the relation of the Vaughans to the Prossers makes it not unlikely that this is the poet's elder son. Miss Morgan describes it as 'a beautiful

son may be the Thomas Vaughan, son of Thomas, of Llansantffraed, who matriculated at Oxford from the Queen's College on
1 March 1722/3, aged 22, and graduated B.A. in 1727.[1]

Henry Vaughan's only son by his second wife, Henry, was 26
years old when he was ordained priest in the parish church of
Mathern on Trinity Sunday 1687, on a title to the curacy of Llansantffraed, by Dr. William Beaw, Bishop of Llandaff, during a
vacancy in the see of St. Davids.[2] On 29 June 1689 he was
instituted to the rectory of Penderyn in the county of Brecon on
the presentation of William Wynter.[3] He held that living till his
resignation in 1713.[4] There is no record of his burial in the
Penderyn registers. When the church was restored about 1880,
some of the memorial tablets in the chancel are said to have been
placed beneath the new tiling of the floor; Miss Isabel Southall
told Miss Morgan that several parishioners could testify to there
having been a mural tablet to Henry Vaughan, the former rector,
before the restoration of the church. He married Janet, daughter
of Robert Walbeoffe, who was the youngest brother or a kinsman
of the poet's friend Charles Walbeoffe; it is not known whether
there was any issue of the marriage.[5]

signature', and she bore no good will to the man whom she calls 'horrid
Thomas'.

[1] Foster's *Alumni Oxonienses* cannot be right in identifying the graduate
of 1727 with the Thomas Vaughan who became a barrister of the Inner
Temple in 1732 and was buried in the Temple churchyard on 30 Aug. 1753.
The barrister, at his admission to the Inner Temple on 2 Sept. 1723, nine
years before being called to the Bar, is described in the Inner Temple Admission Books as the second son of Thomas Vaughan of the Inner Temple, who
was himself admitted on 20 Nov. 1697 as second son of Richard Vaughan of
Penrhyn, co. Cardigan.

[2] 'Henricus Vaughan, literatus, titulo curatus Lansanfread in comitatu
Breconiensi, 26' (*Llandaff Records*, ed. J. A. Bradney, 1909, iii. 38). The age
of the ordinand is given at the end of each entry.

[3] *Menevia Sacra* (by E. Yardley, Archdeacon of Cardigan, 1739–70), ed.
F. Green, for the Camden Archaeological Soc., 1927, p. 349. Foster's *Alumni
Oxon.* wrongly assigns this appointment to another Henry Vaughan, son of
Pendred, of Llandyvock co. Carmarthen, who matriculated at Oxford from
Jesus College on 17 Apr. 1668, aged 18, took his M.A. in 1676, and became
vicar of Trelach-ar-Bettws co. Carmarthen in 1688 and vicar of Clodock co.
Hereford in 1699. *Menevia Sacra*, p. 361, gives 'A.M.' to the Henry Vaughan
instituted to St. Clodock in 1699, but the poet's son was 'literatus' only
(i.e. without a university degree).

[4] 'In August 1713 John Williams was instituted to Penderin on the
resignation of Henrice Vaughan' (Carmarthen Diocesan Registry).

[5] MS. Harl. 2289, f. 81, *cit. ap.* Chambers, II. xix. See also Chambers, II.
xxii and 346–7. Charles Walbeoffe had also a cousin Robert, who may be
Janet's father.

Henry the younger's three sisters seem all to have made happy marriages. Grisell, the eldest, is described in the indenture of 28 January 1688/9 as married to Roger Prosser, and in a later document he is described as a saddler of Brecon town. The Prossers were an old Brecon family; one Roger Prosser was steward of Scethrog Manor in 1612, and Theophilus Jones states that there had been many Prosser tombs in the Priory church, though they were gone by his day. John Prosser of Talyllyn, perhaps a brother of Grisell's husband, was named by William Wynter in 1688 as a guardian, with Henry Vaughan the poet and Hugh Powell, of his younger children;[1] and Grisell's husband named John Prosser as a trustee of his children. Roger and Grisell Prosser's daughter Elizabeth was baptized in St. John's church on 23 December 1686, but she died in infancy and the same Christian name was used for the next daughter, the mother wishing, no doubt, to preserve her own mother's name. Walter and the second Elizabeth were baptized together on 25 June 1693, and were presumably twins. Roger Prosser 'of the town of Brecon, mercer' (the family pursued the trades of mercer and saddler) made an admirable will on 7 October 1707, which was proved by his widow on the following 23 April. He left all his estate 'to my deare and well beloved Wife for maintenance and education of my children'; if she were to marry again, his personal estate was to be equally divided between his widow and their two children. He desired that his father should be maintained 'with sufficient meat, drink, washing, lodging, and clothing, and be allowed twenty shillings yearly for his idle expenses'; and it would best please the testator 'that my Father wife and children shall inhabit and live loving together at my now dwelling-house during my father's life'.

Grisell Prosser did not long remain a widow. On 28 June 1709 she married by licence in St. Mary's, Brecon, Morgan Watkin(s) of Brecon, 'Attorney-at-law & vintner of the old Beare'.[2] By his will, proved on 26 September 1719, he left all to his 'beloved wife Grisell'. Grisell Watkins survived her second husband eighteen years and was buried in the Priory Church on 21 August 1737. Whether her son Walter Prosser married and had children is not known. Her daughter, the second Elizabeth Prosser, married Morgan Davies, only son of Morgan Davies of Cay Jenkin.

---

[1] See above, p. 225.

[2] Register of St. Mary's, Brecon. Strangely enough the St. Mary's register enters the marriage of Morgan Watkin and Grisell Prosser on 28 June 1709, while the same pair are entered in the register of St. John's (the Priory Church) as married on 1 July.

Elizabeth's husband, like her father, was a Brecon mercer. Their children were Thomas (whose baptism is not discovered), Morgan who was baptized on 8 July 1720 and buried on 24 November 1737, and Elizabeth who was baptized on 4 April 1725 and buried on 6 July 1730.[1] Their father died in 1727, and it looks as if there were no descendants in this line unless Thomas Davies, of whom nothing is known, had children.

Lucy, sometimes called Luce, perhaps to distinguish her from her half-sister, is described as 'sole' in the indenture of January 1688/9, but in 1693 as 'now wife to Jenkin Jones of Llangasty-Talyllyn, gent.' He was the third son of Lewis Jones of Trebinshwn near Talyllyn and Elizabeth, daughter of Charles Walbeoffe of Llanhamlach.[2] Lewis Jones, like his kinsman, Jenkin Jones of Llandetty, the itinerant preacher, took the Puritan side and in 1659 was made sheriff of the county, displacing Edward Williams, who was removed during his year of office for his suspected royalist sympathies.[3] Jenkin and Lucy Jones's only child Denise was given the Christian name of the poet's mother; she died unmarried on 29 August 1780, and is the latest descendant of the poet who can be traced. Her tombstone in the north aisle of the Priory Church[4] records her descent from Henry Vaughan, doctor of physic, and gives her age as 92, which must be too old as her mother was unmarried in January 1688/9.

The poet's youngest daughter Rachel was, like her sister Lucy, 'sole' in January 1688/9, but by 1693 was 'wife of John Turbeville of Llangattock, Gent.' One Richard Turbeville was Thomas Lewes's predecessor as rector of Llanfigan. Rachel Turbeville died on 22 October 1727 and was buried in the church at Llangattock, where her father spent his school-days. John and Rachel Turbeville had a son Richard, described as 'of Llanwysc and Glenyrhyd', who died young in 1720, leaving by his wife Mary a son John. This younger John Turbeville's line ends with a daughter Margaret who died without issue on 5 October 1765, fifteen years before her cousin, Denise Jones.

Newton eventually passed to the senior branch of the Vaughans of Tretower, who had already become possessed by marriage of

[1] Miss Morgan extracted these baptisms and burials from the St. John's registers.
[2] MS. Harl. 2289, ff. 70, 157; but Theo. Jones (iii. 194) makes his mother a daughter of John Walbeoffe. [3] Richards, ii. 42.
[4] Theo. Jones (edn. 1809, ii. 71, 544; ed. Bailey, ii. 82, 99) says that Denise Jones is buried in the churchyard, 'near the porch'. The stone was probably brought into the church at the restoration of 1874.

the mansion-house of Scethrog.[1] Charles, son of Charles and Margaret Vaughan (*née* Powell), born in 1705, is shown in the minutes of Scethrog Manor as holding also in 1740 'one Messuage and Lands late the Lands of Thomas Vaughan called Newton'. His son Charles succeeded him in 1777 and on his death six years after without a direct heir, Tretower was sold and passed out of the family.[2] On 29 May 1784 Newton and other free-hold estates were put up for sale by auction at Brecon in one lot. In the advertisement Newton is described as 'all that Messuage Tenement and lands &c. called Try Newidd late in the occupation of the said Mr. Charles Vaughan and now of the vendor', and is said to consist of 'a new built Dwelling-House, a Barn, a stable, a Beast-house and garden and several closes'. The present farmhouse called Newton, situated between Llansantffraed church and Scethrog, to the right of the main road as one goes to Brecon, may be a reduced and reconstructed form of Henry Vaughan's birthplace and home; its external appearance looks modern, but the great roughly-hewn beams which support the ceilings of both floors are evidently old and are either *in situ* or have been transferred from a previous house, Henry Vaughan's home. As the inventory of the Silurist's father shows, Newton in his day had a porch with a chamber over it; the present farm-house has no porch.[3] Miss Morgan maintained that the original Newton was taken down about 1836 and the farmhouse built out of its stones on the same site.[4] The inventory of the poet's father, as has already been argued, suggests a house of only modest dimensions, but it was almost certainly larger than the farmhouse as it now is.

By a deed of enfeoffment dated 16 August 1690, and by a con-veyance of 20 November 1693, the poet assigned the Scethrog cottage and 'the lands called Holly Bush' (Llwyn Celyn) to his neighbour Edward Jones of Buckland in the parish of Llansant-ffraed and to William Phillips, Recorder of Brecon, 'to the use of Henry Vaughan the elder for life, then to the use of Elizabeth his wife for the term of her life, then after their several deceases and the death of the survivor of them to Hen: Vaughan the younger and his heirs for ever'.[5] Whether the younger Henry

---

[1] See above, p. 204.   [2] Theo. Jones, 1911, iii. 185.   [3] See above, p. 18.
[4] 'The fine old manor-house at Newton was pulled down by a stupid land-agent within the memory of man' (Chambers, 1896, II. xx). But Newton was never a manor; it was in the manor of Scethrog. The evidence does not suggest that Newton was 'fine'.
[5] Record Office: Wales 11. 21 and Welsh B. & A., Brecon circuit, Bundle

Vaughan lived there after resigning the rectory of Penderyn, or whether any others of the Vaughan family ever lived there, is not known. This cottage was about a quarter of a mile nearer Brecon than Newton, on the left side of the road as one goes to Brecon. It survived till about forty years ago, after being long in a ruinous condition.[1] A better fate has attended the ancestral home of the Vaughans, Tretower Court. After being used for a farmhouse and farm buildings and falling into much disrepair, it was bought by the Brecknock Society with help from the Pilgrim Trust and afterwards committed to the Office (now Ministry) of Works for systematic preservation and repair.[2]

122, 1696, 25. The name 'Holly Bush' is used in the second only of these documents; it appears there to designate the cottage as well as the adjacent land.

[1] See above, p. 229.   [2] See above, p. 9.

GENEALOGIES

A. VAUGHAN OF TRETOWER

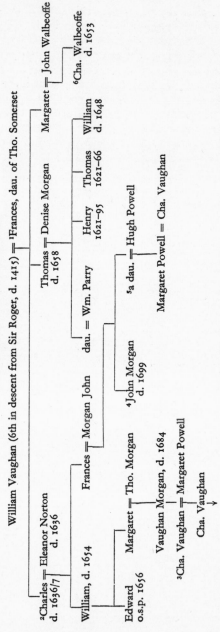

William Vaughan (6th in descent from Sir Roger, d. 1415) = ¹Frances, dau. of Tho. Somerset

²Charles d. 1636/7 = Eleanor Norton d. 1636   Thomas d. 1658 = Denise Morgan   Margaret = John Walbeoffe

William, d. 1654   Frances = Morgan John   dau. = Wm. Parry   Henry 1621–95   Thomas 1621–66   William d. 1648   ⁶Cha. Walbeoffe d. 1653

Edward o.s.p. 1656   Margaret = Tho. Morgan   ⁴John Morgan d. 1699   ⁵a dau. = Hugh Powell

Vaughan Morgan, d. 1684   Margaret Powell = Cha. Vaughan

³Cha. Vaughan = Margaret Powell

Cha. Vaughan

---

¹ By a previous marriage to a Vaughan of Talgarth Frances was mother of Roger Vaughan of Trephilip (Sheriff 1646–7).

² Charles Vaughan married secondly in 1636 Ursula Coningsby (living in 1652).

³ Took his grandmother's maiden name Vaughan. Theo. Jones (*Hist. Breckn.*, 1911, iii. 176) gives Margaret Powell as wife of Vaughan Morgan's grandson, but inconsistently on a later page (iii. 206) he makes the bridegroom Vaughan Morgan's son, which is correct for the reasons I have given on my p. 204.

⁴ Poem on his marriage (M. 617).

⁵ As widow of Charles Williams, her first husband, she inherited Scethrog, which went later through her daughter Margaret to the Vaughans of Tretower. Hugh Powell was rector of Llansantffraed 1668–1717.

⁶ Poem on his death (M. 609).

B. HENRY VAUGHAN'S DESCENDANTS

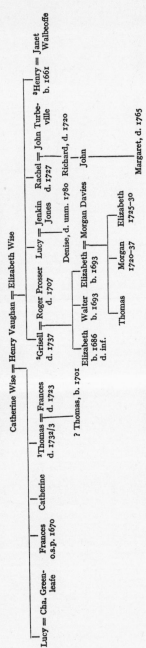

Catherine Wise = Henry Vaughan = Elizabeth Wise

Lucy = Cha. Greenleafe — Frances o.s.p. 1670 — Catherine — ¹Thomas = Frances (d. 1732/3) (d. 1723) — ²Grisell = Roger Prosser (d. 1737) (d. 1707) — Lucy = Jenkin Jones — Rachel = John Turbeville (d. 1727) (d. 1720) — ³Henry = Janet Walbeoffe (b. 1661)

? Thomas, b. 1701

Denise, d. unm. 1780   Richard, d. 1720

Elizabeth b. 1686 d. inf.   Walter b. 1693   Elizabeth b. 1693 = Morgan Davies

Thomas   Morgan 1720-37   Elizabeth 1725-30

John

Margaret, d. 1765

1 Thomas is named after his sisters in Richard Wise's will.
2 Grisell married secondly in 1709 Morgan Watkin, who died in 1719.
3 Hugh Thomas, Welsh Herald, names the children of the second marriage in this order. See above, p. 197.

C. WALBEOFFE AND VAUGHAN CONNEXIONS

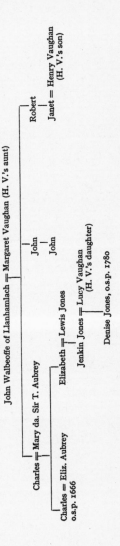

John Walbeoffe of Llanhamlach = Margaret Vaughan (H. V.'s aunt)

Charles = Mary da. Sir T. Aubrey   Robert   Janet = Henry Vaughan (H. V.'s son)

John   John

Charles = Eliz. Aubrey o.s.p. 1666   Elizabeth = Lewis Jones

Jenkin Jones = Lucy Vaughan (H. V.'s daughter)

Denise Jones, o.s.p. 1780

INDEX

PRINTED IN GREAT BRITAIN AT THE UNIVERSITY PRESS, OXFORD
BY VIVIAN RIDLER, PRINTER TO THE UNIVERSITY